To:

From:

Date:

B 83-64-49

Message:

B 83-64-49

Published by Christian Art Publishers
PO Box 1599, Vereeniging, 1930, RSA

© 2019
First edition 2019

Designed by Christian Art Publishers
Images used under license from Shutterstock.com

Printed in China

ISBN 978-1-4321-3086-2

# Traveling LIGHT

## DALENE REYBURN

CHRISTIAN ART
PUBLISHERS

Disturb us, Lord, when
We are too well pleased with ourselves,
When our dreams have come true
Because we have dreamed too little,
When we arrived safely
Because we sailed too close to the shore.

Disturb us, Lord, when
With the abundance of things we possess
We have lost our thirst
For the waters of life;
Having fallen in love with life,
We have ceased to dream of eternity
And in our efforts to build a new earth,
We have allowed our vision
Of the new Heaven to dim.

Disturb us, Lord, to dare more boldly,
To venture on wider seas
Where storms will show Your mastery;
Where losing sight of land,
We shall find the stars.

We ask You to push back
The horizons of our hopes;
And to push into the future
In strength, courage, hope, and love.

ATTRIBUTED TO SIR FRANCIS DRAKE, 1577

# Contents

January:    You Have Reached Your Destination

February:    Passport to Purpose

March:    Home Comforts

April:    Sleeping Under Stars

May:    Baggage and Abundant Life

June:    Nothing to Declare

July:    In Transit

August:    Grace and Gravity

September:    Life on a Shoestring

October:    Go the Distance

November:    Walk Off the Map

December:    Sky's the Limit

January     Read, Live Re...ied Your Destination

February     Passport to Purpose

March     Home Comforts

April     Sleeping Three Stars

May     Baggage and Abundant Life

June     Nothing to Declare

July     In Transit

August     Welcome Or Why

September     Life on a Shoestring

October     Go the Distance

November     Walk Off the Map

December     Go the Limit

# JANUARY

## You Have Reached Your Destination

I think you travel to search and you come back home to find yourself there.

*Chimamanda Ngozi Adichie*

# Anchored

> We have this hope as an anchor for
> the soul, firm and secure (Heb. 6:19 NIV).

*Y*ou're not alone.

On this first day of a new year, you are not alone in your expectation – or your uncertainty. Around the world, women just like you and me are on the cusp of new things. This could be our finest hour – and yet we may be overwhelmed by circumstances, or afraid of where the journey might lead.

As you navigate the seas of a new year, I'm praying this devotional will be the daily breeze in your sails, refreshing you and reminding you that while so much of life is beyond your control, you do get to choose your attitudes and actions – what you do with this moment, and every moment going forward. I pray you'd have Edward Mote's hymn on soul-repeat –

> *My hope is built on nothing less than Jesus Christ, my righteousness;*
> *I dare not trust the sweetest frame, but wholly lean on Jesus' name.*
> *On Christ, the solid Rock, I stand; all other ground is sinking sand.*
> *When darkness veils His lovely face I rest on His unchanging grace;*
> *In every high and stormy gale, my anchor holds within the veil.*
> *His oath, His covenant, His blood, support me in the whelming*
> *flood; When all around my soul gives way, He then is all my hope*
> *and stay.*

Strong God – immovable anchor –
I'm tethering all my hopes to You. Amen.

# Process before proceeding

I don't mean to say that I have already achieved these
things or that I have already reached perfection.
But I press on to possess that perfection for which
Christ Jesus first possessed me (Phil. 3:12 NLT).

Before you head out on the trains, planes and pathways of a
new year, take a minute to ask yourself:

Where will you *keep on* going this year? What did you pack last
year that you need to keep in your suitcase? Are there excellent habits
and relationships that you'll keep on investing in?

Where will you *stop* going this year? Has God shown you some
toxic areas of life best avoided? Are you carrying junk best dumped?
If your bags bulge – heavy with resentment or fear or unresolved
conflict – how can you trash that excess weight?

And then, where have you *never been before*? Is your Father
nudging you to step beyond what feels ordinary and safe – into
something fresh and challenging – possibly scary but almost certainly
thrilling and growth-inducing?

This year you'll be taking another trip around the sun. What are
your expectations? What would make the ride a success?

Here's to the journey of a lifetime.

Heavenly Father, I can hardly wait to find out where
You'll take me this year! Help me process what
You're stirring in my soul, before I press on. Amen.

# First things first

Seek the Kingdom of God above all else,
and live righteously, and He will give you
everything you need (Matt. 6:33 NLT).

Whether you'll be traveling on smooth tar or skidding across gravel this year, guaranteed peace comes from simply determining – each day – no matter what – to seek God first, *first thing*.

It's unbelievably uncomplicated. Very, very difficult, some days. But not complex. It's a matter of addressing your waking thoughts to Jesus. And don't let anyone throw shade because you're not a morning person who is energized by shiny-happy early encounters with God. (You're useful and astute when the morning people are heading for bed and the Kingdom needs *all kinds* of humans.) But as you surface from sleep and your thoughts gather coherence, just offer the day to God. Pray: *Your Kingdom come; Your will be done.*

And as you move through the rushed minutes or the hours of waiting, keep up the appeal – *Your Kingdom come; Your will be done*. You may find it simplifies situations and distills decisions and amplifies God's answers like nothing else, and there's a new freedom to travel light.

God, You first; me second. Maximize my life today,
for Your maximum glory. Amen.

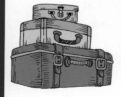

# Already there

God saved you by His grace when
you believed. And you can't take credit for
this; it is a gift from God (Eph. 2:8 NLT).

*I* am usually the first one up in the mornings to brew the
coffee. But first an instinctive daybreak ritual unfolds. I unlock
the kitchen door – and I *stand there*.

There's a rush of un-tasted air, and I just breathe it in. In summer
it's a riot of birds and the promise of heat. In winter the stars are out –
cold air crisp with new mercies.

I haven't gone anywhere or done anything yet. I look my unedited
worst. I haven't necessarily woken up in a fantastic mood. I'm just
standing in the fresh air of a new day, and I just *am*.

That's how God's acceptance feels. We didn't earn or deserve it.
God just receives us – delights in us – cherishes us – without us going
anywhere, or doing anything, or looking our best. It is as if we've
*made it*. His acceptance rushes into our hearts like so much fresh
morning air. And we can just stand there, and enjoy it.

For some, travel is about getting there. For others, it's about the
journey. But what if you saw your life expedition as God does? From
His eternal point of view, you've already arrived.

King of kings, there's no greater destination than Your courts!
And I don't ever need to ask, *'Are we there yet?'* Amen.

# Bite for the road

Jesus answered, 'It is written: "Man shall not live on bread alone, but on every word that comes from the mouth of God"' (Matt. 4:4 NIV).

Jesus' relationship with His Heavenly Father was marked by total, unwavering acceptance. Matthew describes how, as Jesus was baptized, a voice from heaven said, 'This is My dearly loved Son, who brings Me great joy' (Matthew 3:17). God *accepted* Him.

There was more to their Father-Son relationship than just acceptance. There was *sustenance*. Jesus spent regular, intimate time with His Father, drawing away to quiet places to pray (Luke 5:16). In John 4:34, He explains to His disciples, 'My nourishment comes from doing the will of God, who sent Me, and from finishing His work.' He lived in unbroken fellowship with the Father. God *sustained* Him.

And in just the same way, God has entered into relationship with you – He *accepts* you. And He's growing and changing you – He *sustains* you. Quinoa, avocadoes, almonds, broccoli – these are all great superfoods and as far as it depends on your budget and cooking skills, you should totally eat them. But God is your ultimate super-sustenance, satisfying your soul in ways nothing and no one else can, on days when your fridge is stocked and days when it isn't.

Father God, please give me the spiritual sustenance,
the emotional energy, the brain and body zest
to do life well, and to Your glory. Amen.

# Significant sojourner

> Jesus grew in wisdom and in stature and in favor
> with God and all the people (Luke 2:52 NLT).

Jesus lived with the calm, unshakeable conviction that He was accepted by His Father. So can we. Jesus lived knowing that His Father was the source of His sustenance. So can we.

And at just the right time, walking the dusty streets of ancient Israel, Jesus entered into remarkable, significant ministry. And so can we.

It seems God's game plan for Jesus on earth was thirty years of preparation, three years of impact. So if it feels to you as if your life isn't amounting to anything cosmically significant, remember that God's *preparation* of His Son was in and of itself cosmically significant. Don't underestimate how God is preparing you – and what He's preparing you for. *It's all significant.*

What makes the Christian life so different from worldly cultures is that any significant mark we leave on this world will only ever be for God's glory, not ours. C. T. Studd, one of the Cambridge Seven missionaries who traveled to China to break gospel ground in the nineteenth century, said, 'Only one life, 'twil soon be past. Only what's done for Christ will last.'

> Jesus, I believe You accept me.
> I believe You sustain me.
> Help me trust that You're using me
> to make an indelible impact on this world,
> for Your Name's sake. Amen.

# Travel like a boss

No, in all these things we are more than conquerors through Him who loved us (Rom. 8:37 NIV).

From acceptance, to sustenance, to significance, Jesus ultimately moved to achievement. You'd have to agree Jesus *achieved* something. I sometimes picture Him going for a job interview. He's in a boardroom with a bunch of suits and someone on the panel says, 'I see here on your résumé, Mr. Christ, that You "conquered death"? Do You perhaps want to tell us a little more about that ...?' No matter how impressive your credentials, you can't claim to have achieved anything close.

It's only in finding our belonging in Christ, and looking to Him for sustenance, and then leveraging our time, talents and treasures significantly, that we'll be led to achieve our purpose and potential, as we live out our passion and gifting.

This pattern of how God works in our stories – what Frank Lake called the Cycle of Grace that moves from acceptance, to sustenance, to significance, to achievement – is *ongoing* in our lives. We can always enjoy *more* of God's gracious acceptance – lean in even closer for sustenance – pray for greater opportunities to make a significant difference – and continue to do the good works prepared beforehand for us (Ephesians 2:10).

Jesus, if I'm racking up achievements,
let them only ever be a product of my gratitude,
pointing to Your greatness. Amen.

# Wrong way right

> For the wisdom of this world is
> foolishness to God (1 Cor. 3:19 NLT).

Picture living from acceptance, to sustenance, to significance, to achievement – as a circular, *clockwise* movement. Now consider if you (like me) sometimes live the cycle *anticlockwise*. Maybe some anticlockwise thinking has shown up in your life sounding like this:

'I better *achieve* a lot because then I'll be *significant*, and if I can just fake it 'til I make it – if I can just keep *sustaining* some level of achievement and significance – then I'm sure I'll be *accepted* (in this church group, career community or school-mom clique).'

Or, 'If I can just use the right lingo and see the right shows and wear the right clothes and drink the right hipster coffee, then I'm sure they'll think I'm somebody *significant*. And if I can *sustain* all that, they'll be my friend. I'll feel *accepted* – like I really belong.'

But the longer we live anticlockwise – trying to achieve to be accepted – the more we realize we can't sustain it. That doesn't make us feel accepted at all. It just makes us feel like total losers. Which makes us think, 'I better *achieve* more so that – ' And so it goes on. A cycle of destruction, not grace.

> God, show me where I'm trying to impress:
> living from achievement to acceptance,
> instead of the other way around. Amen.

# Right side up parenting

Can a mother forget the baby at her breast and have no compassion on the child she has borne? Though she may forget, I will not forget you! (Isa. 49:15 NIV).

*I* try to praise my kids for the process not the product – rewarding for character not accomplishment. But I still sometimes catch myself parenting from achievement to acceptance, instead of from acceptance to achievement. I send the message: *Do this thing well – achieve! – and you'll get a pat on the back, which will make you feel accepted!*

It's never wrong to affirm our kids. But moms, we're the voice in their heads. (For many of us, our moms are still the voice in our heads, yes?) We're the soundtrack to the lives of our kids. We're the backing vocals singing, *Make sure you're home by 10, well done on winning the match, please set the table, shoo-wah, shoo-wah ...*

But we also need to be the lead vocalist, and the lyrics of the chorus that get stuck in their heads need to be: *Win or lose, I love you. I love being your mom. I love watching you do your best with the gifts God's given you. If God had lined up all the children in the world and let me pick, I'd pick you every time.*

*You're accepted.*

Good Father, help me parent my kids
the way You parent me. Amen.

# Brownie points

The law of Moses was unable to save us because of the weakness of our sinful nature. So God did what the law could not do. He sent His own Son in a body like the bodies we sinners have. And in that body God declared an end to sin's control over us by giving His Son as a sacrifice for our sins (Rom. 8:3 NLT).

Even though we know better, you and I aren't above the cause-and-effect thinking that goes like this: 'If I sign up for all the church committees and join a third Bible study, and if I babysit the pastor's kids for free – then I think I'll be a *significant* Christian and I'm sure if I just *keep that up* for long enough I'll be *accepted* by God.'

Maybe we don't consciously think that, because we've heard it preached enough to know intellectually that we're saved by grace (Ephesians 2:5). But I've sometimes lived it quite differently. I've said I believe that God accepts us and then leads us to achievement, but I've behaved and made decisions as if I believe I need to achieve for Him, in order to be accepted.

Today, could you tear down your mental scoreboard? God isn't counting your points. He's only counting all the ways He loves you.

Savior, show me where I'm exhausting myself
in futile attempts to earn the good graces
You've already lavished on me. Amen.

# Can't help yourself

Just as the body is dead without breath, so also faith is dead without good works (James 2:26 NLT).

You've already reached your destination, in a sense, because your eternal destiny is secure. There's a kick-off-your-shoes kind of wonder and relief in that reality! You don't need to go anywhere, or do anything. Not now. Not yet. Not ever, actually. Mercy floods have washed you into a place of acceptance on the shores of right standing with God. You just get to chill out, and enjoy the fresh air of that most spacious place.

The irony, of course, is that when you relax for a moment in the place of acceptance – when you look around and you realize where you are and how beautiful it is – *you want to go on*. You can scarcely stop yourself. It's the whole grace-works thing that James talks about. We don't have to do a single good thing for God, ever, to earn or deserve His love and our forever with Him. But if we're truly saved by grace, we'll *want* to do good works. They'll be our living, natural, overflowing *I-love-You-back* to God.

Lord, I'm ready to get up and at 'em! I want to fulfill every plan You've made for me. Use me to do the good works that will further Your Kingdom. Amen.

# Priceless

He gave His life to purchase freedom
for everyone … (1 Tim. 2:6 NLT).

*I*t's traditional, in my home country of South Africa, for a man to pay a bride price for the woman he wants to marry. It's called *lobola* and it's given to the bride's father in cattle or cash. There's even an app to calculate it, which I came across browsing the app store once. I wasn't totally comfortable with how the app objectifies women, but I was intrigued nevertheless to find out my worth in cows and South African rand, so I downloaded it and when my husband got home that night I told him he owed my dad some cows.

The app asks you to rate yourself according to age, weight, height, et cetera. (I gave myself a pretty high score for cooking, because I can totally slide some frozen fish into the oven, am I right?) My husband and I had a bit of a laugh. Then he said to me – seriously: 'Think about your *lobola* in God's eyes.'

Not one of us was eligible bachelorette of the year. Yet the *lobola* Jesus paid for His bride, the church, He didn't pay in cash or in cows. *He paid with His life.* We can never attach a price to that. What and how He paid for us, makes us priceless.

Jesus, thank You for the incalculable price
You paid to call me Yours, and set me free. Amen.

# Don't be fooled

> But the LORD said to Samuel, 'Don't judge
> by his appearance or height, for I have rejected
> him. The LORD doesn't see things the way you
> see them. People judge by outward appearance,
> but the LORD looks at the heart' (1 Sam. 16:7 NLT).

When Samuel goes to anoint David as king, Jesse parades his strapping older sons before Samuel. For each son Samuel thinks, 'This *must* be the one?' And for each son God says, *Nope*. Finally Samuel asks Jesse if he's quite sure he doesn't have *any* other sons? To which Jesse replies, 'There is still the youngest, but he's out in the fields watching the sheep and goats.' Samuel says, 'Send for him.' When David is brought in from the fields, God says, *This is the one; anoint him.* (1 Samuel 16:11-12) And the rest is history.

As you focus on the truth that God accepts you – as is, without you doing, trying or being something bigger and better and more impressive or influential – would you remember that He doesn't see you as *you* see you? He doesn't take His cues from you. Thankfully, His opinion of you isn't dependent on anyone else's opinion of you. It's also not dependent on *your* opinion of you. He sees you as you really are.

God, I'm so grateful You know me better than
I know me, and still You love me. Amen.

# Run and re-tell

> The woman left her water jar beside the well and ran back to the village, telling everyone, 'Come and see a man who told me everything I ever did! Could He possibly be the Messiah?' (John 4:28-29 NLT).

When this Samaritan woman encountered the astonishing grace and omniscience of the Savior, she ran back to her hometown to tell anyone who'd listen. Even us, a couple millennia later, we should be always running back to a remembrance and re-telling of how God sees, knows and loves us utterly.

Don't worry about how He'll sustain you, or how He'll lead you into a life of significance, or how much you'll achieve for Him. All in good time. Just know that He knows everything about you – like He knew everything about the Samaritan woman. He hasn't taken His eyes off you for one second of your life. He was there every time someone hurt you or disregarded you. He was there when you got that phone call. That diagnosis. When your kid did that thing you're still embarrassed about. He's kept track of all your sorrows. He's collected all your tears (Psalm 56:8). And – marvelously! – He's started something in you: a good work that He *will* complete (Philippians 1:6).

It's the kind of good news that's worth remembering – and running to re-tell.

Jesus, I'm so happy to have encountered Your total knowing of me. It's mobilized me to make a difference. Amen.

# Worth it?

What do you have that God hasn't given you?
And if everything you have is from God, why boast
as though it were not a gift? (1 Cor. 4:7 NLT).

Maybe you were worth dying for, but I know for sure that I wasn't. God didn't get something super special out of the deal when He shed His blood for me. He didn't say, 'Hmm. We better die for *that* one, because we really need her on the team. She's got a lot to offer the Kingdom so I think we need to get her on board. I think she could add value to our organization.'

We *are* worthy. But our worth, like everything else we intrinsically possess, is a gift from God. It's not something we can brag about because we had nothing to do with it. Our worth comes from the fact that God loved us so much, despite the fact that we had nothing of any real worth to offer Him.

Our worth comes from the astounding truth that He wanted to sacrifice His life for us, *anyway*. His love for us imputes – attributes – *accredits* worth to me and to you. Which means: He doesn't love us because we're worthy. We're worthy because He loves us.

Jesus, Your love fills me up with heavy, glorious worth –
so that I can travel light. Thank You! Amen.

# Relationship before rules

I am the LORD. I will free you from your oppression
and will rescue you from your slavery in Egypt. I will
redeem you with a powerful arm and great acts of judgment.
I will claim you as My own people, and I will be your God.
Then you will know that I am the LORD your God who has
freed you from your oppression in Egypt (Exod. 6:6-7 NLT).

God invites you into relationship with Him, *as you are*. He
doesn't wait for you to prove yourself by traveling towards Him
on specific roads. He treks off road to find you in the middle of your
mess and He says, *I'll be your Dad*.

God didn't give the Ten Commandments, *then* rescue the Israelites. He didn't say, 'Ok, follow these ten rules and I'll consider your
case. Maybe I'll be your God. Maybe not.' He said, 'I'll rescue you from
Egypt. I'll split the sea for you. I'll be your God; you'll be My people.
And *now*, because I love you – because I've set you free and I want to
keep you free – live by this code. It'll bless and protect you.'

Even before Jesus came to roll out the grace plan in our two-
dimensional timeline, His Father was saving sinners by grace, through
faith. It's always been relationship before rules.

Father, thank You for making the first move,
even though I was playing hard to get. Amen.

# Comma before credentials

Paul, called to be an apostle of Christ Jesus
by the will of God … (1 Cor. 1:1 NIV).

The way Paul introduces himself to the churches he's writing to is a powerful non-coincidence. Punctuation is grammatically implied in the original Greek text, so in our English Bibles we have commas and the like. But have a look at Paul's opening statements in every one of his letters: Paul, *comma*, a slave of Christ Jesus … Paul, *comma*, an apostle … Paul, *comma*, chosen by the will of God …

That (implied) comma is weighty. Paul doesn't present himself like this: *This is an apostle of Jesus Christ speaking and I've been chosen by Him and imprisoned for my faith. The name's Paul.* He knew who he was *before* the comma – before his job title and significant achievements.

Think of how people are often introduced, credentials first: *Nominated for six Academy Awards, four British Academy Film Awards and eleven Golden Globe awards, and Oscar Nominee for 2016, we welcome to the stage, Leonardo DiCaprio.*

In the counter-culture Kingdom, who you are before the comma is enough. You don't have to prove your street cred or add gravitas to what God has declared you to be.

God, thank You that You've made me, fully completely,
who I am. Any other credentials are bonus
accessories, to be used by You and for You,
as and when You see fit. Amen

# Chosen

Even before He made the world, God loved
us and chose us in Christ to be holy and
without fault in His eyes (Eph. 1:4 NLT).

Comedian and host of The Daily Show, Trevor Noah, wrote – in all seriousness – 'Being chosen is the greatest gift you can give to another human being.'

Whether or not you get picked or promoted in the way you long to be, in this life, you can take pleasure in the daily confidence of being chosen by God. No other earthly accolade compares. You don't just have a foot in the door. You're *in*. You're walking on the arm of the King who knows your name and He's preparing a place for you that will blow your mind (1 Corinthians 2:9).

When you get comfortable with the truth that you've been chosen to live a new life, you're ok to let go of your agenda, which actually died with Christ. Sure, you've got dreams, goals and big ideas of how you'd love to live out your earthly potential. But all those big ideas come second to the main thrust of your life, which is to enjoy Jesus.

King of kings, help me to cease striving and start
surrendering – remembering that I'm chosen,
I'm beloved, and I belong. Amen.

# Slipstream

I can do all this through Him who
gives me strength (Phil. 4:13 NIV).

*Y*ears ago, traveling to an out-of-town weekend speaking event, I was nervous. I knew very little about the audience I'd be addressing. I had no idea how my message would be received – or how *I* would be received.

As I drove and prayed, God gave me a picture of a motorboat surging through water and leaving an enormous wake. He said to me, *Get into My slipstream. I will power through the water – not you. I will go ahead of you to open hearts – and change them. Your job is very small. I am very big. Just show up. Get behind My power and it will be effortless. Get into My slipstream and you'll see that I've cleared the way. I've done the hard work. They're not even going to notice you or remember you. They will remember Me – and that's the point, isn't it?*

I've clung to that image. It's how I pray about every event, interaction and ordinary day. It's not that life is just easy and effortless if you get into God's slipstream, because the struggle is real and there's going to be resistance and tragedy and things going wrong. But surrendering to God's power helps us remember that – thankfully! – we're just flecks in the wave of history that rolls on all for His glory.

Almighty God, I'm right behind You. Amen.

# Here and there

Acknowledge that the LORD is God! He made us, and
we are His. We are His people, the sheep of His pasture.
Enter His gates with thanksgiving; go into His courts with
praise. Give thanks to Him and praise His name. For the
LORD is good. His unfailing love continues forever, and His
faithfulness continues to each generation (Ps. 100:3-5 NLT).

*I*magine getting to the end of a long, long journey – *finally!* You're
exhausted. Unbelievably grateful to be home. All you want to do
is dump your bags and you're hoping for a hot bath, a hot meal and
your own bed.

For believers, that's kinda-sorta happened. We're *living* in that
place of great and glad satisfaction, because our earthly heritage and
our heavenly homecoming are already established. We're still very
much in the hard traipsing of the long journey – we slog up the hills
and our feet slip on the down slopes – but even in our terrestrial
travels, we carry the soul knowledge of a glorious, guaranteed end to
look forward to, and until we actually, *finally*, get there, we have the
joy of living in two places at once: textured, tangible life as we know
it on these roads we walk, and ultimate, eternal life with the Messiah
who accomplished our redemption.

Jesus, thank You that You walked this
earth before me, finishing Your work so I
could follow freely in Your footsteps. Amen.

# Here we are

*I am not saying this because I am in need, for I have learned to be content whatever the circumstances* (Phil. 4:11 NIV).

No matter where the journey takes us, let's practice being in the now – arriving at the destination of each moment. Try journaling with this sentence (or bring it to mind while driving, riding the elevator or defrosting the fridge): 'Well, here we are today, in two places.'

That sentence can frame your every reality. Meditating on each word of the sentence puts you *in the moment* and helps you make the most of that moment. Think along these lines:

*Well.* It's *well* with your soul. All is as it should be. No purpose of God's can be thwarted (Job 42:2).

*Here.* This beats FOMO because God has you *here*, in *this* place (not somewhere else).

*We.* You're never an island and always part of community. Even if you're lonely, or flying solo, who you are and what you do bumps up against other lives all the time.

*Are.* Present tense. This moment is all you know for sure. Be in it. You can't control the future, and you've left the past behind.

*Today.* You'll be somewhere different tomorrow, so live today well, straddling *two places* simultaneously: the chaos of life and the quiet of His presence.

Father, thank You for being with me,
here, in my today. Amen.

# Beautiful train wreck

> But God is so rich in mercy, and He loved us so much,
> that even though we were dead because of our sins, He gave
> us life when He raised Christ from the dead. (It is only by
> God's grace that you have been saved!) (Eph. 2:4-5 NLT)

A t the risk of sounding macabre, I sometimes think of the gospel like this:

You're on the platform of a train station. Weirdly lured by the thrill of it, you decide to jump down onto the tracks, with all your baggage. There's a train coming at you. Full speed. It's not stopping at your station. You're about to be flattened and you deserve it because you chose to jump down onto the filthy tracks, with your filthy baggage. Jesus arrives. He leaps down onto the tracks. He pushes you out the way and the train hits Him instead. You find yourself free, and safe, standing on the platform. As if you've *just arrived at your destination*.

The words *destiny* and *destination* have the same root in Latin, meaning *to arrive*. Because of what Christ has already done for you, you've already *arrived*. You're standing on the platform. Grateful. Liberated. And your knee-jerk love reaction has you going, 'Now that I've reached my destination, how will I live out my destiny, for You?'

Jesus, let my every action and attitude
be my gratitude for Your grace. Amen.

# Shadow selves

> And the angel said to me, 'Write this:
> Blessed are those who are invited to the wedding
> feast of the Lamb.' And he added, 'These are true
> words that come from God' (Rev. 19:9 NLT).

There isn't a Jesus-follower on the pages of history who hasn't been able to identify with Paul's struggle when he says, 'I want to do what is good, but I don't. I don't want to do what is wrong, but I do it anyway.' (Romans 7:19)

It seems sometimes that we're traveling with rogue tendrils of our temperaments – our *shadow selves*, as some call them. Even though Jesus has invited us to a feast, our shadow selves are the bits we're embarrassed to bring with us. And yet Jesus sees all the bits of us – all the incongruent inconsistencies. The ugly and the lovely parts of us. He sees them all and He died for them all. Regardless of where we find ourselves on the sliding scale of sanctification – which is the part of salvation that happens between justification (repenting and committing to Christ) and glorification (our heaven-bound hope of total restoration) – He says, *Come, come, come. Come as you are.* Nothing stays hidden in His presence. Time at His table will bring our shadows into the light, to be dissipated by His love.

> Jesus, thank You for inviting me –
> *all* of me – to feast with You. Amen.

# All the way

Let your character or moral disposition be free
from love of money [including greed, avarice, lust,
and craving for earthly possessions] and be satisfied
with your present [circumstances and with what you have];
for He [God] Himself has said, I will not in any way
fail you nor give you up nor leave you without support.
[I will] not, [I will] not, [I will] not in any degree leave
you helpless nor forsake nor let [you] down (relax My
hold on you)! [Assuredly not!] (Heb. 13:5 AMP).

Once, for Father's Day, our eldest son wrote a bunch of notes to my husband, Murray. He hid the notes all over the house and Murray would keep on coming across them randomly for weeks afterwards. Amongst the tea bags was scrawled: *Dad, I wouldn't swap you for anything.* Amidst his socks was, *Dad, I think you're cool!* By far the best one – buried in a breakfast cereal – said: *Dad, thank you for never forgetting.* (No pressure!)

Our Heavenly Father never forgets. He never stops watching us. He never stops walking with us. He never stops sending us reminders of His grace-grip on our lives. He sees the end from the beginning – and not a stretch of the journey takes Him by surprise.

Heavenly Father, thank You that
You're in this for the long haul. You're traveling
all the way with me, so I can travel light. Amen.

# IED

But You, LORD, are a shield around me, my glory,
the One who lifts my head high (Ps. 3:3 NIV).

*I* remember being in an area of Mozambique where we were warned not to wander into the bush on either side of the road we were on, because unexploded landmines still lurked beneath the soil and you didn't want to disturb one, by standing on it …

It seems the century we're standing in is one big anxiety minefield. It's as if every other person (maybe you and me?) is walking around with a ticking Improvised Explosive Device of the soul just waiting to go off when stepped on by others' Irritation, Embarrassment and Disappointment.

If we're honest, we're all somewhere on the anxiety spectrum. We need to diffuse our hearts from time to time before they get dangerous. And we need to help others do the same.

God has this to say about irritation, embarrassment and disappointment: He seeks you out and He rejoices over you with singing (Zephaniah 3:17). *He's not irritated.* He entered time and space to get to you, and He advocates on your behalf (1 John 2:1). *He's not embarrassed of you.* You're the apple of His eye (Zechariah 2:8). *He's not disappointed in you.*

Lord, thank You for going ahead of me to
clear the landmines. You are my safety and
the One who lifts my head high. Amen.

# Gone guilt

He cancelled the record of the charges against us and took it away by nailing it to the cross (Col. 2:14 NLT).

*I* would guess you're incredibly supple. You stretch your budget, your schedule, your patience and your caffeine threshold in superhero ways. Your heart is stretched so thin in places that heart-goo seeps through all your inside spaces and sometimes leaks embarrassingly from your eyes.

You bend every which way to please and placate and catch whoever's falling. You love fiercely, and with a tender flexibility that scares and surprises you. And your psyche has plasticized so impressively that you can accommodate vast mental tracts of mom guilt, wife guilt, daughter guilt, friend guilt.

Except, women aren't superheroes. We're actual, human sinners. Guilty as charged. Desperate for grace. And God has dealt with your guilt – so, stop it already. He carried your shame. Why would you ask to carry something unbearably, impossibly heavy – something human arms can't ever stretch around – when Someone else has offered to carry it for you? You don't get to beat yourself up. You don't get to punish yourself because your punishment has already been endured.

On days when you *are* guilty of sinning against others – for real – ask their forgiveness. Restore the relationship. Find each other again in the soft, strong circles of mercy. And move on, guilt gone.

Jesus, You were weighed down
by my shame, so I could travel light. Amen.

# Enough

> I will answer them before they even call to Me.
> While they are still talking about their needs, I will
> go ahead and answer their prayers! (Isa. 65:24 NLT).

Guilt tortures you with accusations that you're always behind on doing and being all you want to do and be. It nags that there's never enough time, never enough money, never enough *you* to go around.

*There's enough time.* There's enough time for the story you're living. But the chapter you're in is part of a much longer plot that climaxes in eternity. Like, we start families, but we don't finish them. Don't feel guilty for determinedly starting something you definitely can't finish. We're all somebody's previous generation. It's a beautiful, humbling thing to build something that will outlast you – something others will finish, to God's glory.

*There's enough money.* Guilt has you believing you're supposed to stretch your stressed out self over every gaping hole. That doesn't model dependency on God. It models delusional self-sufficiency. He knows your needs.

*There's enough you.* God makes sure there's fresh mercy on every breakfast table in every kitchen every morning (Lamentations 3:23). That means, it may *feel* like there's not enough you, but for sure there's enough grace for you not to give up.

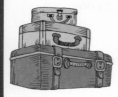

> God, You *are* enough, and You *give* enough!
> Energize and mobilize me with
> that truth. Amen.

# Worth your wardrobe

> I am overwhelmed with joy in the LORD my God!
> For He has dressed me with the clothing of salvation
> and draped me in a robe of righteousness. I am like …
> a bride with her jewels (Isa. 61:10 NLT).

For a school project on recycling, a friend's middle school daughter made an outfit out of trash. She sewed together dozens and dozens of used, dried-out teabags – logos and lettering of various tea companies still visible through the stains – and made a long, layered, heavy, rustling, exquisite dress.

*What if you and I wore the Word of God like that?* What if we dressed ourselves, not in trash, but in the truth that we're wearing heavy, royal robes. That we're not *so last season*. We're *so next season*. So *never-ending season*. Because we're dressed for eternity.

We could sew together verses like so many teabags to remind ourselves and each other to dress like daughters – not orphans – because 'God decided in advance to adopt us into His own family by bringing us to Himself through Jesus Christ.' (Ephesians 1:15)

We might remember to carry ourselves as image-bearers of the Creator-King who sees us, knows us, and calls us chosen people, royal priests, a holy nation, God's very own possession (Genesis 1:27, Jeremiah 1:5, 1 Peter 2:9).

> Father, help me to remember who I am,
> and to dress accordingly. Amen.

# Worth your weight

> Like newborn babies, you must crave pure spiritual milk so that you will grow into a full experience of salvation. Cry out for this nourishment, now that you have had a taste of the Lord's kindness (1 Pet. 2:3 NLT).

*I* still sometimes shop in the kids' department, because I'm not the biggest human. But as far back as I can remember my self-worth has been attached to a number on the scale. It started as an insidious whisper in my little girl ears. It grew to a scream drowning out reason in my teenage and young adult years. And there are still mornings that it's the voice of motherhood and *now-you're-40-something!* shouting from the morning mirror or across the school car park, at dinner parties or ministry events. It's the hiss that I'm not pretty enough. Not tall enough. Not hipster enough. Just, *not enough*.

And I'd bet my best pair of heels that I'm not the only one listening to the lie because there's a thriving global industry blasting it from newsfeeds and plastering it on Pinterest.

Friend, we could roll out a revolution if we started weighing ourselves on God's scales. Because we're heavy with *abundance* (John 10:10). There's so much life crammed into us that it steadies and secures us. We're wonderfully weighted by unsurpassed lightness of being.

> God, thank You for weighting me with worth so I needn't fear the slurs of skin-deep culture. Amen.

# First Class travel

… Christ Jesus came into the world to save sinners …
(1 Tim. 1:15 NIV).

*I* fantasize about being the happy victim of a flight ticket error. 'We're so sorry, Ma'am. It seems we've double-booked your seat. Would you mind terribly if we bumped you up to Business?' 'Well. If you must.'

I've slept on beaches, airport floors and the decks of ferries – which is when the First Class fantasies were particularly vivid. But we'd be silly to attach our worth to a level of luxury. Your worth isn't a stamp on a ticket – a designation of carriage or caste. Your worth is a stamp on your heart.

If life's a journey, we all deserve to be shoved into the luggage hold. But Jesus *rocked* First Class. He deserved free snacks in every high flyer lounge. Then at the cross, He took all our lack of preparation, our too-much-baggage and I-forgot-to-pack-my-toothbrush, our fear, self-centeredness, apathy and immaturity. He was embarrassed on our behalf. Our shame hung all over Him – as if it were His. He squeezed into an overhead compartment with the carry-ons – the place that should've been ours.

*And He handed over to us His First Class ticket.* Not so we could feel superior or complacent. Rather, so that all our travels for the rest of our lives would be characterized by gratitude, freedom and joy.

Jesus, thank You for writing
First Class on my heart. Amen.

# Living eulogy

And you yourself must be an example to them by doing good works of every kind. Let everything you do reflect the integrity and seriousness of your teaching. Teach the truth so that your teaching can't be criticized. Then those who oppose us will be ashamed and have nothing bad to say about us (Titus 2:7-8 NLT).

'Live so that the pastor says nice things about you at your funeral.' This was genuine, well-meaning advice, offered to me as a teenager. It's a little crass maybe, and self-serving. But it can frame how we live – while we're living.

Let's decide to travel well this year, so that we have brilliant stories to tell – and so that people coming after us have even better stories to live. Let's travel well, not because we want recognition, but because we want to beat smooth paths for others to walk. Eyes on Christ, let's travel well so the world looks at us a little wonderstruck and says, 'She travels so light and free. It's almost as if she's already reached her destination.'

Lord, help me live each day the way
I'd want to tell it to my grandkids. Amen.

# FEBRUARY

## Passport to Purpose

The real voyage of
discovery consists
not in seeking new
landscapes, but in
having new eyes.

*Marcel Proust*

# Not for nothing

The Lord will work out His plans for my life –
for Your faithful love, O Lord, endures forever.
Don't abandon me, for You made me (Ps. 138:8 NLT).

**P**eople travel with intention – with *raison d'être*. They travel to see things or learn things. To relax or recuperate or escape or explore. And actually, whether you're on vacation or at home, on a business trip or in an office cubicle – you're traveling, all the time. You're traveling round the sun – through time – all the sunrises and sunsets it takes you to get from diapers to death.

But if you don't know the *intention* of the trip, the travel will feel pointless. It will feel like you're being shunted from airport terminal to airport terminal, hotel lobby to museum to cathedral to beach to … you get the idea. It might feel fun – for a while. The change in scenery might be diversionary and stimulating – to a point. And then it'll get stale and you'll catch yourself wondering, 'What am I doing here? *Is this all there is to travel?*'

Thank God He's pieced together your life's itinerary. And when you begin to visit the places He's picked out for you to discover – your journey gets a whole lot more interesting.

Almighty God, thank You that my life's journey is
not for nothing. You haven't left me purposeless
or directionless. I'm excited and expectant! Amen.

# Just information

'Don't be afraid,' he said, 'for you are very precious to God. Peace! Be encouraged! Be strong!' (Dan. 10:19 NLT).

You could forge a passport – if that was your thing. You could fake a travel document. But no matter what information you fabricated – it would remain just that: information.

*Information does not equal identity.* A name on a travel document – even a photo – doesn't really tell you all that much about the person carrying it. It's *evidence* of who the person is – but it's not *who the person is.*

This is true for you as you travel down all the avenues of life. Your identity is independent from – safeguarded against – any info thrust upon you. This is wonderful, powerful, very good news. It's a great relief. Because if the information you receive is rejection or misunderstanding or misrepresentation – or if the info is that you're hoping to get invited or included or loved and you don't – that information will hurt and it will be difficult to process. It will be hard to capture the data. *But it doesn't actually change anything about who you are, or your standing with God.* You're still utterly beloved. The rebuff or the nastiness – it's just information.

Lord, thank You that I don't have to qualify myself. You've already qualified me to be who You've called me to be, and all You've called me to be is myself. Amen.

# Obedience over impact

For we will be counted as righteous when we obey all the commands the LORD our God has given us (Deut. 6:25 NLT).

When we think of *purpose*, our minds might leap to fantasies of grand ideas and enormous influence. Except really, we'll be judged on our *obedience*, not our *impact*. God is pleased with our surrender to His will and His ways – more than He's pleased with the press we receive. You may never walk out of International Arrivals to be greeted by a crowd of ululating fans. That's ok. You were created to make a difference, not an impression.

That's not to say you won't have grand ideas, or that God won't give you enormous influence. In fact, the more obedient you are, the more likely you are to have that kind of impact. Just keep in mind – as you *go big* – the sobering truth that elevating ourselves always diminishes us. It makes us look silly and people cringe because we're always the last to see our self-absorption.

Dream your dreams. Set your goals. And know that true success is measured in daily, hourly, moment by moment obedience to your Heavenly Father.

God, You *created* purpose! Help me
only ever to look for it in You. Amen.

# Immeasurable, untouchable

Yours, O LORD, is the greatness, the power, the glory, the victory, and the majesty. Everything in the heavens and on earth is Yours, O LORD, and this is Your kingdom. We adore You as the one who is over all things (1 Chron. 29:11 NLT).

Part of our purpose is healthy ignorance. Wholesome unawareness of how God is using His Spirit in us to bless others. You will never know the impact you've had in this life. There's no accurate earthly glory-meter. You may catch glimpses of how God is making something beautiful from your life, but you'll only comprehend the sweeping scope of the stardust you've scattered when you view it from eternity.

And then, you won't be able to touch that glory, and you won't want to. You'll grasp with startling clarity that your life was never about your ambitions – *your* purposes. It was about *God's* purposes in and through you.

> Creator God, would you send enough encouragement
> to keep wind in my sails – but please never send
> the gale force applause that will knock me off course.
> Your glory is the north star I'm sailing for. Amen.

# Serious lightness

> Because of the privilege and authority God has
> given me, I give each of you this warning: Don't
> think you are better than you really are. Be honest in
> your evaluation of yourselves, measuring yourselves
> by the faith God has given us (Rom. 12:3 NLT).

We can all be reactionary extremists. Sometimes we're too flippant about what God has called us to. We don't appreciate the eternal urgency of the lives we lead on earth. We don't appreciate the seriousness of our sin: how it separates us from God, and how much He paid to close the gap. Other times we take ourselves far too seriously. Fear of failure paralyzes us from doing anything at all, or we attach too much gravitas to our own efforts and strengths.

Part of discovering our purpose is learning to balance those extremes: carrying well the tension of not taking ourselves too seriously but simply being willing and available to be used by God as and when He chooses – and living passionately and excellently and with serious intent, for His glory.

What you're doing for God today was inked into God's plans from eternity past. It's a big deal! Concurrently, what you're doing for God today is just another brick in the Kingdom wall. Relax, and travel light.

King of kings, help me never to take myself too seriously –
even as I take You and Your ways very seriously indeed. Amen.

# Irrefutably unseen

My sheep listen to My voice; I know them, and they follow Me. I give them eternal life, and they will never perish. No one can snatch them away from Me … (John 10:27-28 NLT).

One of the thrilling things about travel experiences is that no one can take them away from you. You might accidentally delete the photos or lose the been-there-done-that t-shirts. People might not believe that you really went to the places you said you went to – but none of that matters because you went, and what you experienced changed you.

It's ok that others don't always recognize God's purposes in your life. The work He's doing in and through you won't always be evident to people around you. But there's a golden thread running through your existence, weaving your context and your character around the unique life's work that God has called you to. You're made in God's image and every day you're journeying more deeply into the likeness of Christ.

That reality will last forever, so it doesn't matter if your peeps don't see it or understand it. It's eternal. *It is*, because it is wrought in you by the great *I Am*.

Jesus, thank You that I don't need to be seen
by the world when I'm seen by You. Amen.

# Have training, will travel

> But you are a chosen people, a royal priesthood,
> a holy nation, God's special possession, that you
> may declare the praises of Him who called you out
> of darkness into His wonderful light (1 Pet. 2:9 NIV).

Peter was writing to Christians scattered across the Roman Empire. I'm pretty sure they didn't feel like a chosen people, a royal priesthood, a holy nation. They were being tortured for their faith. But despite their horrific circumstances, Peter reminded them of who they really were – of their royal purpose as God's chosen earthly ambassadors, and of how God had trained and equipped them for that role.

God doesn't call those who are qualified. He qualifies those He calls. And that's not just a cute sound bite (kudos to whoever coined it). It's the story of our lives. We're not expected to labor until someone says we're good enough. God declares us good enough – then we work *from* approval, not *for* approval. He bestows on us fantastic credentials, even when (especially when) things around us seem bleak, so we're fully equipped to spread His fame to a dark and desperate world.

God, remind me that I've already graduated.
Help me live each day as if I really believe
the things You've written on my résumé. Amen.

# Itinerary

> Take delight in the LORD, and He will give you
> your heart's desires. Commit everything you do
> to the LORD. Trust Him, and He will help you …
> The LORD directs the steps of the godly. He delights
> in every detail of their lives (Ps. 37:4-5, 23 NLT).

When I travel I like to keep it simple. Stay in the moment. Absorb the spirit of place. Fly by the seat of my pants.

But traveling through life is complicated. Or is it? What if we simply, habitually, prayed for God to give us His desires, each day, trusting Him to show us the next step? Wouldn't it make life *astronomically* simpler?

Start by praying: *God, what would please You?* He'll answer by fine-tuning the desires of your heart. He'll adjust your tone, your reactions, your choice of words, the current direction in which your decisions are taking you – if any of those things are dishonoring to Him.

The psalmist tells us that God delights in the details of our lives. He directs every step. There's nothing vague about God's itinerary for your life. Ask Him to lay His desires on your heart – then pay attention. What are you *passionate* about, and *good* at? Which ideas haven't gone away? Which situations or encounters clarify your values? How are you pressing on to take hold of that for which Christ Jesus took hold of you (Philippians 3:12)?

What's the next step, Lord? Amen.

# Equations

The thief comes only to steal and kill and destroy.
I came that they may have life and have it
abundantly (John 10:10 ESV).

*L*ast month's devotions focused on our *identity*, and *purpose* is a spinoff of that. If we had to make an identity equation, it might look like this:

*Acceptance + Abundance = Identity*

By that I mean: when we take hold of the truth that we're entirely *accepted* by God – based on nothing we've done to deserve that acceptance but on His love and power alone – and when we've realized that Jesus came to bring us not just life but life in *abundance* and when we've gratefully received that life – we come into a whole new sense of being. A whole new awareness of *identity*.

Once you've owned who you are, and Whose you are, you'll be done striving for belonging and affirmation and purpose. You can get busy doing what God has called you to do. In fact, the *what* becomes clearer when you've settled the *who*. It all begins to add up.

Father, thank You that knowing *who* I am (Yours!)
is so often the obvious and immediate clue to
discovering *what* I should be doing with my life. Amen.

# Noise

> Whoever belongs to God hears
> what God says … (John 8:47 NIV).

Train platform announcements and airport terminal last-calls are notoriously indecipherable. *'This is the final call for passenger hwah-hwah-hwah. Please board at Gate shweh-shweh …'* The information we need most is often a blur of sound or static.

Fathoming our purpose and hearing God's voice in a noisy world can feel just the same. I know I've definitely – more than once – felt lost, alone and bewildered, and you probably have too.

Maybe the thing is to keep still for a bit. Anxiously – recklessly – running between platforms or boarding gates can heighten the hysteria and confusion. Keep from frantically asking, 'Where am I now? Where have I landed? Where am I going? Where am I supposed to be? And where are the bathrooms?' Rather say, 'Lord, I'm here. Find me.' And trust that the ultimate tour guide and the most efficient airport security personnel officer – Jesus – will make His way through the throngs and do just that.

> Good Shepherd, I have no idea where I am. Please meet
> me right here, and take me where I need to be. Amen.

# Purpose precision

> In His grace, God has given us different gifts
> for doing certain things well … (Rom. 12:6 NLT).

As you commit to living out God's you-plan, ask Him to give you wisdom and clarity around your gifts. You're not doing yourself or the world a favor if you're delusional about what you can and can't do, and do well.

That said, He has gifted you uniquely and distinctively, and He has planned since eternity past where, when and how He'll use you: your sensitivity, your razor-sharp creativity, your scintillating personality, or whatever it is you have to offer the world. So ask Him to confirm where, when and how you can position yourself in sweet spots of maximum efficacy.

Next: ask God to help you recognize the lies of the enemy – limiting beliefs you've picked up on your life-travels and added to your baggage. There will always be opposition to your purpose. It's one of the things that makes uncovering it a kind of daring quest. Renowned painter Vincent van Gogh said, 'If you hear a voice within you say, "You cannot paint," then by all means paint, and that voice will be silenced.'

Lord, You're a God of detail and specifics. You don't deal in generics. I trust You to protect me from contesters to my destiny, and to lead me into my precise purpose. Amen.

# Purpose versus perfection

Now all glory to God, who is able, through His
mighty power at work within us, to accomplish infinitely
more than we might ask or think (Eph. 3:20 NLT).

*I*f you're a perfectionist (takes one to know one), please don't
let yourself get in your own way to finding and fulfilling your
purpose. Moses, Elijah, David, Rahab and a bunch of others – they
were all flawed humans who offered all of their imperfect selves. They
just mucked in and followed God regardless.

Living deep and wide into God's purposes for us – walking to the
borders of our inheritance – welcoming the abundant life designed
for us – all of that ushers in wondrous contentment and fulfillment.
But to get to that most satisfying place, we're going to have to get
over ourselves and our impossible personal standards. We're going
to have to get over what others think of us. We're going to have to
get over our Imposter Syndrome that has us paranoid that we'll be
found out – that the world will finally cotton on to the fact that we're
frauds because we're not as perfect as we present ourselves to be.

We will always be broken vessels. But God is strong in us, able to
do immeasurably more than we ask or think, and able to lead us into
His purposes for our lives.

God, this is all of imperfect me,
leaning into all of Your perfect purpose. Amen.

# Final word

> … for it is God who works in you to will and to act
> in order to fulfill His good purpose (Phil. 2:13 NIV).

When you don't get the affirmation, affection, admiration or acceptance from others that you long for – the warm fuzzy feelings that (you think) will confirm your calling – you don't actually have the right to sulk, or doubt. Silence or rejection from others, or having your efforts disregarded or misconstrued – these are not necessarily indications of what is or isn't your purpose.

Firstly, you don't know what's happening in the world of the person to whom you're looking for feedback or verification. Secondly, what you feel (uncertainty, or fear of failure or dismissal) is just that – a *feeling*. And emotions don't actually change the facts about you or your circumstances – or your calling.

Other people's responses can be insightful, and even an indication of the direction we should pick. Just remember: you're fulfilling God's purpose in *your* life – not in the lives of the people commenting or criticizing. Have your trusted advisors who will tell you the truth, then go with your gut. Go with what you know God is prompting you to do. He drew up the plans for your life, and He gets to have the final word.

Jesus, keep me and anyone else from finishing Your sentences. When it comes to my purpose, please have the last say. Amen.

# Purposeful failure

> The godly may trip seven times, but they
> will get up again. But one disaster is enough
> to overthrow the wicked (Prov. 24:16 NLT).

We all know failure is inevitable. More than that, failure is so often the path to your greatest success as a purpose-hunter. Seth Godin says, 'If I fail more than you do, I win.' In other words, if you're failing a whole bunch more than someone else, maybe you're learning and growing and fine-tuning the coordinates of your direction far more effectively.

The key to using failure as a means of moving forward in the present moment – as opposed to wallowing in the past, which helps no one – is to do a few don'ts. *Don't* ask, 'Why me?' *Don't* look for sympathy and *don't* indefinitely keep on accepting condolences from others. *Don't* blame, and *don't* complain.

Even in the midst of horrid, embarrassing, egg-on-face failure, try to call to mind the truth that we have a hope that does not disappoint (Romans 5:5), and we have a God who causes all things to work together for our good (Romans 8:28). Even failure.

Father, thank You that I can offload the baggage
of my mess-ups. Thank You that You will use even
these failures to fulfill Your purposes for me. Amen.

# Excuse or epic?

Even though the fig trees have no blossoms,
and there are no grapes on the vines; even though
the olive crop fails, and the fields lie empty and barren;
even though the flocks die in the fields, and the cattle
barns are empty, yet I will rejoice in the LORD! I will be
joyful in the God of my salvation! (Hab. 3:17-18 NLT).

My son once came home from school prattling unfazed about a class birthday party. There weren't enough party packs to go around, and so he didn't get one.

I was mad. Why *him*? Why should *he* have gone without? I asked him later if he was *really* ok with how things had gone down. I asked, 'So, why do you think you were the kid who didn't get a party pack?' And he said, 'Well, Mom. If not me, why another kid?'

I was pretty impressed by his powerful reminder that the people in the world doing the things that really matter seldom have time to complain about how unfair things are. Mariane Pearl was right on the money when she said that self-pity, even when legitimate, never fails to undermine your strength.

God, help me remember that whatever I'm living –
fair or unfair – I can make it my excuse, or I can
make it a glory story worth reading. Amen.

# Big picture travel

Where there is no vision,
the people perish … (Prov. 29:18 NKJV).

*I*t's possible you're struggling to see a way forward. Perhaps you feel desperate, and strength-sapped. You can't quite see a way to launch yourself effectively into the riptides and rigors of real life.

Traveling with big picture perspective may give you the vision you need. Keep the big picture stuck up on the bathroom mirror of your mental landscape and glance at it every day.

Get perspective on where you are. For example, the parenting season you're in may feel unending and all-consuming. But very, very soon, it will be over. You've still got a huge chunk of life to live post-sleep-training, post-homework, post-Friday-night-youth-group-angst.

Get perspective on legacy. You're leaving one. Get perspective on your journey, and your kids' journeys. A decade or so from now, you're hoping they'll be confident, content grownups who love God and others. Pray big prayers and dream big dreams with that in mind.

Lord God, don't let me lose sight of the big picture, and my small place in the world, so I can keep on traveling light. Amen.

# Small picture travel

> They have made God's law their own, so they
> will never slip from His path (Ps. 37:31 NLT).

As much as travel gives you perspective, it also helps you to be in the moment. It heightens your sense of wonder and awareness of immediate flavors and fragrances. It helps you notice the small. And if we're actually all lifetime travelers, shouldn't we live with that kind of *small* picture perspective too?

Small picture travel is about proximity. *Nearness.* Small picture travel-through-time helps me remember, for example, that when my boys ask me to play soccer and I snap at them – *Not now!* – that's all they see. They see a small picture of what's happening in my day. They haven't just read the email with news that sent my head spinning. All they experience is the *Not now!* Sure, life happens and they'll learn that I can't always drop everything for soccer, but I want to get better at bending low and close, to explain that.

Small picture travel is deep-breath slow-down grace-for-today living. It's responding instead of reacting. It's about routine and spontaneous non-routine, in the small spaces of ordinary life, remembering that routine isn't boring; it's calming. And occasional *change* in routine isn't unsettling; it's stimulating. Noticing the little moments in each day will help us manage a healthy balance of both.

God, let the momentum of my small picture
decisions steer my ship towards big picture shores. Amen.

# Every masterpiece you meet

For we are God's masterpiece. He has created
us anew in Christ Jesus, so we can do the good
things He planned for us long ago (Eph. 2:10 NLT).

At bedtime one night, our eldest (who is visually impaired),
cried because his magnifier is too big for his school desk. He
wishes his books were *normal* like everyone else's and he wishes he
was just *normal* like everyone else. Our youngest (who is not visually
impaired) cried because he wishes he could also have fancy magnifiers
to supersize his homework.

It's all *so unfair*, they said, and I was all out of ideas.

Then a movie line surfaced in my mind: *'You can't blend in when
you were born to stand out.'* Every masterpiece is created to stand out.
That's what separates masterpieces from factory generics churned
out in bulk. And God calls *each one of us* His masterpiece. We all feel
the pain of the chisel chipping away to make us beautiful. We feel the
pain in different places, in different ways. Plato nailed it when he said
we should always be kind, because every person we meet – every
*masterpiece* we meet – is fighting a hard battle.

So here's to daily kindness to our kids, our colleagues, ourselves –
as we allow the Master to do His wise work.

Maker of every masterpiece, make me brave to
stand out for You, however You choose to
display Your workmanship. Amen.

# Purpose in people

Carry each other's burdens … (Gal. 6:2 NIV).

*I* once got a migraine and passed out at my kids' school swimming gala. I don't remember much, except that it was unbelievably humiliating. I do remember hearing faraway voices. Voices looking for my car keys so someone could drive me home. It was so embarrassing. And I was so thankful. I remember thinking, *You can't do a thing on your own. You desperately need these people. Take that, ego!* So later when a friend texted to say she was having pizza delivered to us for supper I swallowed the last of my pride and said, 'Thank you!'

I can crush a to-do list. But when I'm pinned down by pain my list doesn't matter. Incapacity distills importance. I don't think, *Must phone the guy about the dishwasher!* Or even, *Must achieve my great life's work!* I think, *Are my kids safe? Ok cool. I can die now.*

This was just a migraine. No one was dying. But I sometimes look at my dreams and to-dos and think, *If I die tonight, none of this will matter much. What matters more is that I'm at peace with everyone* (Romans 12:18), *and everyone I love most, knows it.* We can't achieve our purpose in isolation. No matter what we're getting right, without right relationships, so-called success is empty.

God, give me right perspectives on
my purpose, and my people. Amen.

# No pride in purpose

John replied, 'No one can receive anything
unless God gives it from heaven' (John 3:27 NLT).

Words are my thing. My bread and butter. My soul oxygen. But when I get a bad migraine, I lose my words. It's terrifying. I can't say people's names. I don't even *know* people's names. I have to think and think and *think* and *fight* to get the sounds out and they sound wrong. (Like, *Really? That sounds weird. Are those my kids' names?*)

In the aftermath of one such skull-crushing migraine, I felt God say – *I give you all the words.*

And there it was. The acute awareness that not one of us has anything we did not receive (1 Corinthians 4:7). If we forget Who our gifts are from and Who they're for, we can too quickly start operating out of our natural abilities and not from God's anointing – His will, His way, in His strength, and for His glory.

This is possibly why church history is littered with brilliant preachers who lose the plot. Dynamic communicators clever enough to come up with inspiring ideas, riding a wave of their own making. We all know those waves crash on the beach. In Normandy. On D-Day. And no matter what our strengths, none of us is above getting shot down in the waves of our delusional invincibility.

Jesus, keep me from getting
proud about my purpose. Amen.

# Meaning and magnitude

Instead, God chose things the world considers
foolish in order to shame those who think they
are wise. And He chose things that are powerless
to shame those who are powerful (1 Cor. 1:27 NLT).

What looks impressive to the world isn't always impressive to God. And what looks insignificant and inconsequential to the world might be of staggering eternal value – or not. The difference hinges on the heart.

We can be simultaneously humbled and comforted by an understanding that, whether we're holding a microphone on a stage before thousands, or whether we're holding a spade on the lawn to scoop up dog deposits, in both scenarios we're wearing His royal robes. Both undertakings can and should be of equal eternal significance. Because we can and should be doing both with a heart bent on honoring only Him.

So, whether we're doing what we do from a stage or the back lawn or behind closed doors, if we're doing it with selfish, egotistical motives – or bitter, cynical mumblings – it's not pleasing to God. Similarly, if we're doing what we do as a love offering to God – an act of worship with Him at the center and us on the periphery – then whether it's done before millions or only One, the impact and importance are eternal.

Father, help me purpose my every feat –
viral or invisible – to magnify Your splendor. Amen.

# Small life, big purpose

Only let each person lead the life that the Lord has assigned to him, and to which God has called him (1 Cor. 7:17 ESV).

*I*'ve volunteered at a few big Christian conferences. Once I was peeling barcode stickers off pot plant holders in the speakers' green room. The next day, Tim Tebow, Robert Madu, the Hillsong band and others would be using the room before and after their sessions. I wondered if any of these celebrities would really notice or care if the price tags were still on the pot plants.

It struck me that as much as I admired the work and influence of these people, they were no more or less important to God than the other barcode-sticker-peeling people filling the room with me now – the other volunteers chatting about their kids, or battling singleness, or offering an encouraging word for me or others, or laughing at YouTube clips.

It struck me that all the ground is holy ground when we're living between God's presence and wherever He has us standing on planet earth. Whether we're holding the microphone or the mop, we each have a story to tell of God's changing grace. We each have a platform to proclaim His goodness.

God, help me see the small spaces of my small
life as big opportunities to spread Your fame. Amen.

# Surrender

Now may the God of peace – who brought up from the dead our Lord Jesus, the great Shepherd of the sheep, and ratified an eternal covenant with His blood – may He equip you with all you need for doing His will. May He produce in you, through the power of Jesus Christ, every good thing that is pleasing to Him. All glory to Him forever and ever! Amen (Heb. 13:20-21 NLT).

When we decide to hitch our destinies to Jesus – surrendering wholly to God – we surrender our ambitions too. We surrender our big ideas about our purpose. We choose to align our lives with *God's* purposes in and through us – happily letting go of what we think that should look like.

That all sounds easier than it really is, am I right? But if we really trust Him – if we believe He is who He says He is and that He loves us, protects us, never leaves us nor forsakes us – then we have to be ok to submit ourselves daily – maybe hourly – maybe again five minutes from now – to His best plans and purposes. It's His Kingdom after all. He made us – and He made us His heirs. It makes sense that He would know better than us how best we can be used.

Father and Creator, I've got a bunch of pictures in my head of what I think You should do with my life. But I'm happy to go with Your designs. Amen.

# Spit it out

Confess your sins to each other and pray for
each other so that you may be healed. The earnest
prayer of a righteous person has great power
and produces wonderful results (James 5:16 NLT).

We'll never be operating in our full, fantastic purpose if there's unconfessed sin in our lives. And sin has a way of showing up, no matter how well we think we're hiding it. The people around you might not know exactly *what's* going on, but for sure they know *something's* going on. Hiding and hanging on to sin has us living with a limp.

It might be the hardest thing for you to submit to the accountability of trusted travel companions. It might take the last shreds of your courage. But don't ever deceive yourself into thinking you don't need the checks and balances of authority and accountability to lead you into your purpose. The truth comes out – somewhere, somehow, sometime. *Every* time. Maybe it's wise to fear the consequences of concealment more than we fear the consequences of confession.

As difficult and awkward as confession will probably be, don't put it off for another day. Come clean. You'll be so grateful you did, and you'll find yourself traveling light.

Father God, it's Your kindness that leads
me to repentance. Give me the courage to
confess my sin and the assurance of Your
absolute absolution. Amen.

# Purpose with humble pie

Not to us, O LORD, not to us, but to Your name goes all the glory for Your unfailing love and faithfulness (Ps. 115:1 NLT).

When we make our endeavors all about ourselves, we'll either experience tremendous performance pressure and self-consciousness, or we'll be arrogant and self-centered. Either way, not pretty.

Thank God there's another option. Adopting a not-about-me approach frees us to *relish* our purpose with ease because we're handing over any results or accolades to the God who initiated our purpose and set us up to walk in it. Our purpose is far more satisfying – and attractive to a watching world – when we serve it with a slice of humble pie.

Humility always seems to usher in remarkable expressions of God's might and magnitude. His cosmic strength is available to us when we're willing to open our hearts and our hands, allow others to see our weaknesses, and admit that we need God to come through for us.

Father, forgive me for all the times I've allowed my purpose to go to my head. Keep me humbly, happily, depending on You to do in me and through me all that You've planned. Amen.

# Only you

In His grace, God has given us different gifts for doing certain things well. So if God has given you the ability to prophesy, speak out with as much faith as God has given you. If your gift is serving others, serve them well. If you are a teacher, teach well. If your gift is to encourage others, be encouraging. If it is giving, give generously. If God has given you leadership ability, take the responsibility seriously. And if you have a gift for showing kindness to others, do it gladly (Rom. 12:6-8 NLT).

*Only you* can be the mom of your kids or the wife of your husband. *Only you* occupy the you-shaped space in your broader family or community.

Andy Stanley would tell you not to give up the jobs that *only you can do*. Prioritize the roles that only you are called to fulfill, because part of your purpose on the planet is to complete those unique assignments. After all, Jesus promised to build His church; He didn't promise to parent your kids.

Without being unnecessarily morbid, consider the parts of your purpose that will *really matter* one day when you're nearing death and eternity. Then make sure you're investing intentionally in those things.

Jesus, keep me from being distracted by things that aren't part of my purpose. Show me how to do what only I can do. Amen.

# Strengths on purpose

They are to do good, to be rich in good works, to be generous and ready to share … (1 Tim. 6:18 ESV).

When my son came home from school with a note about astronaut dress-up day, I broke out in the cold sweat of horrifying insecurities. Because there's nothing like a badly aluminum-foiled bike helmet to expose that you're a rubbish mom when it comes to artsy-craftsy days.

I was reluctant to spend money on an outfit I'd get sadly wrong anyway. We scrounged for anything vaguely astronaut-ish – like silver spray paint and plastic pipes. Not exactly the stuff of NASA.

But mediocre astronaut outfit aside, I realized it's not a bad thing for my kids to know my limitations. No mom is perfect. Not even the perfect ones. And it's a good thing for our kids to learn that no human can possibly fill all their gaps, or endow them with identity or security.

We all have our weaknesses, idiosyncrasies and ill-managed strengths. And we all have stuff that makes us awesome image-bearers of our Creator-King. Let's be women who generously give the next generation the benefit of our strengths, trusting God to temper our course when we buckle beneath failings. Let's live the truth that people are for loving and leaning on. But only Jesus meets our whole soul needs. Only Jesus is our hope.

God, I surrender my weaknesses,
and celebrate my strengths. Amen.

# Knee time

Never stop praying (1 Thess. 5:17 NLT).

*I*f you're keen to figure out your purpose, there's no substitute for prayer.

Sometimes the circumstances will be telling you one thing – like, *Stay!* Or, *Go!* – but when you get on your knees, God says the opposite. I know for sure that if I react to circumstances without quieting myself in prayer and waiting for the still small voice of the Father, I mess up.

Sometimes we also seek God's hand, when He longs for us to seek His face. We want to see Him act within our circumstances – we want Him to confirm our purpose in some tangible, measurable way – when He's inviting us into intimacy with Him so that we can hear His heart.

Don't put off time alone with the King – even if – especially if – you're a little bit afraid of what He might say. He only ever seeks your good and His glory. Trust Him. And let the words of Gene Edwards comfort you: 'Beginning empty handed and alone frightens the best of men. It also speaks volumes of just how sure they are that God is with them.'

Father, draw me into calm and constant
conversations with You. Amen.

# Extraordinary purpose

Trust in the LORD with all your heart; do not depend on your own understanding. Seek His will in all you do, and He will show you which path to take (Prov. 3:5-6 NLT).

We all have days when we want to know how the story ends. We want to know if everything's going to be ok. We want to know if we've heard right – if this really is the purpose – the calling – the life's work we should be pursuing.

Of course, if we knew the outcome of our quiet convictions and brave public decisions – they wouldn't take courage. Knowing the end of the story doesn't take courage. Knowing the end of the story just informs our common sense and we act accordingly. The catalyst for living out an extraordinary purpose is often one act of courage. It may not be a *glamorous* act of courage, but it will be *defining*.

It also might be nothing more than a slight change in posture or trajectory – a slight change that takes tremendous faith in the moment, and will likely put your life on a whole new extraordinary course.

God, I don't want to look back and wonder what
You might have done if I'd been brave enough to
step into the purpose I knew You were calling me into.
Help me see extraordinary opportunities. Give me the
courage to take them, so that I can live regret-free. Amen.

# MARCH

## Home Comforts

Every dreamer knows that
it is entirely possible to
be homesick for a place
you've never been to,
perhaps more homesick
than for familiar ground.

*Judith Thurman*

# Nearly home

> So be truly glad. There is wonderful
> joy ahead, even though you must endure
> many trials for a little while (1 Pet. 1:6 NLT).

There's nothing like the sight of the trail's end to strengthen the legs of even the most exhausted hiker. And knowing you've stopped to fill the gas tank for the last time on the long road trip suddenly makes everyone in the car a little more cheerful. Heading home puts hope in our hearts.

Making the most of our travels through this life is as simple as making the most of opportunities along the road. And what helps us maintain that positive, go-getter headspace is the comfort of knowing that every day that comes and goes is another day closer to finally getting home.

Adventurer and travel writer Dervla Murphy said, 'The further we travel, the less we find we need.' The further we walk with Jesus, the less invested we are in stuff and status. We're more satisfied by simplicity. We find it easier to prioritize. The more we know of the world to come, the less we need from the world we're in. So no matter how drab or spectacular the scenery is on this stretch of your journey, you can look happily ahead to the comforts of home.

Jesus, my compass is set for home, and I can't wait. Amen.

# With-strong

All praise to God, the Father of our Lord Jesus Christ.
God is our merciful Father and the source of all comfort.
He comforts us in all our troubles so that we can comfort
others. When they are troubled, we will be able to give them
the same comfort God has given us (2 Cor. 1:3-4 NLT).

The word *comfortable* doesn't mean *at ease*. It means *stronger*. Comfort doesn't say, *Oh you poor thing!* Comfort says, *You can do it!* Because the prefix *com* means *with*, and *fort* is from the Latin – *fortis* – meaning *strong*. So if you say to someone, *Can I comfort you?* You're saying, *Can I with-strong you?*

If you've lived a bit, you'll know anything worthwhile in life – a good education, a great marriage – will cost you some time, effort and emotional resources. Things that come easy – low-barrier achievements – also come cheap. So if you're aiming for some high-barrier achievements – if you've got big dreams and you need some *with-strong* – tune out the voices saying, *Whatever. Just Netflix and chill.* Listen for the voices saying, *I'm here for you! I know you can get it together and be extraordinary!*

Your kind and tender Father is the source of all comfort and He offers you that comfort without reserve. But He's urging you not just to ease your pain, but rather to seek His strength.

God of all comfort – with-strong me!
Use me to with-strong others. Amen.

# Small comfort

'Go with the strength you have, and rescue Israel from the Midianites. I am sending you!' (Judges 6:14 NLT).

There'll be days when you wake up thinking, *I don't have the strength to get out of bed, never mind make it through the day.* You'll probably be right. You don't have enough strength to make it through the day. *But you've got a little bit of strength.*

When the angel of the Lord tells Gideon to defeat the Midianites, Gideon says, 'No way; I'm such a loser!' The angel calls him 'mighty hero' (Judges 6:12) – even though Gideon really is a bit of loser at this point. Then he *comforts* Gideon, saying, 'Go with the strength you have.'

He doesn't say, 'You've got lots of strength!' Because Gideon doesn't have lots of strength. But he's got a *little* bit. And he goes with that little bit of strength. He keeps on going with it. And he defeats the Midianites.

So there'll be days when you don't have lots of strength. *But you've got a little bit of strength.* Enough maybe to swing your legs over the bed. Walk to the kitchen. Flick on the coffee machine. Go with the strength you have. Keeps going with it. Five minutes at a time. Until you realize you've made it through the day after all.

God, here's the last bit of my strength.
Give me the courage to go with it. Amen.

# Comfortable with discomfort

… The news about His miracles had spread far
and wide, and vast numbers of people came to
see Him. Jesus instructed His disciples to have a boat
ready so the crowd would not crush Him. He had
healed many people that day, so all the sick people
eagerly pushed forward to touch Him (Mark 3:8-10 NLT).

It's tough to strike a balance between self-preservation and martyrdom.

Culture tends to say, *Look out for Number One! You can't love others until you've loved yourself! Be kind to yourself!* This insidious message creeps in through inspirational memes and friends who tell us what they know we want to hear. It sounds true enough. But it also smacks of selfishness.

The opposite is what happens to people in churches, schools, non-profits and families: total burnout from giving themselves over to worthy causes at the expense of all reason and wisdom.

Jesus got it right. He poured Himself out unreservedly for others. Then He rested. He wasn't ridiculous about His emotional energy expenditure. He never burned out – and never made out as if burnout was super spiritual. But He wasn't all about protecting Himself and His interests. He knew that He needed boundaries, margins and emergency escape boats, and He knew that love is seldom convenient. He lived well and wisely within that tension.

Jesus, show me when, where and how to expend
my time and energy, generously and wisely. Amen.

# Comfort gifts

Whatever is good and perfect comes down to us from God our Father … If one of you says to them, 'Go in peace; keep warm and well fed,' but does nothing about their physical needs, what good is it? (James 1:17, 2:16 NLT).

When someone arrives on your birthday with flowers or chocolate, you don't feel guilty, right? Even though you had nothing to do with being born on that particular day. You just receive the gift, gratefully.

Same-same with God's gifts to us, which we do *zilch* to earn. If you're reading this book, you probably live in a bubble of relative luxury billions on our planet will never experience. By global standards, it's unfair. You may think, *How can I be giving thanks for my morning latte, when others are starving?*

The gifts you're giving thanks for in your current reality – they're still *gifts* from a gracious God. Sure, you don't deserve them. Me neither. But we can give thanks for the moment we're in because it is what it is, and it's part of the sufficient grace God gives for each journey (2 Corinthians 12:9). Instead of feeling guilty – which paralyzes – let's turn compassion into conviction – which mobilizes, so we can do what we can with what we have, to bring help and healing – change and comfort.

Father, I praise You for Your lavish generosity.
Give me culture-shifting ideas for using
my resources to comfort others. Amen.

# Home baggage

We love each other because
He loved us first (1 John 4:19 NLT).

Much of the too-heavy emotional and relational baggage people carry has been collected in their homes. Whether you live oceans away from your family, in the same town, or in one another's pockets, it can be tricky to travel light with blood relatives, in-laws or extended family.

Humble yourself before God. And get honest. As much as you need to make space for someone's jagged edges, don't forget that you're also a broken bit of the family mosaic, and people are making space for you too.

It's worth remembering that God grows each nucleus family more and more into its own unique entity. It's beautiful and good. It's His way of decorating the bigger family tree – extending its branches to cast shade for generations to come.

It's also worth remembering that you're free. You can't choose your family, sure. But you're free to choose to be *part* of a family. You're free to participate. And if things don't roll your way, don't surrender your happiness to the situation. Be clear on non-negotiable boundaries. But every now and then, be the bigger person by offering a little finger, and letting the family take your whole arm.

God, I don't want to miss out on tremendous
family blessings. Give me grace and great love for
the tapestry of lives You've sewn me into. Amen.

# Comforting questions

So whatever you wish that others would
do to you, do also to them … (Matt. 7:12 ESV).

Bad questions put us on the spot. They're awkward or confrontational or require a defense. So imagine we started comforting our co-workers, kids or others in our care by asking questions differently.

Maybe we shouldn't ask little people, 'What do you want to be when you're big?' Because if we get kids to pin their hopes on an astronaut or marine biologist, we set them up to ask themselves follow-up fear-loaded questions like, 'Do I have what it takes? What if I'm not enough?' Instead we might ask, 'What do you think you're made for?' This reminds our kids – and their grownups – that there's already something in them they were born for. They can be confident and content, because they're already enough.

Shame-heaping rhetorical questions – 'I hope you're never going to do *that* again?' – don't comfort either. I'd definitely respond better to someone asking me, 'How could you have handled that differently?'

Try asking your people, 'In a perfect world, what would you do with today?' Then work backwards from that, factoring in imperfections, non-negotiable obligations and circumstances beyond your control. Re-nuancing our questions might be all it takes to comfort, instead of condemning.

Father, infuse me with Your kindness.
Help me to ask gentle questions
that lead to life. Amen.

# Vibes

> If it is possible, as far as it depends on you,
> live at peace with everyone (Rom. 12:18 NIV).

**M**any of us women are fixers, are we not? We register and absorb all the vibes in a room and we try to manage and solve the emotions of all around us. This can be a wonderful, healing relational quality, and it can be futile, frustrating and exhausting.

If someone in your family or office space is having a bad day, ask yourself, 'Did I in any way cause this? Where am I at fault?' If you're convicted that you're the cause of some hurt, ask forgiveness, quickly and sincerely.

If you're not at fault, ask yourself, 'Can I do anything to help this person out of their anger or self-pity or emotional lethargy or lousy-mood funk?' Love and serve as best you can, within the realms of what's reasonable.

Then, if there's nothing you can do to turn their bad day into a good day, you may need to graciously leave them be. Don't hand over your happiness to someone else, or allow them to steal your joy.

God, make me like You: slow to anger and abounding in love and compassion! Also, give me wisdom to navigate other people's emotions. I don't want to carry baggage that doesn't belong to me. Amen.

# Immersion

> Each heart knows its own bitterness, and no
> one else can fully share its joy (Prov. 14:10 NLT).

When we travel, we only really have *our* perspective on a place or culture. And every traveler's perspective will be slightly different.

When your travels through time take you to places like an abrasive boss, a sullen shop assistant, an indifferent or openly antagonistic family member – try to remember that you only have *your* perspective on this place you've landed. You don't know fully or exactly what battles your friends, colleagues, or even your kids are fighting. Happily, Jesus is immersed in their worlds, just as He is immersed in yours. Try to greet their negativity the way Jesus would: slow to anger, abounding in love (Psalm 103:8).

The best way to learn a foreign language is through immersion: plunging yourself into the place where that language is spoken, until you learn to swim. Do what you can to immerse yourself in people's pain or preferences, so you can learn the language of their hearts, and bring real comfort.

Lord, give me more than just my limited take on things. Help me see as You see – hear as You hear – and love as You love. Amen.

# Clean comfort

She looks well to the ways
of her household … (Prov. 31:27 ESV).

*I* f we believe that everything is spiritual because 'in Him we live and move and have our being' (Acts 17:28), then that includes how clean or how dirty our homes are. But one state of hygiene isn't necessarily holier than the other, so don't get proud if you're a Martha or feel condemned if you're a Mary (Luke 10).

Our highest priority is to love the people we live with, and it's up to us to figure out what it looks like to create homes that are safe spaces of peace. If love is not selfish, then I definitely can't always get my way. If I could, our home would be perpetually spotless and de-cluttered. Things also can't always be how my boys want them, or the floor would be wall-to-wall unwashed socks.

For others to be at peace (not pestered), you may need to make peace with their mess. Or, you may need to meet their mess (or your mess) head-on – turn it into minimalism – and make space for serenity.

God, give me wisdom to strike the right balance
between regulation and relaxation. Amen.

# Have sanitizer, will travel

> A wise woman builds her home, but a foolish woman
> tears it down with her own hands (Prov. 14:1 NLT).

*I* hate crumbs. Sometimes my boys are still eating their sandwiches and I'm lifting their plates to wipe the kitchen table. I'll always prefer the less-is-more of open spaces, and that's ok. The world needs tidy people *and* laissez-faire people, which is why God created both kinds of human and mostly gets us to marry each other.

Of course, minimalism needn't be clinical; it can be calming. But I know I need to recalibrate when my passion for simplicity and everything-in-its-place gets a little OTT. And OCD.

Wherever *you* find yourself on the home front, trust God to transform you, making you the maker of a home that's (mostly) clean and neat. Beautiful, within the bounds of practicality and imperfection. Doors wide open to anyone He brings.

Run a tight ship (Proverbs 31:27). Just know that when you're dead and gone, you won't want your kids to reminisce, 'Mom always dusted the piano keys! *We grew up clean!*' But rather, 'Mom let us bang out any old wild and tuneless composition. *We grew up free.*' Let's make sure people know that under our roofs there's good coffee, good conversation and comfort. That courage and compassion are valued more than clean counters.

Father, help me remember that
mess is sometimes just a sign of life,
because people live here. Amen.

# Travel mates

I am my lover's, and my lover is mine …
(Song of Solomon 6:3 NLT).

Marriage is a long, beautiful road to walk, and you'll want to be strong enough – as comfortable as possible – for the journey. Get comfortable by living well the tension of complementing each other: filling up with your strengths the gaps created by his weaknesses while never enabling him by constantly covering his tracks. And invite him to do the same.

To know the difference between comfort and co-dependence, in any given situation, ask yourself:

*Is my husband sinning? Do I need to call him out on this thing, because he's better than this and I have the inside track on his life and if I don't hold him accountable, who will?*

*Or, is it that he's just not particularly organized and it helps him if I get stuck in to help, or I'm extra insightful in this particular area and I know he'd appreciate my input?*

To travel far and comfortably in marriage, regularly replenish your own soul. Restore healthy respect for your husband and relinquish inappropriate control. You're not reducing yourself – just loving your man humbly, as you'd expect him to love you.

Jesus, I pray we'd make each other
better and better versions of ourselves. Amen.

# Clothes and close comfort

And the LORD God made clothing from animal
skins for Adam and his wife (Gen. 3:21 NLT).

*A* friend confessed to me once that she was teaching a Sunday
school class when God crashed right into her world. She was
telling the kids how Adam and Eve hid from God because they were
ashamed. 'But that's exactly what I do with my husband,' she told me.
'I hide from him. There are dishes in the sink from three days ago; he's
washing them and I'm failing at this wife thing and I'm ashamed. So
I hide.'

She went on to say that that's not how her husband sees it at all.
He doesn't want her withdrawal (or her dishwashing). *He wants her
drawing close.* God's great grace was that He *made clothes* for Adam
and Eve. He didn't leave them naked and ashamed. He didn't leave
them hiding. He set in motion the plan already in place to send His
Son – not just to cover their shame, but to draw us all back close and
make us holy.

Father, thank You for covering me completely. Help me
to show up and show myself, to love and be loved. Amen.

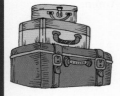

# Comfortable exclusivity

Know that the LORD has set apart His faithful servant for Himself; the LORD hears when I call to Him (Ps. 4:3 NIV).

The word *holy* means *cut out of a template. Framed for a specific purpose.* It means *different* or *distinguished* or *distinct from*. It means *set apart*. Setting ourselves apart – aligning our lives with Jesus because of how He drew us close – that makes us holy, even though we're still wholly damaged and deficient.

Whether or not you get it all right all the time as a wife, you're still a *holy* wife, because you're set apart exclusively for your man. No shame in that. And whether or not you get it all right all the time as a mom, friend, boss, co-worker or volunteer team member, if you're called to those roles, then God has set you apart to fulfill them as part of your life's work and you can steward and enjoy them as holy tasks.

Lord God, strengthen me to do the things
You've set me apart to do, and do them well. Amen.

# Comfortable kindness

> Instead, be kind to each other, tenderhearted,
> forgiving one another, just as God through
> Christ has forgiven you (Eph. 4:32 NLT).

*I*'ve asked my boys about the best girls in their class at school – the nicest girls – the ones they're chuffed to sit next to if the teacher moves the desks around. I ask them, 'What makes her the best girl?' The answer is not, 'She's so pretty,' or 'She's so smart,' or 'She's so thin,' or 'She's so *together*'. The answer, without fail, is: '*She's so kind.*'

Researchers into what your husband really wants from you have uncovered that, shockingly, he doesn't want you to iron his socks or fetch his slippers. He doesn't want a maid or a golden retriever. Really, he just wants you to be nice to him, and nice to the kids.

Your husband married his *best friend*. His *girlfriend*. *You.* Try not to hide behind the crazy and the kids. Try letting the to-do list get a little longer, and just be that girl.

> Father, help me to keep a soft heart towards
> my man. Give me fantastic ideas of ways I can show
> pure, unadulterated kindness, every day. Amen.

# Travel in between

It was also called Mizpah, because he said,
'May the LORD keep watch between you and me
when we are away from each other' (Gen. 31:49 NIV).

*E*leven nights is too long to sleep on different continents,' I told my husband when I was 13553 km away from him. We'd been voice-noting and video-calling and doing our best to keep in step with out-of-step time zones and I was praying on repeat Laban's prayer: *May the Lord watch between us when we're apart.*

Because not one of us – unwatchful – is above the slow sad drift or devastating implosion of a marriage. And maybe watching – and trusting God to watch for us – looks like this:

Don't stop looking into each other's eyes. Because eyes stay the same. The eyes you fell in love with will be the same eyes wrinkle-hugged one day in the face of your aging soul-mate. Look deep into those eyes, and remember.

And do the hard work of soft hearts. Sure, have date nights, have a budget, do random acts of kindness and sexiness. But what makes a marriage work isn't paying accounts on time. (Though it helps.) It's doing the prayerful hard graft of loosening heart soil, to keep resentment at bay.

Maker of marriage, keep us close – soft heart connected to soft heart. And watch between us when we're traveling apart. Amen.

# Still traveling

> And I am certain that God, who began the good work within you, will continue His work until it is finally finished on the day when Christ Jesus returns (Phil. 1:6 NLT).

*Y*ou might have heard people tell you their marriage is over. You might have said it yourself.

Please don't give the enemy an inch (Ephesians 4:27). This might sound lame, but when you know you guys are going to be spending time apart from each other – for business or travel – agree that you'll only uplift each other in conversations with others. That way, you're not making room for the subtle, socially acceptable spousal bad-mouthing that leads to bitterness.

And please – before you give up on your marriage – turn your eyes to the future. Love who your spouse is becoming. Paul assured the Philippians that God wasn't done, and that He would certainly finish what He was busy with in their lives. You're not perfect and neither is your spouse. But one day – yay! – all flaws and weird idiosyncrasies will be ironed out glorious because God has perfection planned for you both and how cool is that?

Do another day of life with your lover, knowing it marks a little more passing of the old. A little more ushering in of the new. A little more Jesus.

God, help me remember that I'm not all I should be – not all I *will* be – and neither is my man. Amen.

# Happiness comfort

… for each one should carry their
own load (Gal. 6:5 NIV).

*I*f your kids are still living at home, you'll know that you don't have much time. You're on the cusp of this one short parental season to love and lead them well. To master the slow steady transfer of life responsibility, from your hands into theirs.

Let's determine to grow kids who believe in their bones that we are responsible to love them, and with all our hearts, we will. But that *they are responsible for their happiness.*

They hold their own happy – as we do, ours – and they need to be sure they're not handing it around expecting others to hold it for them. It's too heavy – too unfair – to expect anyone else to haul it about and hand it back gift-wrapped.

That said, let's try to be fun to live with. Let's find adventure. Make moments. Wrestle entitlement to the ground and grin our victory in grateful, simple thanks. Let's pick experiences over things, character over comfort, and relationships over pretty much everything. Let's choose our own happy, hold onto it, and encourage our kids to do the same.

God, keep me from moping and blaming my misery on
others. Help me carry the happy load of my own contentment,
inspiring those around me to do the same. Amen.

# Decision comfort

Yes, each of us will give a personal
account to God (Rom. 14:12 NLT).

As much as children need to know they're responsible for their own happiness, they also need to know they're responsible for their decisions. Depending on how big your kids are, you may need to do your fair share of handholding for a while yet. But ultimately, it's all up to them. They're on their own journeys and there'll be grace enough.

It's up to us, however, to model integrity. Let's help them hear God's voice above the din of culture. Let's show them how to dig for truth beneath lies and assumptions. And at every twist and dip and hurdle and cliff, let's commit to calling out courage and wisdom from their supple, strengthening hearts.

I suspect it's going to get harder before it gets easier. I suspect that eye-rolling, door-slamming and disagreeing are in our mutual future. I suspect that we'll wonder every other day if parenting is supposed to be this hard. I suspect we're choosing the path of maximum resistance, and maximum reward. But I suspect we will all survive, and be so very glad.

Jesus, I hope and pray my kids and I
will be firm friends on the far side of
these parenting paths. I trust and believe
that though we wait for a late harvest,
it's true that *later is longer*. There'll be
time to feast on the fruits. Amen.

# Over and over comfort

But the Comforter, which is the Holy Ghost, whom the Father will send in My name, He shall teach you all things, and bring all things to your remembrance, whatsoever I have said unto you (John 14:26 KJV).

Some of the best parenting advice we were ever given was, *Figure out what your kids need to hear from you, in order to be shaped by acceptance, not rejection. Then, tell them ten times more than you think they need to hear it.*

As in, if you think you've told them enough? Tell them again. And then one more time. Depending on age, stage of life and temperament, our kids all need to hear different things. But your list might include:

*God loves you. God gifted you. God forgives you, and never forgets about you. God's plan for you is the best plan for you. You're brave and beautiful; handsome and smart. You have what it takes. You've worked so hard. I love you no matter what. I love spending time with you. I'm listening. I respect you (and your opinions, passions and aversions). I'm proud of you. I trust you to think and pray. I trust you to choose a good, kind attitude. I trust you to make a plan. It's so cool that everyone is different.*

God, help me live, love and parent so my kids never doubt Your comfort and acceptance, or mine. Amen.

# Doing family

Children are a gift from the Lord; they
are a reward from Him (Psalm 127:3 NLT).

No matter what kind of a family you were part of growing up –
and what kind of a family you're part of now – 'familying' can
feel like traveling nowhere slowly. Going in circles.

But sometimes there's a moment – a Saturday morning that
finds you all in the pool – or Wednesday morning breakfast hugs
even though the coffee's burnt – a small, unremarkable moment that
defines an on-purpose verb, *to family*.

*To family* means to do the over-and-over of slowly getting somewhere, sometimes by going in circles. We *family* when we keep on
making and remaking circles of mercy. When we keep on finding
each other – forgiving each other – no matter how many times we've
been annoyed or disillusioned. We *family* with the satisfaction that
each time we circle back to ordinary moments, by God's grace we
know and love each other a little more.

When we *start* a family, we have no idea what hangs in the balance.
We have no idea how big the future is, or how to *finish* a family well.
All we can really do is family in the *now* by keeping on choosing brave
over easy, remembering that there is always hope.

God, make our home calm, welcoming, warm
and safe – a refuge for rest and wrestling where
we can learn well how to family. Amen.

# Travel towards

> But I say, love your enemies! Pray for
> those who persecute you! (Matt. 5:44 NLT).

There's a time to travel in circles – to walk the same ways, wearing smooth relational paths of trust and comfort. And there's a time to walk the hard ground of discomfort where stones get in your shoes or you stub your toes, because sometimes we need to walk towards the people who irritate and offend us. The people who disagree with us, or who just *dis* us in general.

It may be time to be honest with ourselves about comfortable friend zones – admitting that the reason we won't step *out of* those zones or *away* from those zones, is fear. It can be terrifying to travel towards someone who is different from us or who threatens our sense of safety in some other way. But sometimes, taking a step towards the thing that scares us most is what changes the world.

Father God, help me see *humans* – not hostility. Help me see potential friends instead of likely foes. No matter how scary or uncomfortable things get, help me to love anyway. Amen.

# Comfy-pants friends

> You were cleansed from your sins when you obeyed the truth, so now you must show sincere love to each other as brothers and sisters. Love each other deeply with all your heart (1 Pet. 1:22 NLT).

*L*ots of proper grownups haven't got friendship totally figured out. Millions of words have been bled into best-selling books about friendship. That speaks of a gap in the market, and maybe a crisis of culture.

Self-preservation (and the high walls that go with it) is a global epidemic. At the same time, social media *tramples* walls, connecting us vast and shallow to thousands of people, and leaving us lonelier than ever.

So, we fill our lives to fill the void, ensuring we have dwindling capacity to take a real interest in anyone not directly connected to whatever we're chasing. Despite our flurries of activity and achievement, we're increasingly insular, and uncomfortable. Instead of being our imperfect, stretchy-pants selves, we squeeze into trendy skinny-jeans friendships that look good or impress others. We get hurt – and hurt others – when we dress up our friendships in what isn't completely honest, or comfortable, or true to ourselves. Let's be better than that: creating safe, breathable, lasting friendships.

Friend of friends, help me accurately assess my friendships: what I've loved and appreciated, what's helped and hurt. Amen.

# Golden rule travel

> Do to others as you would like
> them to do to you (Luke 6:31 NLT).

The golden rule – do for others as you'd have them do for you – is the most beautiful way to travel with friends.

Humility is friendship's secret sauce. It makes us brave to be vulnerable, to forgive and ask forgiveness, to ask for help and offer it. Your friends are made in God's image, not yours. They won't fit your cardboard cut-out. Get comfortable with loving their unique shape and size. Don't guilt-trip. Don't keep score. Friendship isn't a one-for-me-one-for-you competition.

Sometimes you'll need to say hard things that are hard to hear. Only say them if your friend is in danger, deception or denial. Don't begrudge your friend's success. Don't be jealous or threatened. Cheer and say wonderful things about her, to her face and behind her back.

Have tons of fun. Celebrate and respect your friend's temperament and strengths. Protect her dignity when her weaknesses are exposed.

You aren't responsible for your friend's happiness, and she isn't responsible for yours. But – carry each other's burdens any way you can. Be your friend's barista, life coach, prayer warrior, stand-up comedian. Let her know she can hand herself in like an unedited essay. Just read her. No red pen.

> Jesus, help me travel light alongside my friend,
> the way I need her to travel light alongside me. Amen.

# Sensitive traveler

> [Love] is not provoked, does not take into
> account a wrong suffered … (1 Cor. 13:5 NASB).

To be a travel companion without too much baggage, don't be over-sensitive. Yet sensitivity – being emotionally available – is what makes you a great friend. So, don't take things too personally, even while knowing that friendship is *very* personal. Lean on God for wisdom and discernment to strike a happy, uncomplicated balance.

Continually surrender your friendships to God, trusting Him to protect them. Ask Him to bring to mind friends you need to pray for or connect with. Invite. Include. Text. Reply. Show interest. Show up. Be happy with those who are happy, and weep with those who weep. (And eat cake with those who eat cake.)

Judge your friends on their good intentions. Judge yourself on your actions. Promise not to make promises unless you mean to keep them. Only say, 'We should have coffee!' if you totally mean it.

As time barrels on, one or both of you might start living at a different pace, or needing space. Agree that while life blows hot and cold, your hearts toward each other can stay consistently warm. Remember too that we're each the common denominator in all our relationships. If we keep tripping over the same things, they're probably our own feet.

> Lord, help me not to be too serious or intense – even
> as I go about loving my friends with serious intent.
> Amen.

# Winning bread

> Jesus replied, 'I am the bread of life. Whoever comes to Me will never be hungry again. Whoever believes in Me will never be thirsty' (John 6:35 NLT).

Times are tough. Not everyone's free to work their dream job. Maybe that's you? Maybe you're a hard worker willing to leverage all you are, for all you family is becoming. You're a nose-to-the-grindstoner who sacrifices pleasure, possessions and prestige in favor of car services, hockey sticks and weed-killer for the driveway.

God knows the time-money-energy ratio making up your capacity and how there always seems to be too little of at least two of those. And He's the loaves-and-fish miracle provider. You can trust Him to enlarge your heart to cope with all you carry, making a wise way where there seems to be none and pleasantly surprising you with pockets of down-time to reboot, and recalibrate your resolve to be faithful.

Please know with every breadwinning pay check, that Jesus is the bread of life. You're winning bread – and winning others over to Him through thousands of small heroic decisions that few will ever see or know about. You're an extraordinary reflection of Jesus and an extraordinary conduit of His glory.

Savior, I pray for grace to grease the wheels of the daily grind. Help me find the happy rhythm of relentlessly, courageously showing up day after boring ordinary day to do what needs doing. Amen.

✈

# Treading heights

He makes me as surefooted as a deer, enabling
me to stand on mountain heights (Ps. 18:33 NLT).

Whether you're a high-earner or an only-just-survivor, you'll need to challenge culture's lie that you live and then you die, and it would be cool to be comfortable in between. Whatever your financial reality, you can rise above the mediocrity of merely living for luxury.

Ask God to give you renewed excitement to create opportunities for a growing generation – a fresh vision of the future you're shaping and the legacy you're leaving. Trust Him to make good your tenacity to stay in the trenches and fight self-pity and self-preservation, temptation and resentment.

And try to see yourself the way God sees you: a fortress of integrity, protection and provision for those He's placed in your care. In the worry and drudgery of too much month at the end of the money, don't lose your sense of wonder or sense of humor. With every rude awakening of morning alarms wrenching you into new days, be assured the Sovereign Lord is your strength, making you as surefooted as a deer, able to tread upon the heights.

God, lift the shroud of pressure and panic.
Give me Your mantle of peace and perspective.
Settle my soul with Spirit-level equilibrium – so that
deep beneath surface noise and melee and even
helpful God-given adrenalin that gets the job done,
I'd be quiet. Content. Unshaken. Amen.

# Travel trajectory

So encourage each other and build each other up,
just as you are already doing (1 Thess. 5:11 NLT).

As you seek to comfort and be comforted by your people, allow *attitude* and *acceptance* to inform more of your thinking – at home, at work, with your husband, your BFF or your mom-in-law.

Because in every relationship – from inner circle besties to casual acquaintances – we're either focusing on someone's good qualities, or their bad qualities. We're definitely doing one or the other, consciously or not. Acceptance of others' failings, and an attitude realignment towards their fortes, could set those relationships on new and astonishing trajectories. It would be so rad if, in every interaction, we could pause and go, '*I wish this person well*.'

Also, if you're a Highly Sensitive Person (that's me), then you tend to take responsibility for other people's happiness. You internalize conflict. You over-analyze, trying to solve people. But, God places us in relationships, not so we can change others, but so He can change us into more of Him. It's not up to us to renovate people. It's up to us to be Jesus to them – so that when they bump up against us they find themselves in a place of peace.

Jesus, please give me Your attitude towards people,
and help me accept them the way You do. Amen.

# Hard truth comfort

Let your roots grow down into Him, and
let your lives be built on Him. Then your faith
will grow strong in the truth you were taught, and
you will overflow with thankfulness (Col. 2:7 NLT).

A shiny-happy attitude gets you far, but not far enough.
Acceptance brings a needed and beautiful balance. Sure, your
attitude determines your altitude; but acceptance gives you a very
necessary foundation.

I remember one family holiday when our partially sighted son saw
his disability with 20/20 vision. He sobbed his fury into our duvet
because he couldn't see the birds and the wildlife that fascinate him.
'What's the point,' he yelled, 'of just hearing them? What's the point
if everything's a blur!'

When he voices those hard truths, I got nothing. I'm all about
optimism but no amount of positive thinking changes his reality. And
maybe there are hard truths you just need to accept too? Because
the truth always sets us free, even the hard truth. There's something
freeing about the acceptance that unleashes the crucial catharsis of
legitimate grief.

Lord Jesus, help me see as you see.
I pray for peace, and the
grace to accept things that simply
need accepting. Amen.

# Comfortable to overcome

But thanks be to God! He gives us the victory
through our Lord Jesus Christ (1 Cor. 15:57 NIV).

*I* think it takes more faith to suffer well, than to believe God for miracles. It's fantastic, and necessary, to celebrate when God shows up in wondrous ways. But it's also a wonderful, honoring thing to pause, and celebrate the courage of those who overcome hardship – or *endure* hardships from which there's no earthly overcoming. It's also good to learn from them.

Overcomers give more than they get. They know that celebrating how someone else's light shines doesn't dim their own; it just showcases their generosity, humility and untarnished love. Overcomers celebrate others to pre-empt the jealousy, self-pity or disappointment they'll feel if they rely on circumstances to go their way. By giving more than they get, they make their own happy.

Overcomers don't give in; they get comfortable. An old overcomer's prayer reads: '*The longer I walk with You, Lord, I find I have no enemies: only Your gift of chisels etching me deep.*' Overcomers aren't shocked and offended by failure, exhaustion and setbacks. They learn to befriend their menacing mentors. They stop fearing agents of change and growth. They *get comfortable* with discomfort. Mostly, overcomers get comfortable in the arms of the Savior who suffered – and overcame.

Jesus, thank You for overcoming death, so I can
be an overcomer – in this life and the next. Amen.

# Uncomplicated

No, dear brothers and sisters, I have not achieved it,
but I focus on this one thing: Forgetting the past and
looking forward to what lies ahead, I press on to reach the
end of the race and receive the heavenly prize for which
God, through Christ Jesus, is calling us (Phil. 3:13-14 NLT).

Following Jesus isn't always easy, but it's simple. It's as simple as forgetting what lies behind and striving for what lies ahead.

Allow the Holy Spirit to comfort you with the thought that, growing a home or a family is much the same. It's hard work. But if we drill down to the essentials of why we're doing it, it's not complicated. We want our parents, siblings, spouses and kids to remember us not so much for our opinions or our sense of orderliness. We want them to remember us for how we loved. Within the comfort and context of our homes, we want to make sure the roots of love go deep, so that the branches of significance and influence can go wide.

There's uncomplicated comfort and increased capacity for us and our people in the simplicity of a life surrendered to, and strengthened by, our Savior and King.

Lord, remind me that my purpose isn't found in a *what*
but in a *Who* – You! I want to keep on simply striving to
lay hold of that for which You laid hold of me. Amen.

# APRIL

## Sleeping Under Stars

Philosophers can debate the meaning of life, but you need a Lord who can declare the meaning of life.

*Max Lucado*

# Great wide open

And God is able to bless you abundantly, so that in all things at all times, having all that you need, you will abound in every good work (2 Cor. 9:8 NIV).

As you look back over the past few months, I hope you've been reminded and reassured that your identity is settled and secure in Jesus; God is beckoning you into a life of significance and purpose; and He is your comforter – your strength-giver.

This month, the challenge is to carry our renewed strength beyond our safety zones and into the realm of adventure. I'm asking God to loosen us where we're stuck in the ruts of fear or apathy or small thinking.

Let's get out from under what's safe and un-challenging, and get perspective. Whether it's the beach, the mountains, the bush or your backyard – there's something about being out of, and away from, routines and obligations – something about having nothing hanging over you other than the sky. Let's agree to rest, and regroup – and risk. Because getting out and away – really moving beyond our comfort zones – reminds us to live with a sense of intrepid heroism.

God, lead me into a spacious place where I can welcome with arms wide open, the great wide open of an adventure with You. Amen.

# Make the most

Make the most of every opportunity … (Eph. 5:16 NLT).

As a traveler, I've done things I wouldn't do at home. I've slept on train platforms and airport floors and beaches and benches. I've eaten things I wouldn't normally eat and spoken to people I wouldn't normally speak to.

As a traveler, there's footloose freedom to determine that everything is beautiful and worthy of *wow*. I'm more willing to risk, more willing to engage with strangers. There's less to lose. I'm aware that I have a limited time with this person – or in this place – and so I maximize more than usual, with heightened senses.

How might it change our lives – and change the world – if we lived *every day* as if we were travelers in a foreign country? Because actually – no matter where we find ourselves on the planet – *we're travelers in a foreign country*. We're citizens of heaven (Philippians 3:20). We have a limited time with these people, in this place. Trust God to heighten your senses to all that's around you, so you can maximize the moments He's given you at your current coordinates.

Lord, I don't want to waste a moment.
Absorb me in what You're doing all around me.
Amen.

# Unglamorous travel

I have chosen to be faithful; I have determined
to live by Your regulations (Ps. 119:30 NLT).

Part of being willing to pilgrim through life for God – part of
traveling through time on His terms – is answering His call
wherever we are, and going wherever He sends.

That sounds exciting! Or not. Because the call to travel into
days of obedience won't necessarily be glamorous. (Like, I might be
picturing a leisure estate with a sea view – and God might call me
to a seedy highway motel.) But wherever He leads us in our days on
earth, His grace will be new every morning, and enough to sustain
us in whatever He's called us to do and be (Lamentations 3:22-23,
2 Corinthians 12:9).

Plus, we always have the comfort of prayer. So let's pray. Let's pray
until it engages our emotions. Let's be brave to look at the glamorous
and the unglamorous parts of ourselves in light of prayer. And then
let's be expectant – praying about where God wants to take us, the
way John Newton prayed:

*Thou art coming to a King*
*Large petitions with thee bring*
*For His grace and power are such*
*None can ever ask too much.*

Jesus, whether the scenery is boring or beautiful,
I want to go wherever You send me. Amen.

# Anything

> This calls for patient endurance on the part
> of the people of God who keep His commands
> and remain faithful to Jesus (Rev. 14:12 NIV).

Today, would you risk praying the Anything Prayer with me? As in, *God, I'll do anything. I'll go anywhere. I'll stay anywhere. I'll say anything. Anything at all that You call me to be or do – I'll be it and do it.*

It's all the rage to be spirited and up for any kind of challenge. We like to think of ourselves as brave and edgy – and we're secretly disparaging of those who are more cautious, more risk-averse.

But if we're honest, when it comes to saying yes to God, we can be big-talk no-action. When He beckons, we're suddenly not so brave. Also, the thing God is calling us to might not be trendy or admirable. It might be quiet and seemingly insignificant. He might not be placing you on a springboard to greatness. He might be sending you to hidden corners of the Kingdom to comfort the desperate or despairing.

True faith is tested in our willingness to do for God the risky and the radical, as well as – perhaps even more so? – the quiet and the ordinary.

Whatever it is You've made me for, Jesus, I'll do it. Amen.

# No app for that

> Why, you do not even know what will
> happen tomorrow … (James 4:14 NIV).

When you're planning a trip to *anywhere*, you can visit dozens of websites that help you *live* yourself into the places they depict. You can get tons of advice on what to do and see. Tour operator apps and travel agencies can tell you what you totally shouldn't miss, and what you can expect from the cuisine and the culture.

The thing is, there's no app for the future. And that makes traveling towards it scary. We tend to awfulize the future – submitting to our fears, and imagining worst case scenarios – instead of actualizing today by living well where we are – which in actual fact goes a long way towards securing the future.

It's cool to remember that the Word is better than a website. In the details and descriptors of Scripture we have everything we need to take the next step into the future God has mapped out for us.

God, I'm satisfied to travel without an app. Surprise me!
I trust You know exactly where You're taking me. Amen.

# Entitlement interrupted

Don't be selfish; don't try to impress others.
Be humble, thinking of others as better than
yourselves. Don't look out only for your own interests,
but take an interest in others, too (Phil. 2:3-4 NLT).

There's nothing like being inconvenienced to show up my heart's wickedness. Like, there was a day when a friend's kid was sick and she needed me to look after him while she worked. Someone else stopped me for marriage counseling in the supermarket's cereal aisle. Date night with my husband had to be postponed. Plus the dogs dug up part of the garden and brought it into the lounge.

I was indignant. I felt I was *owed* something denied to me. I thought, *Why should I be the one to bend around other people's calendars and concerns?* But God convicted me: I don't *have* to do things for other people. I *get* to. I had no claim to any of the things I was missing out on, or that didn't go my way. I felt entitled, instead of grateful. And grateful is when you really recognize *grace* – which is getting stuff or having stuff you weren't entitled to get or have in the first place.

Jesus, help me be ok with appropriate boundaries,
and also with being interrupted and inconvenienced – so
that I can better participate in the grand gospel adventure.
Help me get out of my own way so I can follow You. Amen.

# Brilliant view

For just as the heavens are higher than the earth,
so My ways are higher than your ways and My
thoughts higher than your thoughts (Isa. 55:9 NLT).

Sometimes we think God should put us up in the Ritz, and instead He has us rolling out our sleeping bags on the gravel. It's hard and cold. Uncomfortable. Unpleasant. It's understandable you'd get mad at God for that. I mean, why is He doing this to you? Why won't He come through for you? Where's the rescue He promised?

But then maybe you look up. And it's just *oh my gosh* ... The boundless brilliance of a million stars glinting above you in the ink of night. If God had booked you into the Ritz? It would probably have been all about Netflix and room service. And you would have completely missed out on the vaulting luminosity of His cosmos.

It's in second-choice places of disturbance, discomfort and pain that we see the intensity of God's love and presence – His person and His purposes – most clearly. Get yourself a great sleeping bag and get ready to roll it out under any lovely sky of His choosing.

Father, thank You for only allowing pain to slip through
Your fingers so that it can fall on me like stardust,
displaying Your splendor. Amen.

# Expectation management

… may He equip you with all you need for doing His will.
May He produce in you, through the power of Jesus Christ,
every good thing that is pleasing to Him (Heb. 13:21 NLT).

Before a family holiday, we always have an Expectation Management Discussion. We all get a chance to say one or two things we're hoping to achieve or enjoy during the time away. Like, *I would love one long walk on the beach, all alone.* Or, *I want to go fishing in the lagoon.* Or, *I want pizza for supper at least once.*

This goes a long way toward avoiding tension and disappointment. We try to make sure everyone in the family gets their One Thing (or maybe Two Things) – then whatever else does or doesn't happen, we roll with it and relax, because we've settled our expectations.

Since we're all traveling through time, all the time, wouldn't it be wise to do some expectation management, every day? It might help to decide before you go somewhere how things are going to go down. Like, *I don't feel like going to this party – but I'm looking forward to one good conversation with one person.* Or, *Kids, you can pick fries or a milkshake. Not both.* There may be pre-event fallout but there'll also be time to gather yourselves before it all goes live.

Lord God, help me manage my expectations
so I'm realistic and expectant. Amen.

# Routine and non-routine

> God created everything through Him, and
> nothing was created except through Him. The Word
> gave life to everything that was created, and His
> life brought light to everyone (John 1:3-4 NLT).

Routine is essential for making the world go round. Without routine, things fall apart. And yet a break from routine – a spontaneous change in the rhythm of the humdrum – stimulates and sparks life in beautiful ways. So, routine is always the springboard for spontaneity. Without routine, so-called spontaneity would just be random. Without routine, haphazard happenings would just be instability and unpredictability.

Jesus had a routine. He regularly drew away to quiet places to pray (Mark 1). He ate with His disciples. He went to the temple. And He broke out of routine. He healed on the Sabbath (Mark 3). He raised the dead (John 11). He made breakfast on the beach for His friends (John 21).

Routine, and non-routine, are essential for marriage, parenting, work, leisure, food and friendship. It's ok to embrace both. Because there's something settling and satisfying about having dinner on the table at the same time every night – and there's something marvelous and magical about sometimes eating it in a tent in the garden. Let's make space for both.

> Jesus, show me how to live well, so that I'm
> not erratic or dangerously unpredictable, but
> happy to seize moments, and lighten up. Amen.

# Coram Deo

You will show me the way of life, granting
me the joy of Your presence and the pleasures
of living with You forever (Ps. 16:11 NLT).

*Carpe diem* – seize the day – has shaped the worldviews of maximizers and enthusiasts for millennia. It's about making the most of every opportunity and living an extraordinary life.

But sometimes in seizing the day – catapulting ourselves into all that we crave – we sacrifice wisdom on the altar of desire. There's an even more beautiful concept: *coram Deo*. It means *in the presence of God* and it protects the trajectory of our lives by steering us towards wisdom rather than hedonism, adrenalin or a need to prove ourselves.

Chara Donahue shares from her journey: '*Carpe diem* screams, "Chase pleasure! Follow the flesh." This eventually yielded heavy fruits of internal disharmony, confusion, and a constant lust for more. Living in the face of God, living *coram Deo*, is where I learned to lay hold of wisdom. Soon the fruit of the Spirit, true peace, true joy, and true love, were what emerged from my life. In the face of God I flourished. In the lust for more I withered … The urgency of the moment hijacks our tomorrows, and though another day is not guaranteed, chances are it will come.'

God, earth-side, YOLO is a real thing. Help me
live fully! But remind me to live always in Your
presence, where I'll really live forever. Amen.

# Go be still

For to me, living means living for Christ, and dying is even
better. But if I live, I can do more fruitful work for Christ.
So I really don't know which is better (Phil. 1:21-22 NLT).

One of the tough things about being human is that we're
spiritual beings trapped in very unspiritual bodies. We're dust-
to-dust flesh-and-blood growing older by the day – yet we know
there's more to life, and more to come. We know that what we do on
earth matters in eternity, and we look forward to total renewal and
restoration. We're body-bound and heaven-spun.

*Coram Deo* – living in the presence of God – helps us carry this
tension. If we focus too much on either one of our realities (physical
or spiritual), things get weird. We need to be acutely aware of the Big
Picture – patiently waiting for it to unfold timeously and gloriously
– so that we'll act immediately and obediently in the Small Picture –
doing with urgency all we can within our circles of influence, to make
a Kingdom difference. As we *go* and make disciples (Matthew 28:19),
we're simultaneously *still*: knowing that He is God (Psalm 46:10).

Lord God, with You, all things are possible. Ready me
for Your purposes, even as I rest in Your promise. Amen.

# Hug God, tiny me

For the LORD your God is the God of gods
and Lord of lords. He is the great God, the
mighty and awesome God … (Deut. 10:17 NLT).

*I*'m the poster child for Type A personalities. I easily fall into the trap of making my own plans, living my own life, doing it my way, and being in control.

So God often needs to remind me of His enormousness. He needs to take me to the end of myself – where real life begins. Because at the end of my very small self I get to a spectacular, panoramic view of a world which is all about living for Him, and others. Making big plans to fashion a tiny little life wrapped around just me – isn't big at all.

Let's be glad we serve an immeasurable God – closer than breathing yet spanning the stars and all eternity. Let's be glad that He and His ways are wholly beyond our comprehension, let alone our control.

Almighty God, I'll never see Your bookends because You have none. I stand in awe of Your unfathomable, unreachable greatness and I can't believe Your power lives in me. Thank You! Amen.

# Are you game?

Therefore, gird your minds for action, keep sober in spirit, fix your hope completely on the grace to be brought to you at the revelation of Jesus Christ (1 Pet. 1:13 NASB).

Whether you're bookish and indoorsy or energetic and outdoorsy – or a combination of both – you need a spirit of adventure for the Kingdom work God has set you up to do.

Encouraging every mom, youth pastor, Sunday school teacher and God-follower, Jack Klumpenhower writes, 'Jesus tells us that the work of proclaiming God's Kingdom is dangerous. It takes courage. It demands earnest prayer. It's more about faith than giftedness, and it requires no resources other than those God provides. It's a high-stakes spiritual battle, using supernatural weapons. Anyone willing to engage the fight on this level is needed for the cause. Such an adventurer will reap a rare mix of power, humility, and wide-eyed joy.'

Don't shy away from the grand venture of saying yes to a cause so much bigger than you. You won't regret throwing yourself into the global – even intergalactic – project God promises to complete (Matthew 16:18, Philippians 1:6).

Jesus, make me brave and keen to say yes to any operation You launch! I want to get on my game face, for Your Kingdom and Your glory. Amen.

# Unboxed

It is for freedom that Christ has set us free.
Stand firm, then, and do not let yourselves be
burdened again by a yoke of slavery (Gal. 5:1 NIV).

Maybe you've been boxed? Or maybe you've tried to box others – like your kids or your husband, your friends or employees? Mostly we box to feel in control (of our own insecurities). We fear not measuring up to what we assume others expect of us.

I don't believe God is in the box business. In nature, things that get boxed – in eggs, wombs, cocoons – are only there for a season – and then they come out, and really live. God is all about freedom. And maybe it's good to recognize that we and others are made uniquely. There's no one quite like you. There's no one quite like your son or your daughter or your husband or friend. God made us diverse to demonstrate that there's freedom in following a strong Savior who was anything but conventional.

No one flourishes under the iron fist of a control freak. Also, no one flourishes under the weirdness of superfluous, over-the-top, out-of-whack praise. Let's encourage instead of criticizing, and affirm instead of inflating unrealistically. That feels more like freedom, yes?

God, I want my life to reflect, in every way,
that You've set me free. Amen.

# Fear-free zone

Christ has set us free to live a free life.
So take your stand! Never again let anyone
put a harness of slavery on you (Gal. 5:1 MSG).

*I*f you're brave enough today, ask yourself what it is that's enslaving you. What's keeping you from venturing forth – looking up and out – marveling at the stars above you and the possibilities ahead? Christ set you free to live a free life. Are you living it?

Mostly, we're ensnared by insidious, vice-like fear, not so? Maybe your heart's pinned down by fear of the future. Fear that there won't *be* a future – for you, for your kids. Maybe you fear for your personal safety, or you fear people's opinions. Maybe you fear the pressure to perform. Or perhaps you've forgotten you're actually *free* from the crippling power of sin.

Nothing is impossible for our God (Matthew 19:26). Get help. Talk to someone. Enlist people to pray for you. Fear is not the boss of you anymore. Neither is sin, and neither is anyone else or their opinions. Only Jesus holds that rank in your life. And He has set you *free*.

Lord Jesus, remind me every hour of today that,
like the song says, *I'm free, free, forever, amen!*

# Wonder

> May the God of hope fill you with all joy and peace
> as you trust in Him, so that you may overflow with
> hope by the power of the Holy Spirit (Rom. 15:13 NIV).

The first time I slept outside for a whole night, I was twelve, and freezing. We were too close to the river. The ground was stony and punishing and it was absolutely exhilarating. The great starry silence above awoke fresh wonder in me.

We don't need to sleep under the stars every night to sustain our sense of wonder. But man, we need to be sure we never lose it. And one way of guaranteeing we don't is to lean into what renders *others* wonder-struck.

For a year or two when he was little, our youngest son was passionate about zebras. So I collected zebras wherever I went. I took photos of zebra sketches in doctors' waiting rooms and zebra cushions in home décor stores. We took detours past the reserves in our city that boasted small zebra herds, hoping for the reward of a sighting. The greater reward was hearing my boy thanking Jesus at bedtime 'for all the zebras in our day'.

Whether it's zebras or today's lunch in a zip lock bag – there's wonder right now, right where you are.

> Creator God, give me eyes to see the
> stripes and strands of wonder You weave
> into all of life, all the time. Amen.

# Quench

> Rejoice in our confident hope. Be patient in
> trouble, and keep on praying (Rom. 12:12 NLT).

Enthusiasm is so often the mark of an extraordinary life. Because that word – *enthusiasm* – comes from the Greek word *entheos*, which means *God within*.

But there are those on earth and elsewhere who don't want to see God's Kingdom come. The enemy of our souls doesn't want our lives to flourish. He doesn't want our enthusiasm – the thrill of God-in-us – to spill over onto the parched ground of a wretched, desperate world.

Yet that's exactly what God's called us to do. We're called to be the tall glass of something cold for withered, un-watered souls. It'll take courage and commitment, but we simply can't allow the cynics and the snide remarks to embezzle our joy. Ask God for wise ways to go on the flood offensive – inundating the dry spaces you fill with undeniable, un-ignorable joy.

God, fill me to the brim and keep on filling,
so that Your love quenches those whose thirst
has made them scornful and skeptical. Amen.

APRIL 18

# Abundance in the dust

> We can rejoice, too, when we run into
> problems and trials, for we know that they
> help us develop endurance (Rom. 5:3 NLT).

We live in Africa and we try to take our boys into the wilderness as often as possible. One year, the bush was decimated by a devastating drought. Waterholes had dried up. Trees were leafless. Where grass had been only dust remained. Despite the fact that much of the game had perished in the waterless heat, we had the privilege of more sightings than ever before. There was no long grass for the animals to hide behind. And they were all on the move in search of water.

When life is uncomfortable and difficult and we're tramping through parched land – it's often then that we see God's abundant blessings. Because when life is stripped of the trappings of plenty and ease, we see the hand of God. We even see His face. When life is fat with prosperity, the ample goodness of the Lord is all around us, all the time, and yet somehow we don't notice. It takes opening our eyes wide and honest in a place of need, to clear our vision.

Heavenly Father, You're so kind. Thank You for compelling me to seek You, and find You. Amen.

# Seriously un-serious

So go ahead. Eat your food with joy,
and drink your wine with a happy heart,
for God approves of this! (Eccles. 9:7 NLT).

*I* have a friend who is intentional without being intense. I always walk away from our conversations with a heightened sensitivity to the work of God in the world and how He's inviting us to be part of it. She's kind, wise and intuitive like very few other people I've met. She thinks and feels deeply enough to be able to bring just about anything to the surface, with a single question. Which means, she counsels me without me realizing that I'm being counseled.

She's also very funny, and she never takes herself too seriously. She's beautifully British but there's nothing stiff-upper-lip-ish about her. When she talks about being intentional without being intense, she's describing exactly the effortless Christ-likeness she lives. I want to be more like that.

We serve the God who created happiness, pleasure and delight. He's also the God who takes holiness so very seriously that He bled for us – intentionally enduring agony so we could be emancipated from sin. Let's not be flippant, but let's definitely be free to travel light.

Great God, I'm sobered before Your serious majesty.
I'm celebrating Your kindness and compassion. Amen.

# Thrill

When you go through deep waters,
I will be with you (Isa. 43:2 NLT).

One particular camping trip with our boys, we set up our tent next to the river and waded in right away. Standing thigh deep in said river, I called the farmer's wife from my cell to say we'd arrived. I asked her, 'Is it really safe to swim?' 'Sure,' she said. 'My kids swim in the river all the time. It's clean. Of course, there are hippos in the area. They've been spotted upstream and downstream of the campsite, so keep a lookout. But I'm pretty sure you'll be fine.'

Oh right. Hippos. *Hmm*. We swam nonetheless, though I swam while casting furtive glances across the water. But we swam because there was something thrilling about the risk. Something stretching and strengthening for my boys whose urban world is so safe, so measured. There was something freeing about splashing over rocks knowing that no one was logging my exercise on an app, and that Africa's most dangerous beast could've been snoozing in the reeds.

We couldn't see our feet or the crabs or the rocks (or the hippos) but we clutched hands and kept going, equal parts desperate for adventure and terrified of the unknown – because that's what brave feels like. It's the exhilaration of stretching taut your capacity. It's a whole lot of honest-to-God pretending while you push through panic – and it's fantastically survivable.

Strong God, thank You for wading with me
into the waters, and giving me guts. Amen.

# Inflexibly flexible

Walk with Me and work with Me – watch how I do it.
Learn the unforced rhythms of grace (Matt. 11:29 MSG).

Getting out of your comfort zone and into an adventure zone recalibrates the soul for simplicity and flexibility. It reminds us that we need to be absolutely inflexible on the important stuff, and absolutely flexible on absolutely everything else.

As Jesus-followers, we need to prioritize relationships, inflexibly. Life is too short to do anything but love people, and love God. And we dare not budge from the perspective we get, on His magnitude, when we're barefoot beneath stars and sun.

But, we need to be flexible about how our coffee is brewed. Flexible about the kids making a fort in the lounge with every single piece of bedding in the house. And occasionally, we shouldn't get our knickers in a twist about the disproportionate vegetable to marshmallow ratio.

Some days, it's ok to be flexible about dirt, discomfort and our own agendas, and allow weather or whim to dictate the rhythm of the day. We might ask, *What's the worst that can happen? And if it does happen, does it matter?* (Of course, some things really do matter. But many things really don't.) Consider allowing yourself, today, the flexibility to experience the freedom of unbridled happiness.

Jesus, help me to be inflexible in my resolve to be more flexible, simply embracing the adventure around me. Amen.

# Be wise under the skies

… make the most of every opportunity (Col. 4:5 NIV).

Before you step into the adventure of today, be still. Breathe. You need to be strong to find common ground with others, and to dig into your capacity for creativity and decisions. Be still, and know that He is God (Psalm 46:10).

Be slow. Slow to empty out all your words on another. Slow to un-cage your rage when things don't roll how you hoped. Wait. Be sure your response is the cure not the cause. 'A gentle answer deflects anger, but harsh words make tempers flare' (Proverbs 15:1).

Be quick. Quick to give, and forgive. Quick to listen wide open and soft to the hearts of others. Quick to offer your help, your seat, your sandwich, your suggestion or solution.

Be careful. You can say *anything*. Ask *anything*. Tact, timing and tone are key.

Be free. God has already paid your life's ransom. You *are* free. Now stay that way. Which means, don't get trapped in tangles of unwise choices. Rather, obey. Not to earn God's favor or anyone else's, and not because obedience is the gravy train to success. Obey because that *is* success, and simple freedom.

God, give me all the wisdom I'll need for today's adventure.
Amen.

# Brave heart

'I knew you before I formed you in your mother's womb.
Before you were born I set you apart and appointed
you as My prophet to the nations' (Jer. 1:5 NLT).

Standing beneath the same sky as Goliath, David said to him,
'You come to me with sword, spear, and javelin, but I come to
you in the name of the Lord of Heaven's Armies – the God of the
armies of Israel, whom you have defied' (1 Samuel 17:45). David
wasn't outsized, out-speared or outsmarted, because he knew that
no one could outdo his God. You, too, can be brave to step into big
tomorrows, because the tomorrows come one at a time and you'll
meet a big God in each one.

And in your courage, be kind. Live outside your skin enough to
know what the world feels like coming up against someone else's. Be
prepared to pray hero prayers. Be prepared to say with the psalmist,
'I am counting on the Lord; yes, I am counting on Him. I have put my
hope in His word' (Psalm 130:5). And be you. Of the seven billion
people on earth, you only get to be one of them. Do the best you can
at being the only you. He calls out the stars by name. He'll call out the
treasures He's placed in you.

God, please kit me out for kindness and courage. Amen.

# Not what I pictured

Consider it pure joy, my brothers and sisters, whenever
you face trials of many kinds, because you know that
the testing of your faith produces perseverance. Let
perseverance finish its work so that you may be mature
and complete, not lacking anything … Blessed is the one
who perseveres under trial because, having stood the test,
that person will receive the crown of life that the Lord has
promised to those who love Him (James 1:2-4, 12 NIV).

Sometimes we have a picture of how we should behave and
how life should work out as a result. We memorize Scripture
– and so we should. We might read the best books and apply them
practically – and it's a brilliant idea to do that. Knowledge is power,
for sure.

And yet if you've lived a bit, you'll know that spiritual maturity isn't
gauged and appraised on perfect behavior; it's measured in terms of
persevering faith. No amount of intellectual know-how can plough
the heartland that produces a crop of righteousness and stalwart
devotion. It's the onslaught of life in all its beauty and hardship – and
it's your response of faith, and more faith, and continued faith time
and again up and down steep and slippery slopes – that results in
robust reliance on our great God.

Father, things aren't going as I planned. Help my
faith! Help me trust that though this is not
what I pictured, You're producing in me
something better. Amen.

# Feel all the feelings

> Rejoice in the Lord always. I will
> say it again: Rejoice (Phil. 4:4 NIV)!

Perhaps the older you get, the more you struggle to *feel* things. You don't *feel* Christmassy, the way you did as a kid. You don't get excited for your birthday like you used to. And maybe you don't *feel* what you once felt, about what Jesus did for you.

Considering the desperate state of the globe, more than ever we need to *feel* irrefutable truth. We need to notice and glory in the beauty of lights and food and music and every other good gift: the multi-sensory here-and-now reminders of the extravagant wealth God ushered into our poverty – the radiance He shone into our darkness.

We need to *feel* relief and gratitude that truth is always the perfect plumb line between the pendulum extremes of liberal and conservative. Let's be so steeped in truth that we wouldn't swing to the side of all things insubstantial, feel-good, flaky and fake. Let's be so steeped in truth that we wouldn't swing to the side of all things Spiritless, straight-jacketed, law-bound and unadventurous. Because then, the truth, the whole truth and nothing but the gospel truth will produce in us well-founded, wild emotion. It will burst our hearts with joy. Flood our lives with peace.

> Jesus, where I've grown bored and blasé –
> shake me awake! I stand in awe of You! Amen.

# Who are you (not)?

The One who calls you is faithful,
and He will do it (1 Thess. 5:24 NIV).

Maybe what keeps you from living adventurously – from being and doing all God's called you to be and do – is the fear of being found out. There's a voice you hear sometimes that says things like, *You're not who they think you are. You can't really do what you say you'll do. Who are you to claim to be able to do this or that?*

That voice is the sound of the very real fear that maybe you're not all you're cracked up to be. But girl, you need to start telling yourself the truth. Yes, you're a weak, broken human with flaws and a fickle heart and yes, you're too easily swayed by pride and fear and a host of other sins. Me too. We're great sinners – but we rest in the grace-grip of a greater Savior. He's bigger than your faults and your feelings of inadequacy. He's big *in* you and *through* you. In fact His bigness is manifested most beautifully when we authentically lean on Him in our weakness (2 Corinthians 12:9).

After all, who are you to say God's power may be big – it's just not big enough to work through you?

God, the calling You've placed on my life sometimes
scares me. Help me to fake it 'til I feel it –
trusting You every step I take. Amen.

# VIP

> … to them I will give within My temple and
> its walls a memorial and a name better than
> sons and daughters; I will give them an everlasting
> name that will endure forever (Isa. 56:5 NIV).

People with big titles stay in fancy hotels. People with no titles sleep under the stars. What if, knowing your title and feeling secure in it meant you didn't need to chase bigness to prove how big you were? Maybe if you knew your title – *really knew it* – it wouldn't matter who else in the world knew it or didn't know it – respected it or discarded it.

You might know what it feels like to be the most important person in a room. You might be a CEO, a member of Congress, a PhD or the President. Yet the greatest title that can ever and will ever be draped gloriously over your life is Child of God. And the extraordinary thing about that title is that it was a *gift*. You couldn't slave for it, buy it or sleep your way to the top for it.

Once you know your title, it won't matter where you sleep. Knowing your title doesn't lead to arrogance or complacency or compromise, but to life-changing hope. And knowing your title will give you the confidence to follow Jesus on any adventure.

Jesus, thank You for rebuilding my reputation.
I'm excited to be exactly who You say I am. Amen.

# New day

> Therefore, since we are surrounded by such
> a huge crowd of witnesses to the life of faith, let us
> strip off every weight that slows us down, especially
> the sin that so easily trips us up. And let us run with
> endurance the race God has set before us (Heb. 12:1 NLT).

Sleeping under the stars gives us front row seats to a new day. We're the first to greet the dawn. It requires a little more courage than bedding down indoors, but sunrise makes the discomfort worthwhile.

Spiritually, it's a new day for our generation. We could ride on the momentum of previous generations and call it courage – but it's not. Courage is an everyday, growing, decision-by-decision, sunrise-by-sunrise thing. That means, while we might benefit from a rich spiritual inheritance, we'll need to make our own sacrifices, not just relying on the sacrifices of those who've gone before. We need to be courageous enough to cut away contemporary realities that have us tangled, so we can run into the new day, possess all God has for us and leave a legacy.

You might be weighed down by unhealthy friendships. Or social media. Maybe you're continually tripping over the ropes of comparison. What can you drop or cut loose, to walk free into the dawning God-venture ahead?

> God, help me throw off entitlement,
> apathy or addiction – and make a
> difference in this new day. Amen.

# Call it what it is

If we claim we have no sin, we are only fooling
ourselves and not living in the truth (1 John 1:8 NLT).

Being under a big sky strips away pretenses. The sweeping
perspective of the arcing firmament helps us see things more
clearly. It's the same with our souls. Looking up to our great God
leaves our sin no place to hide – though hiding it is exactly what we
too often try to do. Not only is this ridiculous, and futile, but we're
also committing spiritual malpractice by not calling it what it is: *sin*.

Loads of us are keen to change the world, yet we're unwilling for
God to change us. More than anything we need to stand still under
God's bigness and allow Him to heal our souls.

This is not a quick fix, but it's *so* worth doing. Because if there's
a discrepancy between our inner world (what's really going on in
our hearts) and our outer world (the way we project or perform or
pretend), our *whole* world will cave in.

Holy God, who am I kidding? Keep me honest
about my sin: naming it, so we can nuke it. Amen.

# Look up. Look back.

You hem me in behind and before, and You
lay Your hand upon me (Ps. 139:5 NIV).

An all-encompassing panorama of the stars above helps with viewpoint. In looking up, we're somehow better able to look back and remember all God has done for us. Just as He's keeping the stars suspended and planets circling, He's ceaselessly doing enormous things in the background of your life, without you even realizing it.

There's also nothing like stars to remind you of the majesty of God – to remind you that He's greater and more powerful than anything you face. The God who hems you in behind and before is always bigger than any giant pacing on the peripheries.

What your Savior did *for* you is always bigger than whatever has been done *to* you. And He's not done displaying His brilliance through the stars, and you.

Savior and star-maker, remind me to look up –
to regain perspective on Your majesty. And remind me
to look back – in awe of what You've done. Amen.

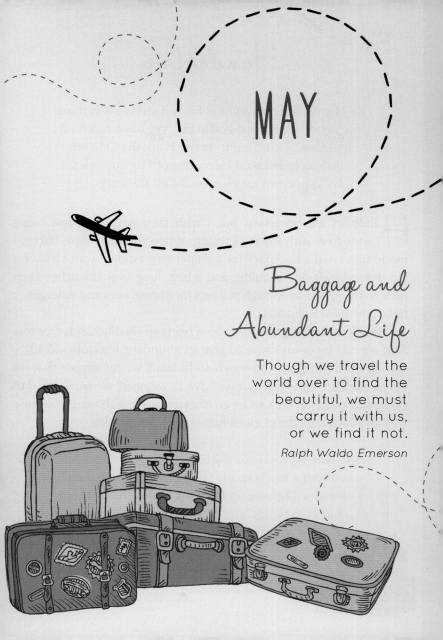

# MAY

## Baggage and Abundant Life

Though we travel the world over to find the beautiful, we must carry it with us, or we find it not.

*Ralph Waldo Emerson*

# Hands-free

> By His divine power, God has given us everything
> we need for living a godly life. We have received
> all of this by coming to know Him, the One who
> called us to Himself by means of His marvelous
> glory and excellence (2 Pet. 1:3 NLT).

Handbags are necessary, but I wish they weren't. I love being hands-free, with no stuff to lug. When my boys were babies I made sure I had a backpack for a diaper bag. I didn't want to have a kid draped over one shoulder and a bag slung over the other. Even now, if my outfit has enough pockets for phone, keys and emergency headache pills? Brilliant.

There's something splendid about being spiritually hands-free too. And we *can* be. Jesus came to give us abundant life (John 10:10) – spilling-over, filling-up, too-much-to-fit life. If we remember that we are so filled up with Him that we have all we need, we won't need to cart extra baggage. We can let go of cases laden with issues, because we carry within us the glorious fullness of sufficient life.

> Lord, teach me how to collect and carry life's precious
> souvenirs. But keep me from carrying more than
> I categorically have to. Keep me hands-free – kitted
> out completely with all I need for life. Amen.

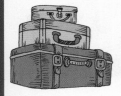

# Maximize

Then people brought little children to Jesus for Him to place His hands on them and pray for them. But the disciples rebuked them. Jesus said, 'Let the little children come to Me, and do not hinder them, for the kingdom of heaven belongs to such as these' (Matt. 19:13-14 NIV).

*I*f you're a maximizer, you're probably intent on sucking the marrow from every moment and opportunity. You're also excellent at making rods for your own back. You're quick to beat yourself up for not achieving all you've set out to achieve. I only know this because, on a day when I have, say, eleven things on my to-do list, I'm appalled if I only achieve three of them. As far as I'm concerned, if that day were a test, I'd flunk.

But it's possible that what really happened on that un-maximized day were some amazing – slow – deliberate – moments with my kids. And some pausing in the margins of a busy day to listen to a friend. And maybe the better test question to ask is, 'Am I maximizing each moment, *relationally*?' Answering *yes* to that will have you passing the abundant life test with flying colors. Relationships don't always fit into tidy calendar slots, but they're the stuff of life. It's our community and connections we should be maximizing most of all.

God, remind me that not everything crucial to life can be ticked off a list. Amen.

# Garden self

Now the man and his wife were both naked,
but they felt no shame (Gen. 2:25 NLT).

A friend asked me once, 'What would you have looked like in the Garden of Eden?'

That's quite a thought. What would *you* have looked like? I don't mean the naked you. I mean, you, *pre-sin*. What's the best, most beautiful version of you – without pride or fear or selfish ambition or jealousy or anger or greed or – fill in every single sin-blank?

If we can get a glimpse of what might have been – and what God might be shaping in us as He restores us over all our earth-side days until that final transformation into our eternal, glorified selves – that might change how we act and react. How we treat others. What we say and how we say it. Decisions and discernment. In weird, difficult, tense, spotlight moments, ask yourself: *What would the Garden of Eden version of me do?*

And when others misunderstand you, reject you, insult you, offend you or disregard you, pretend a little. Treat them like you would in eternity, where you and they will be perfect.

Jesus, remind me that You see the garden me. You've eradicated my sin: renewed me and restored me. Amen.

# Bedrock

> … He set my feet on a rock and gave
> me a firm place to stand (Ps. 40:2 NIV).

As a kid I loved boulder-hopping and rock-clambering and I still do it any chance I get. My best is climbing up and onto smooth outcrops of volcanic granite. Even better if the rock is sun-warmed but there's shade enough from the day's heat.

That experience always resonates somewhere in my soul because it reflects our reality as Jesus-lovers. The firmness beneath our feet is the bedrock of Christ. We stand on the Rock of our salvation: unshakeable ground.

When we remember we're standing on solid rock, we don't need to hang onto other people for balance. We don't have to rely on them to hold us up or support us, because we're entirely comfortable, steady and stable. The rock is beneath our feet all the time, so we're not focused on ourselves or our feelings of security. We're able to enjoy and appreciate wholeheartedly the people in our lives, without setting them up for failure by expecting their love to make us feel safe.

God, show me who I'm leaning on unfairly or unrealistically. Thank You for putting terra firma beneath my feet. Amen.

# Family formula

Love one another with brotherly affection.
Outdo one another in showing honor (Rom. 12:10 esv).

We can't fit life and God into formulas – but sometimes they're helpful to concretize our thoughts. And a formula for unity – the belonging we long for – might look like this:

*Forgetfulness + forgiveness + friendship + faith = unity*

*Forget* yourself. C. S. Lewis brilliantly said that humility isn't thinking too much of yourself (arrogance) or thinking too little of yourself (the self-absorption of self-deprecation); it's just not thinking of yourself at all. For unity to flood in and fill the cracks of alienation and hurt, we need to forget ourselves, and pour out who we are and what we've been given, to bless others.

*Forgive.* Choose daily – or hourly – to *let people go*. Break the links that have those folks chained to your heart, so you can walk free. Do you still need to rehash the offence with anyone who'll listen? You probably haven't forgiven. Try saying over and over, of the people who have hurt you, 'I wish them well. I wish them well. I wish them well.' Until you mean it.

Practice selfless *friendship* by considering others more important than yourself, and pursue *faith*. Lean heavily on His great strength to empower you in your great weakness.

Father, we're a family united!
Help us live like that's true. Amen.

# Sweet porridge

You prepare a feast for me in the presence of my
enemies. You honor me by anointing my head with oil.
My cup overflows with blessings (Ps. 23:5 NLT).

*I* love the fairytale of the magic porridge pot. A little girl and her
mom are awfully poor. A mysterious old woman meets the girl
in the forest and gives her a magic pot. All she has to stay is 'Cook,
little pot, cook!' and the pot makes the sweetest porridge. The girl
goes out for the day and her mom doesn't know that when she's had
enough porridge she needs to say 'Stop, little pot.' So the pot keeps
cooking – overflowing – flooding the village – the countryside – as if
it wants to satisfy the hunger of the world.

Even if porridge is not your jam, the sweet abundance coming
from the magic pot is how I picture the abundant life Jesus gives us.
It pours out of us – and it just keeps pouring. The faster we live that
life – pouring it into the lives of others – the faster He fills us up.

We all have days – even years – when we feel as if the life has run
out of us. We've nothing left to give. Let's preach gospel to ourselves,
to remember the reality of the abundant life the Redeemer has
poured into us. It never runs out.

Thank You, Jesus, that You fill me and You keep on filling. Amen.

# Stuffed

How excellent is Thy lovingkindness,
O God! (Ps. 36:7 KJV).

When you've had a great meal, you don't think about food. Your hunger is satisfied – so you're unaware of it. In the same way, when you're filled up with satisfying life, you don't obsess about you and your life and how things could be, because you're content – *satiated*. You're able to focus on others, pouring out your life in comfort and companionship.

And the unparalleled characteristic of Jesus' abundant life in us is that *it leaves no room for anything else*. When we enjoy the assurance that we're brim-filled with the good life of a good God, there's no more space for fear. No space for pride or arrogance. No space for shame, insecurity, neediness, lack of affection or affirmation or approval, jealousy, greed, comparison, insults.

None of those things can get stuck anywhere in us because we're full up with life. We simply don't have space for them.

God, I couldn't eat another thing!
Thank You for filling me up. Amen.

# *Luxury life*

All glorious is the princess within her chamber;
her gown is interwoven with gold (Ps. 45:13 NIV).

*I*ndia's royalty lost their official powers with national independence in 1947, but they're still a stunning example of almost unthinkable opulence.

A royal wedding will showcase lavish spectacles like elephants in gold headdresses, camels adorned with embroidered artworks and week-long festivities including thousands of people. In the Indian culture, royalty carries tremendous value. There's worth attributed to royalty. And because of this *worth*, there is jaw-dropping *abundance*.

You might not be an Indian princess, but you're royalty in the most profound, cosmic sense of the word. You've been adopted by the King of kings – clothed in the colors of His royal courts. That's abundance. All your shame has been stripped away and replaced with sumptuous – unearned – righteousness. There's more than enough of it in the King's storehouses. Your God-imputed worth results in staggering plenty.

My God and King, thank You for these
royal threads! Help me wear them well. Amen.

# Crowns laid down

You will be a crown of splendor in the LORD's hand,
a royal diadem in the hand of your God (Isa. 62:3 NIV).

Once when we were living in England, I saw a member of the royal family in our local supermarket. The store had just opened an organic produce section and he was there to endorse it. I was struck by how *normal* His Royal Highness was. Completely down to earth. That's what impressed me.

The people I'm most drawn to are always humble. Unassuming. And *secure*. Because they're secure – knowing who they are, and Whose they are – they don't need to keep telling you. Imagine a plain-clothes president picnicking with his family in the park. You'd be a little gob-smacked, right? Impressed. Humbled. You'd be less impressed if you saw him dining out with his cronies at a Michelin star restaurant, flaunting his power, influence, wealth and connections.

Knowing our worth – knowing we're really royalty – means we're quite comfortable to lay down our crowns before the throne of the God who bestowed them. We don't constantly need to polish and parade the bling tiaras of our accolades or applause or affirmation or appreciation. Knowing we've already received all those crowns from the only One whose approval matters means we don't need approval from everyone else.

King of kings, I'm so grateful for the crown You've placed on my head that I'm leaving it here at Your feet. Amen.

# Carry your bags

But they will have to give account to Him who is
ready to judge the living and the dead (1 Pet. 4:5 NIV).

*I*n *The Horse and His Boy*, the third of *The Chronicles of Narnia* by
C. S. Lewis, Aslan, the great lion (and allegorical Christ), scratches
the girl, Aravis, with his enormous claws. Her friend Shasta is peeved.
He accuses and interrogates Aslan: 'Then it was you who wounded
Aravis? ... But what for?' Aslan replies, 'Child ... I am telling you your
story, not hers. I tell no one any story but his own.'

Every breathing human has a little, or a lot of, baggage. Now and
then we get a glimpse of the baggage someone else is carrying – a
glimpse of what God is doing or apparently not doing in another
person's life. But He wants to draw our eyes to the story *we* are living.
We're not responsible or accountable for the stories of others. He
doesn't owe us an explanation for the blessing He bestows or the pain
He allows in another's journey.

You probably have more than enough unpacking and sorting
and refolding to do in your own life, from your own bags. You can
confidently leave the contents of another's suitcase full of stories to
the One who wrote them.

God, thank You that I only have to live my own story. Amen.

# Carry another's bags

We who are strong ought to bear with the failings of
the weak and not to please ourselves (Rom. 15:1 NIV).

To say that we each live only our own story, *and* that we should
carry one another's burdens, is not a contradiction. We don't
need to understand fully God's work in another's life; we just need
to serve them. Carrying one another's burdens doesn't mean being
held accountable for others' decisions or directions or destinations.
It doesn't mean becoming co-dependent by enabling someone who
isn't taking responsibility for his or her life. It just means seeing a need
– and stepping in to do what you can to meet it.

Carry someone's bags by praying for them, or mowing their
lawn, or being kind to their difficult kids. Sure, you might be putting
yourself at risk by carrying their bags – just as you're at risk in an
airport when someone asks you to carry their bags and those bags
may or may not contain illicit drugs.

And sure, carrying someone's bags is seldom convenient or comfortable. Carrying the baggage of our sin to the cross wasn't convenient or comfortable for Jesus, either.

Jesus, today, please show me whose bags
I need to carry, to help them travel light. Amen.

# Drama-free queen

> So get rid of all evil behavior. Be done with all deceit, hypocrisy, jealousy, and all unkind speech (1 Pet. 2:1 NLT).

The world loves drama. Drivers rubber-neck at accident scenes. Sensation sells the news. There's something in all of us that's drawn to a spectacle.

And yet, you wouldn't want to be called a drama queen. We all know it's not an attractive quality – to be *that* woman, always hustling for the scoop and slightly unhinged with hysteria.

As a woman who travels light, you need to drop the drama baggage. And the best way to do that is to pick up wisdom. That means, in those situations where you're tempted to give in to the weird stimulation of sensationalism, rather ask yourself: *What's the wise thing to do?*

Considering what I've seen, heard and experienced in the past – considering my present context and the truth about my current circumstances – and considering what I'm hoping to achieve in the future, or the story I hope to tell one day – what is my wisest (and possibly less dramatic) move, right now?

God, I don't need to be in on all the action or the scandal.
Give me wisdom to make my next move. Amen.

# Important people do

The LORD looks down from heaven on the entire human race; He looks to see if anyone is truly wise, if anyone seeks God (Ps. 14:2 NLT).

*I*t's a lie that important people get to do important things. *Truly* important people are those *already doing* important things. That's what makes them important. The fact that they're doing things of eternal value – things bigger than themselves – that's what sets them up to leverage their influence. They're not just elevated by *self*-importance, or *inherited* importance. They're also free from scandal and sensationalism – because they're not focused on themselves and the next rush. They're focused on others, and on somehow improving the world.

Of all the people you know, or know of, who do you consider important? Are they just *self*-important – or are they *really* important? Are they just celebrities – or have they garnered significance because they're making a significant difference?

God, help me forget about *being* important. Show me how to *do* important things – for Your Kingdom and glory. Amen.

# Skinny

That is why I tell you not to worry about everyday
life – whether you have enough food and drink,
or enough clothes to wear. Isn't life more than food,
and your body more than clothing? (Matt. 6:25 NLT).

Friend, you and I need to get thin. We live in a fat, flourishing
world that needs to be *thinned out* – like how you'd thin out a
veggie patch to make space for everything to grow.

Wayne Muller writes, 'Thinning is … making space for life. We plant
so many seeds, and they seem so small, so benign, they take up hardly
any space at all. But everything, as it grows, needs space. Children,
a home, a career, a project, a hobby, a spiritual practice, everything
needs space, and everything needs time. And as each grows, each one
takes from the other, until nothing grows beneath the surface, it is all
foliage and greenery aboveground, and no nutrition beneath. Sooner
or later, it all withers from lack of nourishment.'

I'm thinking we need to be much thinner wives, moms, friends
and co-workers, to model this for the world. Let's not crowd our lives
with things and stuff and busy-busy all teeming for headspace and
heart space and leaving us confused, exhausted and unable to find
the wonder and the wisdom.

Lord, show me where and how I need to thin out my life. Amen.

# Success story

Love never fails (1 Cor. 13:8 NIV).

Real success is a lifelong aspiration towards what Henri Nouwen called *downward mobility*. Nouwen was once invited to the White House. Hilary Clinton had been reading his work on gratitude and forgiveness, and he was asked to provide counsel during tricky times. He declined. He sympathized with the Clintons' sorrows, and appreciated that they were prioritizing spirituality, but he had a disabled friend who needed him at the time. 'There are others who can go to the White House,' he said.

That's downward mobility – and a crazy classification for success. Yet God-defined success is a lowering – not a ladder-climbing. Going to the White House isn't always wrong – so long as our going makes us more like Jesus who was over-qualified to wash feet but did it anyway, with great love. Nothing's beneath us. People who realize that are the kind of humans we all love best.

'Love never fails,' writes Paul. *It works every time*. It's always successful. Love never leaves the heart that loves or is loved, the same. It changes us and others. Even if the shop attendant glares at your kind hello, her heart is surely better affected, even if unwittingly, than if *you'd* glared at her. Love is our highest triumph and achievement, guaranteed to outlast every other success.

God, I pray for resounding success as I
dive low to live and love like You. Amen.

# Not another step

Moses said, 'If Your presence doesn't take the
lead here, call this trip off right now' (Ex. 33:15 MSG).

Moses didn't want to take another step into the desert without
the assurance that God's presence would lead them – and
hem them in from behind (Psalm 139:5).

Daily praying this prayer for God's presence helps divest us of
the baggage that weighs down our decision-making around which
direction to take. If you're a Jesus-follower then the Holy Spirit is in
you, so of course you take His presence with you wherever you go.
But what Moses is talking about here is more than God's indwelling
presence in the hearts and minds and lives of believers.

It's the dispensation of grace that accompanies us when we're in
the center of His will, doing and being what He's called us to do and
be, and going where He's called us to go.

Heavenly Father, before I step into today, align my
path with Your strategies and perfect plans. Amen.

# Midlife crisis

He has also set eternity in the
human heart … (Eccles. 3:11 NIV).

Maybe you're wondering if there's more to life than this – or if this is as good as it gets? Because you're sleep-deprived and soul-depleted from kid-raising and you're not even sure you have interests of your own anymore. Your body can't do what it used to do and doesn't look how it used to look.

People say you're just getting comfortable in your own skin but you long for a tighter fit. You scaled the rock face of career with sheer grit and guts only to emerge on the plateau of mediocrity for a lukewarm, perfunctory pay check. You're juggling kids and crazy but beneath all the frenetic – monotony seeps insidious. You're living with an acute case of full-blown, terminal life.

And you're coming into fullness. A new, beautiful depth of experience. When you were younger you only saw half the truth – that there's hope, beauty and possibility in this world. Now you're living the privilege of older and now you have a fuller picture of the truth: yes, there's hope, beauty and possibility in this world, but their transient manifestation is just a stunning reflection of the hope, beauty and possibility of an everlasting future.

God, this is more than a midlife crisis.
It's eternity in my heart. Thank You!
Amen.

# Hard

Look, I am sending you out as sheep
among wolves. So be as shrewd as snakes
and harmless as doves (Matt. 10:16 NLT).

*I*t's possibly occurred to you that Jesus-followers have to carry the heaviest bags of all. (It's occurred to me anyway.) Maybe Christians have it harder than most. All around you are folks who don't value morality or accountability so they're doing whatever (and whoever) they want or swiping the plastic for debt dressed in bling because their worldview allows them to have a spectacular – necessary – *deserved* – personal crisis and loving Jesus can feel boring and exhausting and – *is it worth it?*

You're not the only one living with raw questions and half-baked answers. You're not the only one comparing your real to the highlight reels of Fake-book and reeling from the realization that life really is hard, like God and your parents told you it would be.

Be brave. Jesus never said following Him would result in an easy life. In fact, often when we follow Jesus, life *does* get harder. But the suffering we endure now is daily racking up in eternity a weight of glory that far outweighs our earthly experiences (2 Corinthians 4:17).

Jesus, I'm finding it hard to live righteous. Help me trust
You that a lifetime rooted in joyful obedience results in a
rich harvest of freedom from the entanglements of sin. Amen.

# Beat defeat

Finally, be strong in the Lord and in
His mighty power (Eph. 6:10 NIV).

To defeat defeatist thinking that says life is hard and getting harder, *find wonder again*. And refuse to lose your sense of awe at who God is and how He splashes splendor across the skies and our hearts.

Keep hunting for beauty. Keep scratching out thank-You-God moments in your journal or your Instagram stories, even if people think you're weird. Keep teaching your kids and your colleagues to notice and revel and reach for the mystery. All this present glory tugs at our sleeves – points eagerly to the unfading glory to come. Don't let the sadness wash over you for what might have been. The best is yet to be.

And *get dirty*. Dig deep into the life soil of your kids and your community. Don't be afraid to get your hands muddy for Kingdom causes bigger than you. Live unveiled, unfettered, unhurried. Sow generously all God has sown in you.

Jesus, I praise You that wonder is weightless, and service sets us free. Help me travel light with those truths in mind. Amen.

# Baggage to beauty

He does great things too marvelous to understand.
He performs countless miracles (Job 5:9 NLT).

When you feel weighted down by your circumstances, you won't necessarily make sense of the heaviness by unzipping it all and rummaging through it. Rather, in the midst of difficulty, determine not to grow weary of doing good. In due time you'll reap (Galatians 6:9). In due time, you may even *have* more time. And new direction and opportunity. Don't give up now.

Paul – persecuted – wrote, 'We now have this light shining in our hearts, but we ourselves are like fragile clay jars containing this great treasure. This makes it clear that our great power is from God, not from ourselves. We are pressed on every side by troubles, but we are not crushed. We are perplexed, but not driven to despair. We are hunted down, but never abandoned by God. We get knocked down, but we are not destroyed' (2 Corinthians 4:7-9 NLT).

You're not the only one facing what you face, friend. But there is Only One who can turn your doubt and disappointment into deeper devotion, your drudgery into dreams, your despair into post-traumatic growth. He's your courage to face what isn't fair. He's the catalyst for lasting change. He is your hope.

God, I know You can turn baggage into beauty. Take the
mess of my burst-open bags and make a miracle of me. Amen.

# Head spread

… we take captive every thought to make
it obedient to Christ (2 Cor. 10:5 NIV).

*I*f you've spent even five minutes in the last 24 hours wondering
(or mildly obsessing over) what someone thought about what
you said, did or texted – this is for you.

Paul says we shouldn't let trash talk spew from our mouths.
We should only say what's helpful, encouraging and strengthening
(Ephesians 4:29). But what comes out of our mouths starts in our
heads, which is why Paul also says we should make every thought a
happy prisoner of Jesus.

So I'm asking myself, *What rumors am I spreading in my head?*
I dare not believe everything I think. When I'm critical of others, I
know it has more to do with lies I've told myself, about me. Because
we talk ugly about others when we feel ugly about us. We undermine
others when we're insecure or jealous or we've forgotten that God is
holding us in the palm of His hand.

You can't control the stories other people tell. You *can* control the
stories you tell yourself. Tell yourself the true stories God tells about
you. Like, He delights in you, calms your fears, and sings over your
life (Zephaniah 3:17), and you can hide in the shadow of His wings,
knowing He'll fulfill His purposes for you (Psalm 57:1).

Lord, shine a truth laser on the lies that
have darkened my thinking. Amen.

# Rumor to revolution

> Do not let any unwholesome talk come out of
> your mouths, but only what is helpful for
> building others up according to their needs,
> that it may benefit those who listen (Eph. 4:29 NIV).

Sometimes rumors are all in the mind; sometimes they're real. Yet, what other people think of you is none of your business. Their private thoughts about you are just that: *private*. Don't waste time and energy fretting. They may not be thinking about you at all. Seriously, they probably *don't have time*. People's abrupt responses or lack of interest are, mostly, because they're swathed in their own stress and they *just can't even*. There's not a lot of emotional capacity going around these days, for people to stop and show you they care.

But revolutions start with crazies like us who think it's possible to break the cycle of disinterest and apathy. Remind yourself that the people you're trying to impress aren't watching anyway. Make right with people you've wronged. Be real, trust God to protect your reputation, and smile.

It'll hurt at first – like hiking with blisters. You put your boots on and think you'll never move again. You hobble for a mile or two. Then you walk those blisters in. You absorb the pain and start noticing beauty. You realize the rumors aren't running wild anymore. And you're running free.

God, work Your wonders in rumor-ridden relationships. Amen.

# Kid baggage

> I remember your genuine faith, for you share
> the faith that first filled your grandmother Lois
> and your mother, Eunice. And I know that same
> faith continues strong in you (2 Tim. 1:5 NLT).

Maybe, like Timothy, you grew up in a healthy home: well-balanced and well-loved.

Possibly, you grew up spoiled and entitled. You got your way and anything else you wanted, but never the gifts of grit and gratitude.

Or, you grew up ignored, abandoned, disregarded or abused. No one understood what made you tick. Fear and despair hung heavy over your home.

Sadly, both absurd privilege and tragic deprivation can lead to a narcissistic adult life. And we all carry childhood bags we need to open up and sort. Some of our baggage must be burned. Some should be washed, ironed, folded and put away. Some needs to be lovingly held up to our cheeks so we can smell the good memories and appreciate the legacy.

Be brave. Unzip your childhood. God was there in every moment. Whether you believed in Him or not – acknowledged Him or not – He never took His eyes off you. He shares in the happiness, and He's willing to carry the heaviness.

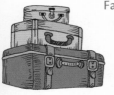

Father, thank You that nothing in my past slipped through the safety net of Your sovereignty, unbidden. My childhood is part of the story You're writing with my life. Amen.

# Dread to dreams

> So after you have suffered a little while, He will
> restore, support, and strengthen you, and He will
> place you on a firm foundation (1 Pet. 5:10 NLT).

*I*f you're weighed down today by the future you imagine – if
what's ahead is more dread than dreams – *don't fear what isn't
real*. I've lived miracles I thought would never happen. And maybe
there are unthinkable miracles for you to live too.

A decade ago – processing what it would look like to raise our
visually impaired son – we thought we'd never be able to take him
hiking. At best, he'd be partially sighted. At worst, he'd be completely
blind within five years. We'd have to become an indoorsy family,
giving up whole bits of our great-wide-open selves to make life work.

And yet, a couple years ago we took our son hiking. He relied on
his walking stick. And he couldn't see the bushbuck crashing past us
through the ferns. But he whistled for a robin outside our hut one
morning, *and the robin whistled back*. It was one of those parenting
moments that aren't spectacular to anyone else, but miraculous to
kid-raising you.

I'm praying that this very day – this day that is the tangible now
of a future you once feared – God would surprise you with His love,
and show you a miracle.

God, remind me that You carve paths through
the future that seem impossible today. Amen.

# Optimism for the win

… while we look forward with hope to that wonderful
day when the glory of our great God and Savior,
Jesus Christ, will be revealed (Tit. 2:13 NLT).

*I* hiked a lot in my teens and twenties – fueled by hopes, dreams,
irrepressible optimism and an unshakeable belief that the future would be better than the past. Nowadays, though my backpack
still fits just fine, I know the future *isn't always* better than the past –
if we think *better* means *happier* or in sync with what *we* think is best
for us, or best for those we love.

But sometimes the future *is* happier. I would even say *mostly* it is.
And a future rendered to God – lived in the slipstream of His power,
wisdom and love – is bigger, richer, deeper, wider, and fantastically
colored-in outside-the-lines. The future reroutes us from our naive,
two-dimensional ideals, and in that, God blesses us to bless the world.

Don't give up. Today is a slice of the future that once gnawed at
your gut. Now it's here, served with a side of supersize grace. Each
single-minded one-foot-in-front-of-the-other will get you to the next
breathtaking view – and eventually, eternity. Relax into the rhythm
of the road and know that ours is a future that's free and everlasting.

Jesus, I can't wait to find You in my future! Amen.

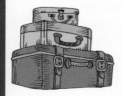

# Bumped

A gentle answer deflects anger, but harsh
words make tempers flare (Prov. 15:1 NLT).

We all get bumped. We bump into people who offend us. We bump into ourselves – surprised by the jealously or resentment we feel at another's success. We bump into failure we hadn't forecast. We bump into diagnoses and tax implications and alarming news reports.

No matter how much we're building stability into our lives, we can control very few of these bumps. We can only control our reactions and responses when something knocks us off kilter. Amy Carmichael said, 'For a cup brimful of sweet water cannot spill even one drop of bitter water, however suddenly jolted.'

When we're bumped, abundant life should come sloshing out of us. That doesn't mean we have a sickly-sweet smiling comeback line even when the struggle is real. It just means we live guilt free because the Prince of Peace who took our shame to the cross rules in our hearts and relationships. It means we choose to walk in forgiveness, gratitude and unmoving trust in the God who doesn't allow anything to touch our lives without His permission.

God, help me to respond wisely – not react rashly –
when I bump into life. And when people bump up
against me, surprise them with Your presence. Amen.

# Blanketed

> I put on righteousness as my clothing; justice
> was my robe and my turban (Job 29:14 NIV).

You've probably seen kids playing make-believe with dress-up clothes – putting on skits and imagining castles and crowns. You probably remember playing make-believe yourself.

I recall watching a home-play performed by a giggle of girls in shorts and t-shirts. One girl disappeared under a blanket to change from pauper to princess. The blanket was a wriggle of excitement – the odd limb emerging – then the covering was flung off and the princess materialized, tiara and all.

That's exactly what God's grace does *to* us, and *for* us. It blankets us – so we're changed. It covers sin and self completely – so we're transformed into the royalty God declares us to be. His grace is always *changing* grace, so an encounter with it will always leave us dressed different: covered and crowned.

Lord, I don't want to fall for emotionalism or
make-believe. I long for Your real, wrap-around,
life-changing, world-altering grace. Amen.

# Beautiful boundaries

The boundary lines have fallen for me in pleasant places;
surely I have a delightful inheritance (Ps. 16:6 NIV).

A friend told me how she had to share the treasured workspace of her study, with her two kids. They were all over her things – using up her space and her stationery and her patience. So she bought some colored ribbons, measured out three spaces, and pinned the ribbons across the workspace to mark the boundaries of their individual areas. She got them their own stationery and turned it all into a celebration.

She was astounded at how those boundaries brought *life*. They taught her kids how to fill their space – just *their* space – and how to fill it well, beautifully and appropriately. Once they understood what was theirs to own, they did a great job, managing their allotment.

We tend to see boundaries as negative restrictions: *this far and no further!* We feel guilty about setting up boundaries in our lives. And the boundary guilt is particularly acute when it comes to relationships. But actually, boundaries give birth to beautiful things like order, respect, responsibility and breathe-easy love.

God, show me where the lines in my relationships
or responsibilities have been unhealthily blurred.
Teach me how to lay down beautiful boundaries
that result in greater love and life. Amen.

# Everything's ok

They do not fear bad news; they confidently
trust the LORD to care for them (Ps. 112:7 NLT).

*I* often get rattled by global and local fear-mongering media outlets. The news is seldom good, right? I start wondering if I'm missing something. Should we pack our bags and go? Should we batten down the hatches and stay?

I also get rattled by my own ambitions. What if I haven't achieved enough yet? Worse still, what if I never do?

What helps me on those days is a few simple sentences I say to myself amidst deep breaths. I say to me, 'All your dreams have already come true.' Because they have. If I think about the things that will really matter to me at the end of my life? They're already in place, because I'm at peace with my people. And then I say, 'It's a beautiful day in (whatever place I am), and I'm standing with my feet on the ground.' Because we're all just under the same big sky and God made the weather today every place you are and if we have food and covering, we can be content (1 Timothy 6:8).

God, help me not to live always waiting for the
other shoe to drop. Help me remember both shoes are
snug on my feet and I stand on the Rock that is You. Amen.

# Slave

But now you are free from the power of sin and have
become slaves of God. Now you do those things that
lead to holiness and result in eternal life (Rom. 6:22 NLT).

*I*f you're addicted to drugs, alcohol, pornography or anything else, God can set you free. (Yip. I just went there.)

The power of His voice called the boundless universe into existence. He's entirely strong enough to break the power of a chemical, an image or a euphoric feeling. God wants to deliver you – because He wants to be your only Master. He doesn't want you enslaved to anything but His great love.

Your deliverance might be immediate. Or it might take years. But He's a thorough physician. He will complete the good work He starts in you (Philippians 1:6).

Addictions are also cultural phenomena – and every addiction isn't as obvious as drug abuse or alcoholism. Some addictions are even trendy. (I'm looking at you, coffee.) It's like, if your kids walked in on you snorting cocaine? They'd be horrified. If they caught you scoffing chocolate, they might just ask for some. The consequences of a cocaine addiction are way more traumatic, but you may be equally enslaved to chocolate, coffee, or something else fairly benign. Just sayin'. And preaching to the mirror.

Jesus, I want to lose my addiction baggage. Show me
if there is any obsession, habit or unhealthy dependence
that I need to dump forever at Your feet. Amen.

# Unburdened

He personally carried our sins in His body on the
cross so that we can be dead to sin and live for what
is right. By His wounds you are healed (1 Pet. 2:24 NLT).

*I*n John Bunyan's classic allegory *The Pilgrim's Progress*, Christian
– the protagonist – gets to the cross, where he loses the heavy
burden he's been carrying. It rolls off his back, and rolls away down
the hill. He's baggage-free at last.

Perhaps you remember a time in your life when there was a
dramatic rolling away of the burden. Maybe the day of your salvation
stands out as a life-watershed moment. Or maybe you recall a season
during which there was a slow, steady sorting through and rolling
away of your sin-load.

But actually, we need to be shedding our burden at the foot of the
cross *every day*. We collect baggage all the time, through things we
see, hear and experience, and through the effect that relationships
have on us. Sometimes old baggage that we thought we'd dropped
claws its way back. Take it to the cross.

Father, I'm so filled up with abundant life! I'd be a fool to keep on
carrying the burden of sin and self. Take it from me, please. Amen.

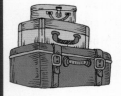

# JUNE

## Nothing to Declare

Travel makes one
modest. You see what
a tiny place you
occupy in the world.

*Gustave Flaubert*

# Live in the light

And we all, who with unveiled faces contemplate the
Lord's glory, are being transformed into His image
with ever-increasing glory, which comes from
the Lord, who is the Spirit (2 Cor. 3:18 NIV).

The world is bent on human rights, and so it should be, because for far too long far too many people didn't have any. And you absolutely do have the right to privacy. Some things are sacred and special and need only be shared with a trusted few, or a trusted one, or God alone.

Yet as believers we have a mandate to live in the light – with 'unveiled faces'. The truth is, no one walks away from Jesus because of Jesus. They walk away from Jesus because of people who say they follow Jesus, but who aren't taking seriously the responsibility of living pure lives. So maybe it shouldn't worry us that Google knows everything about us, because we should have nothing to hide.

In fact, the notion of large corporations violating our privacy by trawling through our Facebook accounts or messaging platforms might even excite us, because maybe in the words and photos and memes and likes, they'll come across something of Jesus.

God, I want to live in the light, so that anyone
looking at my life will see You, lit. Amen.

# Evening offering

Say to the people: This is the special gift you must
present to the LORD as your daily burnt offering.
You must offer two one-year-old male lambs
with no defects. Sacrifice one lamb in the morning
and the other in the evening (Num. 28:3-4 NLT).

A mentor of mine encouraged me years ago to give God an
evening offering. The idea comes from the Hebrew practice
of morning and evening sacrifice (but without the burning lambs).
Before drifting off to sleep – when my brain is sifting through the day
and slowing down – I try to remember to ask, 'Lord, what pleased
You today?' And then, 'Lord, what didn't please You today?'

You'll be amazed how the day's moments will surface almost
immediately: the God-honoring moments of love or difficult
obedience or *not* saying the thing you really wanted to say – those
things that pleased Him. And then those things that didn't – the
harsh word to your husband, the coveting or impatience or greed.

Leaving at the King's feet the things that delighted Him helps you
not to get proud. It reminds you that you did them for Him anyway,
not for you. And leaving at His feet those things that *didn't* delight
Him helps you repent quickly – running into the reprieve of His grace
and forgiveness.

Yahweh, thank You that I'm not defined
by today's success or failure, and that
tomorrow I'll wake up to new mercies. Amen.

# Even if

'If we are thrown into the blazing furnace, the
God whom we serve is able to save us. He will
rescue us from your power, Your Majesty. But even
if He doesn't, we want to make it clear to you, Your
Majesty, that we will never serve your gods or worship
the gold statue you have set up' (Dan. 3:17-18 NLT).

*A* few years ago, I got a fantastic job offer. On paper, I was a fool
not to accept. But I got heart palpitations just thinking about
it. I knew, as attractive as the proposal was, it wasn't God's will.

I had nothing tangible to show for what *was* God's will – nothing
much more than a strong gut feeling. And if my gut was wrong and
He didn't come through for me, I'd end up looking incredibly stupid. I
realized, *This is what obedience really feels like!* It's choosing anyway to
obey – *even if* things don't work out.

Millions of men and women throughout history have lived or led
without vindication – and that might be the story you and I are living
too. We might never be the hero the world finally recognizes and
applauds. *Even if* we die having not seen the fruit of our blood, sweat
and effort, it's actually ok. God sees.

Father, I'm committing to obedience. In this life or the next,
I know You'll clear my name, and claim me as Yours. Amen.

# Just say no

This is what the LORD says: 'Stop at the crossroads and look around. Ask for the old, godly way, and walk in it. Travel its path, and you will find rest for your souls. But you reply, "No, that's not the road we want!"' (Jer. 6:16 NLT)

*I* wonder if the reason many more people today struggle with depression is because we live in an age of abundant choice – each choice laden with perplexing, complicated, latent consequences.

We face a plethora of overwhelming options, and to live in-the-light lives, we need to pray for some clarity on what we should and shouldn't be choosing. Let's be intentional about seeking wisdom and simplicity, because sure, we can do anything, but we can't do everything, and we certainly can't do it all, have it all, and be it all, today.

It may be easier for you to manage your *yeses* well, when you can get it right to disinvest from what people might think of your *no*. Sometimes it's important to consider the impact of a decision on your reputation, and sometimes you need to take ownership of your capacity and your unique context, and *just say no*.

God, I want to say *yes* to You today. Give me wisdom and courage, kindness and courtesy, so I can say *no* if I need to, in a God-glorifying, people-honoring way. Amen.

# Get over it

> Obviously, I'm not trying to win the approval
> of people, but of God. If pleasing people were my
> goal, I would not be Christ's servant (Gal. 1:10 NLT).

Part of traveling light – and living in the light – is getting over the fear of displeasing other people.

Most of us like to think of ourselves as strong and independent, knowing our own minds and not needing validation or affirmation from others. And yet, if we're properly honest, we cringe when things we say come out wrong and we wonder and worry about how our decisions might be received. The humbling thing is that worrying about what others think – wondering if we measure up to their expectations – *that's just pride.*

Ordinary, everyday life is a bit like public speaking. A lot can go wrong on the day. You don't know for sure who your audience will be and how your message will be heard. Perhaps the best thing we can do, to live with confidence and courage, is get over ourselves and aim all our sayings and doings at the audience of One: the only audience that really matters. Let's focus first on connecting with Him – then on communicating with others.

Jesus, I want to live to please You. If I get to
please people as well, that's just a bonus. Amen.

# No one's watching

For we speak as messengers approved by
God to be entrusted with the Good News. Our
purpose is to please God, not people. He alone
examines the motives of our hearts (1 Thess. 2:4 NLT).

One way of living in the light despite the risk and vulnerability of doing so, is remembering that those you're trying to impress probably aren't particularly interested in your efforts. Instead of showing off, get behind God. Trust Him to go ahead of you to open hearts and grace spaces for you to follow Him into, boldly.

You'll probably be your truest self – your most relaxed and most beautiful self – when you're living as if only God is looking on. A day or two from now – three weeks from now – and certainly an eternity from now – no one will remember or be focused on your magnificent success, your mishaps or mistakes. And if you survive a mortifying moment? It'll be a great story to tell.

Father, please take away my self-consciousness. Make
me casual and comfortable – calm and confident – like a
daughter in her Father's house should be. Amen.

# Display

Bring all who claim Me as their God, for I have made them for My glory. It was I who created them (Isa. 43:7 NLT).

All of life is art. God even calls us His masterpieces (Ephesians 2:10). Art needs an audience, but an audience of One is enough. A painting hangs in a gallery for anyone and everyone to see. It's not ashamed. It's also not aware of who walks past to ogle, or ignore. It's not aware of itself or its onlookers. And therein lies the beauty.

You're a work of God's genius creativity and you're on display in the Kingdom gallery. Know that the Artist Himself admires you unblinkingly. He looks on with generous love. It's a glorious thing to live with an awareness of just that, and nothing else.

Great Creator, I'm humbled that You would craft me uniquely, and delight in displaying me for Your glory. Amen.

# Hope declared

And this hope will not lead to disappointment. For we know how dearly God loves us, because He has given us the Holy Spirit to fill our hearts with His love (Rom. 5:5 NLT).

*I*magine for a moment how our homes, our cities, our countries or the world would change if, before customs officials and everywhere else, we lived with nothing to declare, other than our hope in Jesus.

If you tend towards optimism, it's easy to put your hope in a bunch of other things. And if you tend towards pessimism, you're probably more likely to lose hope altogether. Both options lead to disappointment.

But Paul tells us there's a hope that *does not disappoint*, and His name is Jesus. So, if we've been disappointed – and of course we have been, and of course we will be again – our hope was in the wrong thing. It's ok to be disappointed. It's inevitable. But let's decide today to keep on declaring the truth that there's still, always, the hope that does not disappoint.

Jesus, it's such a relief that no matter what happens in this world, I will always have hope, because I will always have You. Amen.

# Keep it real

Seek the Kingdom of God above all else, and He
will give you everything you need (Luke 12:31 NLT).

Social media is a stunning invention. I'm so grateful for the way it connects people and gives us a means of instantaneously sharing news, sharing love, and sharing Jesus. But Facebook, Instagram and other platforms have seen to it that we're frothing to let the world know what we're doing, and how beautifully or perfectly we're doing it.

Maybe one of the secrets to traveling light is to slide your screen off a little more often. Keep your head down, and work at doing real life as wonderfully well as possible. What is God saying to you, today? What's the work He has cut out for you, today? Do it. Take seriously your personal holiness – becoming more and more like Jesus.

Seek first the Kingdom. The rest will take care of itself. And when you lift your head there will be fruit hanging low and ripe from your beautiful branches. Better than pixels – it'll be ready for actual people, to actually pick.

God, let's keep it real. Help me to be authentic:
not pretending perfection, but rather just living,
loving and doing life for You. Amen.

# Declaring others

I have not stopped thanking God for you.
I pray for you constantly … (Eph. 1:16 NLT).

The most effective way out of the heaviness and darkness of self is to celebrate someone else. I heard it said once of an eminent leader: 'He makes other people the hero, which is what all great communicators do.' And you're communicating all day, every day.

Through loud opinions or disinterested silences – you're sending a message to the world around you. Your every action and attitude says something about your values, priorities and state of being.

Could you step out into the spotlight on the stage of today and sing someone's praises? Take the focus off yourself. Make another human the hero. Be an excellent communicator by declaring the loveliness of someone else.

Almighty God, let the message of my life be loud and clear.
I want to be all about honoring others and glorifying You. Amen.

# Word worship

For I am not ashamed of this Good News about Christ.
It is the power of God at work, saving everyone who
believes – the Jew first and also the Gentile (Rom. 1:16 NLT).

When our youngest son was five years old, he asked me, of someone who had come to visit, 'Is he a Christian?' I said, 'Um, I think he is.' Surprised, my son replied, 'Oh. But he never really talks about God?'

No one had overtly explained it, but he'd somehow absorbed the truth that *we talk about what we worship*. Without faking it or contriving our piety, we can naturally give it away – who or what we worship – with our words.

Solomon writes, 'Do not be quick with your mouth, do not be hasty in your heart to utter anything before God. God is in heaven and you are on earth, so let your words be few' (Ecclesiastes 5:2 NIV). While we should unquestionably choose our words well, when we do use them, they should reflect a world view in which God is on the throne.

Jesus, teach me how to season my
conversations with the flavor of You. Amen.

# Special Snowflake Syndrome

So humble yourselves under the mighty power of God, and at the right time He will lift you up in honor (1 Pet 5:6 NLT).

Urban Dictionary defines a Special Snowflake like this: *A person who believes they are different and unique from everyone else because of something they are or do. This thing they are or do, most commonly is something many, many other people are doing. Special Snowflakes almost always have a superiority complex.*

Society has pretty much created a generation of Special Snowflakes. We and our kids are told how particularly gifted we are. How marvelously irreplaceable. It's a bit like George Orwell's *Animal Farm*, in which all animals are equal, but some are more equal than others. Special Snowflake Syndrome croons that all people are special, but *you are more special than most*. And believing it makes us unpleasant to be around.

Humans are reactionary. The pendulum of culture always swings way too far one way, and then the other. People who grew up feeling squashed down – seen not heard – want to raise up kids who are seen, heard *and* given a unicorn. And yet our Kingdom work is to keep on keeping on being the voice of reason on a planet of crazy extremes. Let's suspend radical truth dead center, to steady us and others.

Great God, take me down a notch, where I've bought into the lie that I'm something superior. Amen.

# Set apart

You made me; You created me. Now give me the
sense to follow Your commands (Ps. 119:73 NLT).

You needn't be a Special Snowflake to know that you are unique.
You're never-before, never-again. God says, 'I knew you before
I formed you in your mother's womb. Before you were born I set
you apart ...' (Jeremiah 1:5 NLT). He says that He made all the inside
and the outside bits of you (Psalm 139:13), that every hair on your
head is numbered (Matthew 10:30) and that He has plans for you
(Jeremiah 29:11). That should completely blow each one of our small
snowflakey minds.

It's not that God *needs* us. He's the all-sufficient sustainer of the
universe. It's just astounding and humbling and so very exciting
that He sees fit to make us, love us and use us as part of His coming
Kingdom on this planet. God has created a position for you in His
organization. Just like everyone else, you've been set apart for a
marvelous, God-designed purpose.

God, I can't believe You'd want to use me uniquely
to spread Your name and Your fame. Thank You for
delighting in making me different. Amen.

# Unique like everyone

For you are a holy people, who belong to the LORD your
God. Of all the people on earth, the LORD your God has
chosen you to be His own special treasure (Deut. 7:6 NLT).

*E*ach one of us is head-to-toe unique. And yet, we're not *uniquely*
unique. You're unique, *like everyone*. So don't feel uniquely
superior. God doesn't owe you something because you're peerless.
The only one entitled to anything in your relationship with God, is
God. He's entitled to His glory.

What's more, we all get to decide for ourselves what the practical
outworking of our faith looks like, as lifestyle. If you decide to be an
edgy, organic Christian who doesn't do church, that's cool. Know
that there are others like you, and you're not extra special or extra
spiritual. If you decide to get into the flow of a mainstream (live-
streamed) Sunday thing that serves cappuccinos, that won't get you
a special dispensation of grace. If you lean into meditative vibes, you'll
be another trendy contemplative, of many.

Jesus paid a high price for your freedom. Your one unique life is
about living that freedom with humble joyful thanks, in all the ways
you know how, to make His name great. That is all.

Lord, help me never lose focus on the grand and
unified aim of believers everywhere. Help me live
my unique calling excellently, making space for
others to live theirs. Amen.

# Not about you

O LORD, our Lord, Your majestic name fills the earth!
Your glory is higher than the heavens. You have taught
children and infants to tell of Your strength, silencing
Your enemies and all who oppose You. When I look
at the night sky and see the work of Your fingers –
the moon and the stars You set in place – what are
mere mortals that You should think about them, human
beings that You should care for them (Ps. 8:1-4 NLT)?

Your uniqueness isn't about you.

You get to do your very own life's work and live out your
very own shimmering destiny. But whether you're hilarious, smart,
sensitive or gregarious: all of that loveliness points to your King. The
small white miracle that is each inimitable snowflake doesn't point to
the greatness of the snowflake.

It points to the greatness of the One who made it. Your startling,
powerful uniqueness points to the genius of the One who encoded
your DNA. Your unique gifts are *yours*, but not *for you*. They're to be
used for others, and for the glory of God.

God, thank You that we're all distinct from one another, but not
divided. I want to live that individuality in such a way that it
increases the influence of Your Kingdom on earth. Amen.

# Declaring dependence

O Lord, I give my life to You (Ps. 25:1 nlt).

*I*ndependence is standing on your own two grownup feet, knowing you're responsible for your life. Independence asks, 'What comes next?' then bravely commits.

The Bible doesn't actually have much to say about independence. It does talk about how in Christ we're *independent* from sin (Galatians 5:1). It does talk about working *independently* with our own hands for our own money (2 Thessalonians 3:10) – not being lazy or leaning into the destructiveness of co-dependence.

But mostly, the Bible talks about dependence, and dependability. Throughout the God-story, we read about our desperate *dependence* on a Savior, and how His character forged in us makes us *dependable*. The Word pours stories of community, communion and companionship. Stories about how we're created to need each other's strength and trustworthiness. Stories about how the world will wonder Who we follow. They'll watch us loving each other. And they'll know (John 13:35).

Independence is important. It's right-sized self-assurance that lends us the stability to be dependable. But we dare not let independence mutate into arrogance or self-sufficiency, thinking we're invincible, or above needing the help or accountability of others. How cool, rather, to be known for our courageous dependability on our Redeemer.

Lord God, make me dependable,
and wholly dependent on You. Amen.

# Traveling older

> … Though our bodies are dying, our spirits
> are being renewed every day (2 Cor. 4:16 NLT).

*I* got my first gray hair at 28. I was horrified. The graying has been gradual. Insidious. There's been no absolute *coup d'état* – the brunette clings to power – but the troops in gray gather momentum and ferocity as I advance through the decades.

I have options. I could throw into my monthly grocery cart a box of medium-brown color, to keep the enemy at bay. I could get highlights to conceal the enemy and start down the potentially slippery slope of turning into a fake-blonde forty-something-year-old, secretly pitied as mutton dressed up as lamb. Or I could surrender. Go gray.

Whatever option you or I choose to go with when the time comes, I'm not so stressed about going gray, and you shouldn't be either. It is what it is. Sooner or later, it happens to everyone.

Original sin kick-started the tick of time that counts us all down to age and death and no one can slow it. That's ok. The end marks the beginning and the best is yet to be. Nothing like an eternal mindset to expose the silliness of vainly fighting an inevitable war of attrition – frantically trying to look younger than the person in the trenches next to us. Be your beautiful self.

> Father, even as time takes its toll, rejuvenate
> my spirit to reflect my eternal reality. Amen.

# In your skin

> Don't be concerned about the outward beauty of fancy hairstyles, expensive jewelry, or beautiful clothes. You should clothe yourselves instead with the beauty that comes from within, the unfading beauty of a gentle and quiet spirit, which is so precious to God (1 Pet. 3:3-4 NLT).

The color of your skin, your eyes or your hair doesn't define you. A wise someone said, 'If the world was blind, how many people would you impress?' The mark you'll make on this page of history has little to do with how awesome you look to those around you.

So let's just stop it. Let's stop being insecure. Stop comparing. Your worth – stunning daughter of the King clothed in royal robes – was settled at the cross. Stop trying to find it in the opinions of others.

For sure, make the most of what you have. Feel beautiful and be the best version of you. Worship God with how He's put you together, and don't judge how other women are doing that.

Be a great steward of your beauty within the reasonable limits of time, money and product availability, tempering that with the truth that compromising on what's good, right and wise almost always points to idolatry.

God, do a complete makeover of my insides –
so much so that it would show on my outsides. Amen.

# Celebrate

Gray hair is a crown of glory; it is gained
by living a godly life (Prov. 16:31 NLT).

*A* lovely gray-haired young mama friend of mine says she's going with Proverbs 16:31. She's seeing gray hair as a sign of the wisdom that comes from evaluated life experiences – like she's earned it and she could and should be proud of her silver streaks. She's celebrating.

So, beautiful woman midway through the adventure of life, there's no shame in flashes of white light where before there was only dark. Remind yourself that, possibly, you earned those stripes all the nights you paced the passage willing your babies to sleep. *Sleep.* Oh please God SLEEP. Maybe you earned them that year your kid got teased a lot or all the many years you waited for your dream guy or those months that went on far longer than the money did.

Remind yourself that, probably, it's just genetics. And that's ok too. God birthed you into this family with these genes at this time in this place. You're created for His purposes and for His glory, genes and all. And it's all pretty wonderful.

Lord, help me live each season of this
life gracefully, and with great delight. Amen.

# Impressed

So we make it our goal to please Him … (2 Cor. 5:9 NIV).

*Y*ou're seeing specific faces, aren't you? You're not just worried about what people will think. You're worried about what *certain* people will think.' Perceptively, my husband said this to me after a work deadline I'd slaved to meet had been shifted on – with good reason – meaning that the visible fruit of all my invisible work was still months away. It wasn't actually a big deal. Except, in my world on that day, *it was a big deal.*

But my husband was spot on. My hopes were flying high above the bright horizon of expectation. Then they weren't. And the disappointment was less about delayed income, and more about not having something to show – *sooner!* – for months of lonely laptop time during which it must've appeared to people whose high opinion I covet that I don't lead a very productive life.

My husband also (diplomatically) reminded me of the value of submitting to people who know more than us (even about our areas of expertise). And of being grateful (even grudgingly) for checks and balances in place to protect us – because we're seldom the smartest, wisest, most experienced person in the room.

In our efforts and endeavors to impress, let's simply keep in mind the face of our Savior.

Jesus, I love You best of all. I want to impress
You with every part of my life! Amen.

# Little pencil

We are the clay, and You are the potter (Isa. 64:8 NLT).

Mother Teresa wrote, 'I'm a little pencil in the hand of a writing God, who is sending a love letter to the world … He does the thinking. He does the writing. He does everything and sometimes it is really hard because it is a broken pencil and He has to sharpen it a little more.'

She was all about being the little pencil. She wasn't even a high-lighter. A glitter pen! She was a *broken* pencil and she knew ultimately there'd be no trace left of her in this world. Only the marks of *Him*. And she was totally ok for Him to do the writing.

You and I absolutely have to get out of our own way so God can work out – not *our* purposes – but *His* purposes, through us. Hundreds of sisters in Mother Teresa's order were never venerated for their sacrifice. It's possible – even *likely* – that you and I will serve and sacrifice unappreciated. And that is *so* fine.

When we surrender to the only God who can make something meaningful of our lives – when we stop investing so heavily in our ambitions and agendas – it's remarkably liberating. Disentangled from self-interest, we're fantastically free to go where He sends, and do as He does.

God, take what lead is left in this
little life. Do all the writing. Amen.

# Love-defiant

> Whoever does not love does not know
> God, because God is love (1 John 4:8 NIV).

Traveling in any shape or form – on business, vacation or through life – we'll definitely meet weird people. People hard to love. We should consider, then: *What sad thing happened to this person? What happened today? Last night? Ten years ago? What choice does he regret? What sort of journey led her to this emotional or spiritual space?*

God wastes nothing – least of all our every human interaction. Love never fails (1 Corinthians 13:8), so even though we might walk away from love-defiant people feeling ineffective, God sees the heart. He sees *our* hearts, genuinely loving and respecting the love-defiant. But He sees the love-defiant person's heart too. And if enough people heap love on the love-defiant – the genuine, relentless affection of the Father who runs to us, to rescue us – it might all add up to some kind of wonderful tipping point.

We tend to underestimate the power of God's presence – forgetting we take it with us wherever we go. And so *wherever we go* maybe we've got to ask ourselves, *What does love look like, in this place, at this time?*

Lord, let it be that whoever I interact with today, I leave them somehow different, by choosing to love. Amen.

JUNE 23

# Catch the light

Those who look to Him for help will be radiant with joy; no
shadow of shame will darken their faces (Ps. 34:5 NLT).

Diamonds are multi-faceted. That's what makes them sparkle
and shine as they catch the light. Bits of them have been cut
away, polished, and angled into different surfaces.

Your life is multi-faceted too. You may be a wife, mom, friend,
sister, daughter, employer … And you're thinking, *All those facets of
my life don't make me sparkly; they make me exhausted.* Me too! But
don't lose heart, or stop dreaming. God is shaping you. Polishing you.
Cutting away bits of you to make something beautiful as you trust
Him to position you in those different arenas, for His glory.

God calls us to shine in all facets of our lives – and maybe He's
convicting you in one particular area? Maybe all He's asking is that you
surrender to Him your work, your finances, a particular relationship
or the area of authority you've been given – whatever comes to mind
as you think about your many-faceted life. What catches the light
and gleams?

And what has become dull and unpolished? We're sometimes
our most beautiful when we're most vulnerable. Could you take one
beautiful step towards polishing what needs a new shine by asking
one trusted friend to pray for you – for that facet of your life?

God, polish every facet of me, until I shine. Amen.

# Diamond reset

Remember to observe the Sabbath
day by keeping it holy (Ex. 20:8 NLT).

My sister took her wedding ring to a jeweler, because she could feel that the diamond was loose and she didn't want it falling out in the sink or the garden and losing it forever. The diamond needed to be glued in again – *reset*.

Friend, we need to be reset too. In fact we need to be reset so badly and so often that God commanded we do it once a week. And if we're going to continue to live the multi-faceted lives we're living, and live them beautifully, we have to rest, and reset. Finding a slot in your week to Sabbath intentionally is crucial – perhaps more so than ever.

It might help you to rest better if you remember that, just as every diamond is unique – cut and polished differently – God uses us all in unique ways, in different seasons. He displays us in different ways, at different times, and that's ok. You can do anything, but you can't do everything. And certainly not all at once.

Heavenly Father, help me to humble myself,
and to take time out to rest. Amen.

# Fierce diamonds

You must be compassionate, just as your
Father is compassionate (Luke 6:36 NLT).

Diamonds are the hardest natural substance known to man. They can be fierce. Only another diamond can scratch a diamond. And sure, lots of things in life can scratch *us*. But for the sake of the metaphor (in which we're the diamonds), let's take this as a warning to treat all the other diamonds in our lives with deep love and great respect, because we're unbelievably powerful. Our words are powerful. The social circles we make that include and exclude, are powerful.

Diamonds are also kind of mysterious. When the movie *Blood Diamond* came out, I was horrified. Like, *what if I'm wearing a blood diamond?* My husband bought my wedding ring from a jeweler at the mall but we don't know the full story behind my diamond. Where in the earth was it formed? Was it mined by child soldiers with guns?

Let's decide to stop being so fierce. Let's treat one another's stories gently, *because we don't know them fully*. Decide to see the beauty in others, knowing that allowing them to sparkle doesn't diminish our own light. And all of us should be sparkling our sparkle for the common Kingdom cause, so we should hope and pray all the women around us shine as brightly as possible.

God, make me gentle, believing the best about
others, because I don't have the full story. Amen.

# Hard as diamonds

> So, my dear brothers and sisters, be strong and immovable. Always work enthusiastically for the Lord, for you know that nothing you do for the Lord is ever useless (1 Cor. 15:58 NLT).

The word *diamond* is from the Latin *adamans* from which we get adamant: unshakeable, immovable, inflexible, unwavering, uncompromising, resolute, resolved, determined, steadfast.

Ultimately, spiritual maturity isn't measured in terms of perfect knowledge or perfect behavior, but in terms of persevering faith.

Jeremy Courtney tells the story of how he and his family moved to Iraq after 9/11, and then to Syria, just to be Jesus to a devastated people. Jeremy founded the Pre-emptive Love Coalition. Their mission is that, wherever there's violence and war, they're the first people there and the last to leave. He talks about seeing people, instead of seeing problems – about moving into a neighborhood and loving the way Jesus loved. In doing so, he and his wife and his young children have been shot at by snipers and there isn't a day when he isn't afraid. But, he says, 'You move fear to the passenger seat. You keep driving. And you love anyway.'

That's unshakeable, immovable, inflexible, unwavering, uncompromising, resolute, resolved, determined, steadfast, firm *diamond* faith.

> O God, give me rock hard, glittering, world-changing faith! Amen.

# Darkness, heat and pressure

> We are pressed on every side by troubles,
> but we are not crushed. We are perplexed,
> but not driven to despair (2 Cor. 4:8 NLT).

Diamonds are formed in a unique and specific way. To make a diamond, you need extreme pressure, incredibly hot temperatures, in the dark, for a long time. Diamonds form at a depth of at least a hundred miles below the earth's crust, in volcanic magma. When volcanoes erupt they shoot the diamonds up towards the earth's surface where they can be mined, or picked up in river silt.

Have you experienced – at some point in your life, or now – intense heat and pressure and stress in your life? Do you feel like God's left you in the dark, and like it's gone on for far, far too long? Paul writes, 'We are pressed on every side by troubles, but we are not crushed.' When you're pressed on every side, it's possible that God is forming something beautiful and unbreakable – un-crushable – in you.

Paul doesn't say, 'We're pressed on every side by troubles and *it's awesome! We're loving it*.' He just says, 'We are not crushed.' Breathe deep even as the pressure mounts. He will not let you be crushed.

God, I feel like this thing is squeezing the life out of me.
Help me believe that You won't let it finish me, and You
won't leave me in the darkness, heat or pressure forever. Amen.

# Diamonds are a girl's best friend

For you have been given not only the privilege
of trusting in Christ but also the privilege
of suffering for Him (Phil. 1:29 NLT).

*I* don't say this flippantly, but it's possible we need to see darkness, heat and pressure as a gift. A friend. We can *befriend* suffering because it's part of our royal inheritance as daughters of the King who really suffered, for us.

I'm not telling you to cheer up because Jesus wants you for a sunbeam. Befriending suffering doesn't mean that suffering isn't devastating. It's just that suffering doesn't define you or God.

Job is a great example of someone who lived a fantastic life, and suffered unbelievably. He went through intense heat, darkness and pressure, for a good long while. God didn't stop loving him, counting the hairs on his head, or holding together the universe. But Job still suffered. The rocks around his life were pressing him on every side. He didn't feel sparkly and strong. He felt shocked, sad and angry.

But in the end – *before* God restored everything (Job 42:12) and while he was still a hot mess – Job recognized that his hope should be in God, not in the geological conditions of his life. So in the end, the heat, pressure and darkness didn't shake his identity or his relationship with God.

Father, help me befriend suffering because
of what it produces in me. Amen.

# Faith like diamonds

He will keep you strong to the end so that you
will be free from all blame on the day when
our Lord Jesus Christ returns (1 Cor. 1:8 NLT).

*I*magine we rose to the challenge of being faithful and faith-filled women of God: women with faith in a Creator-King who thought to magic diamonds in the dark depths of the earth, some of which haven't even yet been discovered.

God is growing things in the dark all the time. He's begun good works already that will play out, to His glory, years from now. He's working things out secretly in our lives that we may never even notice or know about. He's using our faith today to build legacies we won't live to see. We know He'll ultimately and eternally complete His work in us (Philippians 1:6). He won't leave us in the dark, the heat and the pressure because Jesus gave His life to present us – the church – to Himself glorious, without a single blemish: holy and without fault (Ephesians 5:27).

We can also enjoy the truth that His great faithfulness in our lives sets us free to enjoy being faithful friends, wives, moms, bosses, daughters-in-law, fill-in-the-blanks. We don't have to get defensive in any one of our multi-faceted roles, because we've got a faithful Defender.

O God, why do I ever doubt that You've got this thing? Amen.

# Diamonds are forever

For this God is our God for ever and ever;
He will be our guide even to the end (Ps. 48:14 NIV).

*I*n our culture, diamond rings symbolize covenant. When your boyfriend proposed, put a ring on your finger and suddenly became your fiancé, he was entering into more than a contractual agreement. He was entering into a covenant with you.

When it comes to covenants, lives are at stake. In the Hebrew tradition they'd cut animals in half as a way of saying, 'If I don't keep my covenant with you, may this be what happens to me. You can cut me in half.'

We could *never* have kept covenant with God. He knew that. He's the great Covenant Keeper, and so He said, *OK, I'll be the sacrificial lamb. I'll be cut and killed. Let this happen to Me – on your behalf – so that I can be your forever.*

God was there at your beginning and He'll be there at your end and then He will be in your eternity. Maybe we can let our diamonds remind us of what's to come. The diamonds we wear, the diamonds we want – they're beautiful – but man, we ain't seen nothin' yet.

Jesus, I have nothing to declare,
except that I'm Yours forever. Amen.

# JULY

*In Transit*

Wherever you go
becomes a part of
you somehow.

*Anita Desai*

# Hurry up and wait

Yet I am confident I will see the LORD's goodness while
I am here in the land of the living. Wait patiently
for the LORD. Be brave and courageous. Yes, wait
patiently for the LORD (Ps. 27:13-14 NLT).

Airports are all about hurry up and wait. Hurry! Get there on time to check in for the next flight! Then wait …

And if someone were to ask me, 'What's the hardest thing about being a Christian?' I'd say without waiting: 'Waiting.' It seems no matter what our life's circumstances, God makes us wait. His chief concerns are His glory, His Kingdom, and transforming us into His likeness, so I have to believe that waiting contributes to all that. It renders in us a kind of transformation that nothing else does.

So we wait for Him. We wait for others. We wait for dreams to come true and desires to be fulfilled. We wait for clarity and resolution, help and healing. We wait for eternity.

Now and then God surprises us with a swift orchestration of events and we go, 'Whoa! That was fast! God's really moving!' But mostly, He works unhurriedly – because we're quick to forget and slow to trust. Or because He's fashioning unseen, background plans, or crafting in us the beauty of patient surrender.

God, show me if I should wait passively –
letting go entirely and waiting for You to work –
or actively – by working while I wait. Amen.

# Obscurity or exhibition

So whether you eat or drink, or whatever you do,
do it all for the glory of God (1 Cor. 10:31 NLT).

The hardest thing about waiting can be not knowing what God is up to. We're not sure if or when we'll see the results or rewards of our efforts, and if those efforts even matter.

Like, perhaps you have a platform of international influence. Or perhaps you're scanning barcodes at a checkout. In the eyes of the King who has welcomed you into His royal household as a child and heir – both of those activities are of absolute and equal significance. You don't know what hangs in the balance of either of those pursuits. But God sees your heart in moments of great public recognition, influence or authority. And God sees your heart in small moments of obscurity and anonymity. Both kinds of moment might carry enormous Kingdom significance, your obedience reverberating in eternity. And both kinds of moment might mean nothing. Those moments might be empty, wasted bits of life – if your heart harbors selfishness or pride.

Whether God has you waiting for the next big thing, or in the midst of a big thing, just as much is at stake. Live those moments as if every small or big thing is a Kingdom thing.

Lord, whether I'm winning, or waiting
in the wings, I'm going to do it for You. Amen.

# Mandatory transit

Then Jesus said, 'Let's go off by ourselves to a quiet place and rest awhile.' He said this because there were so many people coming and going that Jesus and His apostles didn't even have time to eat (Mark 6:31 NLT).

Sometimes waiting is forced upon us. We don't get a say about when we wait, or for how long. And sometimes we need to be intentional about building into our lives times of transit – times to rest, and reset, and allow our souls to catch up with our bodies.

Our culture is bent on sweeping us into all things fast and frenetic, because that makes us feel successful, and because it makes us spend more money on things that help us cope with the pace and the pressure.

We don't need to believe the lie that if every waking moment isn't filled with something measureable or profitable, we're being idle. The Kingdom way of traveling light is counter-culture. Instead of being maniacally industrious at the expense of health and reason, we can exhibit calm, and rest, and unforced rhythms of grace (Matthew 11:28-30).

Jesus, take over my calendars and agendas. Give me ways and wisdom to block out chunks of transit time – waiting on You, waiting on others. Amen.

# Catch your breath

Be still before the LORD and wait patiently for Him;
do not fret when people succeed in their ways,
when they carry out their wicked schemes (Ps. 37:7 NIV).

Transit time will help you to recalibrate. It's really ok to give yourself a break, just once in a while. You can't change the bed sheets and people's minds and the world, all in one day. It's ok not to multi-task (which is really nothing more than task-switching – which lowers productivity). Rather, do each slow steady thing as if it's the only thing, and do it excellently.

There's a lot of noise out there, and in our heads. Mahatma Gandhi said, 'Speak only if it improves upon the silence.' Breathe more deeply, more often. And pause before you re-enter the fray, so the truth can steady you: there's enough time today to do God's will.

Life is not an emergency and God is not in a rush. The things you're trying frantically to achieve in these hours may not ultimately matter. Waiting around for just a little bit, to catch your breath, is just fine.

God, don't let me get ahead of myself – sacrificing my
strength and emotional wellbeing on the altar of productivity.
I'll worship You, and walk at Your pace. Amen.

# Transit un-wasted

And we know that God causes everything to work together for the good of those who love God and are called according to His purpose for them (Rom. 8:28 NLT).

When you find yourself in the in-between – a season of waiting, deliberating, or being subject to debilitating unknowns – it's still possible to live joyfully and intentionally, making sure that this time isn't pointless or insignificant.

For a start, don't begin a day until it's finished on paper, and surrendered to God in prayer. Plan *something* helpful and meaningful, every day, despite the tedium of the wait you're enduring, and despite the uncertainty you face.

By consistently setting small goals you can confidently ensure that you never have a 'zero day' – a wasted, utterly unsuccessful chunk of life spent and forever behind you.

Faith, a positive attitude and maximum effort go a long way to ensuring that you don't become lethargic in the great transit terminals of life. Waiting needn't equal stagnation. It could be a joy-infused time of rest, and preparation.

God, thank You that You're the God who wastes nothing. Redeem this unused time. Turn it into something unusually useful – for Your glory. Amen.

# Mission in transit

The earth is the LORD's, and everything in it. The world
and all its people belong to Him (Ps. 24:1 NLT).

God's plans for you might be sensational and alluring. *Or not.*
Even if your life feels like one big transit lounge and today
looks the same as yesterday and tomorrow promises more of the
same, God is present in every corner of the globe. He cares for you and
your people in your ostensibly hum-drum circumstances as much as
He cares for anyone else in any other small spot of this planet.

Holly Gerth writes, 'God doesn't value a far-off *there* more than an
ordinary and near *here*. And every *there* for us is someone else's *here*.'
Other people's callings can seem exotic – missionaries in far-flung
places, or big-platform influencers. Yet we're *all* missionaries and influencers because we're all on foreign consignment, waiting for the
call home to heaven (Philippians 3:20).

Holly goes on to say, 'We do not have to go anywhere but *to Him*
in order for us to be useful in His Kingdom. For those called to step
on a plane or a train or boat, go with the blessing of God. For those
called to stay in a kitchen or a conference room or at a desk in a class,
stay with the blessing of God.'

God, I'm amazed and excited that no matter where
You have me standing, I stand on holy ground. Amen.

# Wait for yes

Wait for the Lord and keep His way … (Ps. 37:34 esv).

Some years back, after too many unnecessary *yeses*, I took stock of what I should and shouldn't agree to, for the sake of my family and my sanity.

I was showing signs of being addicted to approval, so I started asking myself, 'Am I agreeing to this meeting or event or coffee date out of genuine concern for the people involved, or because it makes me feel good to be needed?' I decided, in that season, to assume the response to every request or prospect was *no*, unless God gave me a clear directive that it was *yes*. It didn't feel selfish, because God also made it clear that with every *yes* I should be laying myself down for another – the way He would.

If you're human, you've probably wrestled with saying *no*. But hopefully God is pointing out your blind spots and the places you're stuck, and you're learning the importance of boundaries and shaking off the impulse to say *yes* to every invitation or opportunity.

Living in the *no*-zone isn't an unwillingness to serve. Rather, it's a way to wait on God for the very best *yes*, and a way to make all the *yeses* more intentional acts of worship.

God, help me create margin to think and better
steward my gifts, by waiting wisely for the right *yes*. Amen.

# Temperament in transit

Now there are varieties of gifts,
but the same Spirit … (1 Cor. 12:4 ESV).

*I*'ve battled to make sense of the difference between self-preservation, and pouring yourself out in service.

Because burnout is not God's will. It's a result of our mismanagement (an overuse and abuse) of our strengths, opportunities and time. It's a sign that we've given in to the tyranny of the urgent, or an obsession to please people.

And laziness is not God's will. It manifests as selfishness, poor stewardship of our time and talents, procrastination, or utter neglect of important responsibilities.

The truth lies in the state of the soul. If you're a maximizer, you need to manage your days with margin enough for unhurried time with God and others. Go out of your way to find quiet and solitude. *This will require dying to self.*

If you're laidback, you need to live your days to the limit, making the most of opportunities. Go out of your way to use the gifts you've been given. *This will require dying to self.*

God, in travel and transit, use my temperament for Your glory.
Teach me where and how to step it up or tone it down. Amen.

# Leave some

When you harvest the crops of your land, do not
harvest the grain along the edges of your fields, and
do not pick up what the harvesters drop. Leave it for
the poor and the foreigners living among you.
I am the LORD your God (Lev. 23:22 NLT).

The Hebraic crop farming tradition was not to reap right to the edges of every field for every last scrap of grain, but rather to leave some grain for the gleaners – the poor or the destitute – to collect. It was a way of living wisely and generously, and it can inform much of our thinking around boundaries and not burning out.

I'm a hell-for-leather time capitalist, but I'm learning that I don't have to fill every waking moment of a day with productivity. An idea you could try – to check where and how you're in the unhealthy habit of picking up every last scrap of grain along the edges of every last field – is to picture your life as a field of wheat.

Picture a field of all your relationships, all your work and ministry and home obligations – ripe for the picking. It's a no-brainer that you'll reap the rewards of your covenant relationships (God, your husband, your kids).

But besides those, pause to pray about what other life-crops are yours to harvest, and what you'll leave to bless someone else.

God, show me what to take, and what to leave. Amen.

# Placed not abandoned

Be strong and courageous. Do not be afraid or
terrified … for the LORD your God goes with you;
He will never leave you nor forsake you (Deut. 31:6 NIV).

Times of waiting can feel horribly like abandonment. Perhaps you're waiting to meet your dream guy. You're waiting to fall pregnant. You're waiting for a visa or a promotion or an invitation. You're waiting for healing or happiness. And it's easy, in times when what you long for is elusive or entirely absent, to assume that God has forgotten you. That He has stopped loving you, and stopped being in control of your life. That He no longer has your best interests at heart.

Let this truth be the wind in your sails: He will never forsake you or move on without you. He will never show up late or overlook a promise. Instead, this hard time of waiting, it's His *placement* of you in the perfect incubator of His plans. He's never *not* transforming you into the image of His Son (Romans 8:28-29).

Jesus spent thirty years in preparation for three years of preaching. Same-same with us. Most of our lives are spent preparing, and that's ok. In fact, it's so very good. God's not done with you because you still have life and breath to read these words. You're being placed, not abandoned.

God, thank You that You position me –
right here where I am – in the waiting. Amen.

# Disharmony or dissatisfaction?

You will keep in perfect peace all who trust in You,
all whose thoughts are fixed on You! (Isa. 26:3 NLT).

Living in transit can be hellishly frustrating. Waiting for the thing we're waiting for can be disappointing and dissatisfying. It can even be idolatry – if we want the waiting to be over more than we want God's will to be done.

But it needn't be any of these things. *Active* waiting can involve perfect peace.

Some prayer, discernment and self-reflection will no doubt reveal what kind of transit you find yourself in. Maybe your frustration is a disharmony that needs to be resolved – a restless stirring to push through in a particular area because of what God is about to do – in which case, active waiting means doing all you can in the direction of what you believe to be God's will, within the scope of your knowledge and influence.

Maybe you still simply need to wait patiently for God to act – in which case, active waiting means loving and serving God and those around you, just where He has you and with the resources currently available to you. This will take your mind off the waiting, and before you know it, it may well be over.

God, as I wait, give me ways to resolve
the disharmony, or dissolve the dissatisfaction
in a generous measure of Your peace. Amen.

# In utero

> You watched me as I was being formed in
> utter seclusion, as I was woven together in
> the dark of the womb (Ps. 139:15 NLT).

A friend expecting her third child told me she was going to ask her doctor to induce labor, because she was tired of being pregnant. Tired of waiting for her baby's arrival. I could totally relate. Pregnancy can feel super long. But I thought, *We're even rushing our children from the womb! We rush their entrance into a rushed world!*

People *prefer* us to be busy and stressed and run off our feet and worried and weary – because it makes them feel better about the fact that they feel all those things too. Our world's workforce doesn't generally promote the slow stock-taking of inner reflection. Where God is asking us to linger, the world says hurry. We're a society of instant gratification and we hate to wait.

Wherever, right now, you're experiencing the hindrance or aggravation of waiting, remember that if our children didn't get nine months of dark, quiet womb-transit, they wouldn't survive. Pray, pray, pray into your future hope. Then simply wait on God as He makes you wait.

> God, give me patience to let stillness
> and seclusion do their work. Amen.

# Parenting in transit

She carefully watches everything in her household
and suffers nothing from laziness. Her children
stand and bless her … (Prov. 31:27-28 NLT).

Raising kids can feel like one long season of limbo. Of course we
see changes in our children as they grow – too fast – and grow
into the people God has created them to be. But mostly, there are
few massive or immediate rewards. The rewards are more of a slow
dawning – moments of realization that *oh-my-word* there's actually
been a bit of progress.

But as the minutes, months and years tick by until our kids' in-
cubation in our homes comes to an end, there are ways to wait dy-
namically – ways to invest in their future.

Write out crafted prayers for your kids. Journal the advice you'd
love to leave them. Read to them at any and every opportunity and
for as long as they'll listen. Ask questions every day. Make time for
face time – real face time – involving their actual faces.

Then, when the wait is over and they embark on their own big
wide world adventures, the wait will have been so worth it, because
they'll be set up for success.

God, help me take full advantage of the
transit time I have with my kids. Amen.

# Walking nowhere

… be prepared in season and out
of season … (2 Tim. 4:2 NIV).

*I*'ve always been a walker. When we were kids, my sisters and I used to walk blocks and blocks with our mom, a daily walker. One of my sisters and I, we still walk together in the early mornings. I like to leave the car parked as much as possible when I travel, walking everywhere to smell things – bump into things – and imbibe the spirit of place that doesn't come at your senses from the air-conditioned insides of a bus.

There's something about being in the going – journeying with purpose – enjoying the rhythm of every heel strike and the expectancy of arriving.

Yet sometimes, we walk and get nowhere. Invigilating an exam once, I paced the gym between rows and rows of desks where high-schoolers hunched over questions. Walking that patch of floor, I covered three kilometers. It felt utterly pointless because I wasn't traveling anywhere – until I reframed it, and began to pray for those kids.

Sometimes life feels like you're just pacing between desks, covering the same ground, hardly raising your heart rate. But friend, you're getting fit for something. You're getting time on your feet that will stand you in good stead, literally, when you need to stand up for something, run for someone, or go where God sends.

God, whatever is beneath my feet, help me to walk well. Amen.

# Stalling

Jesus responded, 'Didn't I tell you that you would see God's glory if you believe?' (John 11:40 NLT).

*I*f I think of the times of transit that I've experienced – or that I still find myself in as I write – they mostly have to do with situations that I know God could fix. He could intervene. He could heal or change or move or provide in some way – and yet He chooses not to.

Today you might be asking, *Why doesn't God do something about this situation?* I don't have the answer. But I do know He *can* do something about it. And I know sometimes He waits before He acts. And I know that – meanwhile – in the waiting – you can trust Him.

We place our hope in what we depend on. Keep depending on God. If it seems to you He's stalling? As if He isn't coming through for you quickly enough? Don't start depending on someone else or something else to fulfill your hopes. His ways are perfect, and all His ways are just (Psalm 18:30).

If God seems to be inattentive, uncooperative or late: know that somehow, somewhere, in some way, you will definitely see His glory.

God, help me to be patient and to trust that
You'll come through at the perfect time. Amen.

# You now, you later

Instruct the wise, and they will be even wiser. Teach the righteous, and they will learn even more (Prov. 9:9 NLT).

*A*nn Voskamp says, 'I know there *feels* like there's only one of you. The you right now. The one who Feels All The Things. But believe the impossible things, because it's true: There are two of you, really. The Short-Term You – and the Long-Term You. The Now-You – and the Becoming You. The Immediate You. *And the Ultimate You* ... Sometimes the short-term Immediate You *cannot have what she wants – so that the long-term Ultimate You can be who she wants to be.*'

Where you're standing now on the road through life, the *now* you is learning things and leaving things behind, collecting and collating ideas and experiences that will become the *ultimate* you.

You need to love both the immediate you and the ultimate you – choosing wisely and well what you do to and with the *now* you so that the *later* you is a beautiful version too.

God, in all my deciding, help me bear in mind that who I choose to be today will influence who I am tomorrow, and beyond. Amen.

# Fenced off

*You must keep My Sabbath days of rest and show reverence for My sanctuary. I am the LORD (Lev. 26:2 NLT).*

Once a year, a marathon that winds through our city includes our street. Thousands of runners come past our house. We stand on the driveway in our pajamas and watch.

It's a picture of the Sabbath. We're ring-fenced from the rush and running of life barreling on oblivious. It makes me think, *Tomorrow, we can join in again. Catch up – or not. We don't have to be fast or busy today. The world can be fast and busy for one day a week, without us.*

To institute a weekly Sabbath, make some rules. Fence off one day a week. It can be any day. Sunday might still work best for you, but if that's a day filled with happily serving others, you might want to shift it to Saturday, or Friday afternoon. Set a couple of specific boundaries, but don't make it complicated, legalistic or unrealistic. Like, you might simply decide not to open your laptop, or not to go onto social media on your phone.

When we decide to Sabbath intentionally, the world really does still spin on its axis, even without us swinging in to add to the momentum.

God, help me trust You enough to accept that it's really ok to do as You say, and take a day off. Amen.

# Break some rules

The LORD is my strength and my shield; my heart trusts in Him, and He helps me. My heart leaps for joy, and with my song I praise Him (Ps. 28:7 NIV).

For about a year, we drew on the dining room table on Sunday nights. We started doing this the second Sunday of the year, quite by accident. I subsequently bought a dozen rolls of brown paper, and it became something of a Sabbath tradition. We drew ridiculous pictures (like, 'This is Dad with his hair on fire and I'm standing on a chair and roasting a marshmallow on his head ...' *raucous laughter*).

As a rule, one doesn't draw on the dining room table. But this is one of the ways we try to break out, on the Sabbath, of what's done or not done, *as a rule*. As a rule, no one has three helpings of ice-cream. As a rule, no one has time to go bike riding or bush walking or lawn cricketing on a Sunday.

So we try – just once a week – to get out and do those double-chocolate-caramel-swirl, under-the-sky things, because a twenty percent effort to rest and refuel can make an eighty percent difference to our energy and enthusiasm in the week ahead.

God, show me where I'm rule-bound, and how I can rest. Amen.

# Posture

> He makes me lie down in green pastures,
> He leads me beside quiet waters … (Ps. 23:2 NIV)

*I*f you do happen to have obligations on your Sabbath day – because life is full, and full of variables – *change your posture.* God knows, the world needs both Marys and Marthas, which is why God created both. But on the Sabbath, you don't have to carry yourself the way leaning-forward, in-control, get-it-done Martha did. You could choose to carry yourself the way un-defensive, at-peace, let-me-listen Mary did (Luke 10:42).

I'm trying to change how I think about church or family get-togethers or any other kind of invitation I've chosen to accept, on Sabbath days. If I go somewhere with an attitude of rest, or host someone with an attitude of rest, it's not a chore.

I'm choosing to include these people or places in my Sabbath celebration of a good God who gives good gifts, like opportunities to hang out with amazing people.

God, help me recognize moments in which to steer
conversations towards green pastures and quiet waters. Amen.

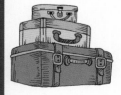

# Set reminders

> Because the Sovereign Lord helps me,
> I will not be disgraced. Therefore, I have set my
> face like a stone, determined to do His will. And I
> know that I will not be put to shame (Isa. 50:7 NLT).

Not to be overly dramatic, but rest requires a hardcore commitment. You've got to set your face like stone. I have a downtime alarm that goes off at 9:30pm every night to say I should start thinking about bed, because life will keep right on happening in the morning, accompanied by brand new mercies (Lamentations 3:23).

Four times a year, my family and I do two or three days of deep rest. It gives us space to go, *Are we all ok? Where have we come from? Where are we going? Let's catch our breath before we carry on.* Every ninety days is also a good time to back up your files, clean up your clouds, use up everything in the freezer and start again. It's astoundingly – surprisingly – restful.

Those rhythms might not work for you, your family or your circle of friends, but for sure, if you don't actively plan some means of rest, somewhere in your schedule, you won't be running your life; your life will be running you.

God, rest is rebellious in this non-stop world – an act
of resistance to trends. Help me to be brave and
intentional, and make sure it happens. Amen.

# Enough is enough

> And this same God who takes care of me will supply
> all your needs from His glorious riches, which
> have been given to us in Christ Jesus (Phil. 4:19 NLT).

*I*'ve got an Enough Habit, which reminds me, 'I get enough (fill in the blank).' Like, *I get enough food, I get enough stuff, I get enough green grass, I get enough attention, I get enough sleep, enough love.* That kind of contentment has restorative power.

The Enough Habit also helps me relax enough to be outrageously happy in *this* moment – which is, *enough.* The Enough Habit might make it easier for you to say things like, 'I'm loving my kid in this phase, or at this age. Just look at him. *In this moment today*, he's so cute, so carefree, so into dinosaurs.'

The prophet wrote, 'The Lord will guide you continually, giving you water when you are dry and restoring your strength. You will be like a well-watered garden, like an ever-flowing spring' (Isaiah 58:11). Today and always, God gives you enough.

God, You are more than enough, and You supply more than enough to meet my needs. I can't thank You enough. Amen.

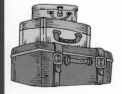

# In the middle

May the God of endurance and encouragement grant you to live in such harmony with one another …. (Rom. 15:5 ESV).

Life happens in three stages: beginning, middle and end. While God is definitely in all three stages, the middle bit is the longest and the hardest.

Becky Beresford writes, 'Our middles are just as important as our beginnings and ends. Sometimes we wish we could bypass the middle and fast-forward to the final chapter where our prayers are answered and our desires fulfilled. But we have such a kind God, and He doesn't waste a single second in our life. He doesn't push the pause button when we feel like life stops moving. He is always working for the good of those who love Him, and that includes you.'

I don't know what you're in the middle of, but you're not alone. Everyone you know or meet is in the middle of something. When I remember that, I feel less sorry for myself, and more compassionate towards the people God scripts into my day.

Also, every time you meet the eyes of another human, he or she is in the middle of a life heading either for heaven or for hell. None of us knows when our middle might abruptly turn into our end. Let's take opportunities to make sure that we and others are ready.

O God, meet me in the middle! Help me to make it count. Amen.

# Stress to stillness

When I refused to confess my sin, my body wasted
away, and I groaned all day long (Ps. 32:3 NLT).

*I* got shingles over Easter some years ago. Elisabeth Elliot said
that we're not laid aside by illness, *but called aside for stillness.* I,
however, didn't get the first stillness memo so the shingles reared its
painful head for round two.

A stress-related illness was humbling evidence that I hadn't
trusted God with the tension of writing deadlines and other jagged
edges of ordinary life. The forced stillness gave me space to reconsider
how I managed my time and responsibilities. It reminded me that I
had only myself to blame for any stress that had lodged in my mind
and infiltrated my body.

We're holistic beings. David knew that his decisions had a direct
effect on his health. Even in our sophisticated century when we
should know better, stress is the biggest killer. We have to become
thought-wranglers (2 Corinthians 10:5). Cognitive neuroscientist Dr.
Caroline Leaf maintains that the effects of negative thoughts look
structurally different, in the brain, from those of positive thoughts.
We are what we think (Proverbs 23:7), and we are how we talk, and if
we want to learn to be still, and stress-free, we need to hold tight to
the reins of our runaway thoughts.

God, strengthen my mind to think upon –
and rest in – Your magnificence. Amen.

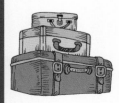

# Rebel

This is my command – be strong and courageous!
Do not be afraid or discouraged. For the LORD your
God is with you wherever you go (Josh. 1:9 NLT).

*I*f you need rest, rebellion is a real game-changer.

Rebel against the martyrdom culture that wears busyness like an honor badge. Thinly masked self-pity makes us look old – like bad make-up. And Paul writes that as people who love Jesus, we should be getting younger and younger (2 Corinthians 4:16).

Rebel against bad language. There are plenty of very raw, very real reasons to be stressed. There are also plenty of ways we talk ourselves into it. We reiterate our anxiety and rehearse our complaints until our language shapes us and we start to live as frenetically as we describe ourselves to be.

Rebel against false guilt, which says we're slackers because *surely* we're not doing, being or carrying as much as so many others. (Except, only God is watching our lives *that* closely. Would we feel as guilty – or be as stressed – if we really lived for an audience of One?)

Rebel against trudging forward in exhausted half-steps because *resting is so lame*. Truth is? Resting *feels* like three steps back, but it may give us a dozen strides forward. And we should do whatever it takes – heck, even rest! – to travel light.

God, help me be brave to stand up to
worldly fads, and find my rest in You. Amen.

# Balance

Therefore, if anyone is in Christ, the new creation has come:
The old has gone, the new is here! (2 Cor. 5:17 NIV).

C. S. Lewis described believers as 'glorious ruins.' Wrecked, damaged, fickle and flawed. But loved, redeemed and renewed, with eternity in our hearts. Despite our roofless walls and crumbling arches, we possess an unearthly, incongruent beauty, because of how the light shines through the cracks in our capacity.

As we seek to wait well – to find rest in the middle of life – we need to balance the earthly and the eternal. The limitless God who spoke out light and split the sea lives in limited me, and you. His infinite creativity, infinite love, dwells in our finite hearts and minds. It is what it is, and what it is, is a mystery.

Alli Worthington writes: 'When God created us, He created us with a limitless capacity to love others and … stretch our talents to be used for His glory. He also created us with a body that needs rest, and He placed us in a universe that has a limited number of hours in each day. When we operate under the belief that we can do it all, we're forgetting how God wants us to rely on Him. We're adding so much extra "noise" to our lives that we can't hear His voice speaking our true calling.'

God, do the limitless in limited me. Amen.

# Accept

For the LORD your God is living among you. He is
a mighty savior. He will take delight in you with
gladness. With His love, He will calm all your fears.
He will rejoice over you with joyful songs (Zeph. 3:17 NLT).

*A*fter his hockey practice one week, our visually impaired son
told me some of the other boys didn't want him on their
team. 'Because then they will definitely lose the match,' he told me.
He was more matter-of-fact than indignant, and I was grateful that
he loosened his words right there in the school car park, instead of
leaving them tightly heart-wedged.

He said, 'I guess I don't really blame them,' cause I do kinda
suck.' I told him he was super brave even to try, and that I was more
concerned about his heart than his hockey. I want him to know that
God doesn't put up with him or me or any of us out of pity, irritation
or obligation, but that He reaches out and picks us for the team and
no one can kick us off.

So much stress thaws out warm when we accept that we're
*accepted* – made worthy by God's lavish love. Let that truth straighten
your back and lower your stress today as you keep on keeping on in
the middle of life.

God, I'm so glad and grateful that for You, I don't
have to perform to be promoted. Amen.

# Healing in transit

> Lord my God, I called to You for help,
> and You healed me (Ps. 30:2 NIV).

*I*t's hard for me to talk about healing, because I'm a mom of a kid who needs healing, and healing hasn't happened. We've prayed. Nada. Other people have prayed. Zilch. Still others have anointed our son with oil at big loud healing gigs resulting in exactly zero healing. We've wracked out our angry grief – clutching hands and bits of sanity. We've fasted and begged, *Come on, God! You'd get so much glory from this!*

So I don't understand everything about healing, but here's what I do know:

We don't pray for healing enough. Maybe because we can't bear the not-enough-faith guilt or the disappointment of our prayers 'not working'. Maybe because too many pseudo-Christians have fake-healed too many times. Maybe because we don't want to treat the Creator of the universe like a genie in a bottle, there to do our bidding, ease our pain, and give us our way.

Yet, we *should* pray for healing, because God heals and because He's never told us to stop praying for healing. He heals in might and power. He takes away cancer, AIDS and holes in babies' hearts.

We should pray for healing as fervently as we pray for wisdom – with absolute assurance that God hears and answers according to His perfect will.

God, I don't understand Your ways.
I trust You anyway. Amen.

# Faith in transit

For we live by faith, not by sight (2 Cor. 5:7 NIV).

When it comes to healing, we're called to live by faith, as we are in every arena of life. It takes faith to trust that God can / does / will heal. It takes faith to trust that if / when / because He doesn't heal, every time, He's still infinitely kind, wise and powerful.

Obviously, we don't give God His power. God's work isn't dependent on our fickle faith. He doesn't wring His hands going, 'Oh! The healing power has gone out of Me because they don't have enough faith!' He heals to *bolster* our faith, more than *because* of it. He heals even when no one knows and no one is looking, and sometimes – most times? – often times? – He lets brokenness run its course.

I have no idea why. But I do know He's faithful, and perfect in powerful love.

It's also comforting to remember that healing gives us a glimpse of God's Kingdom, which is Now and Not Yet. We're in a glorious dispensation of grace and Holy Spirit power – but we ain't seen nothin' yet. If you don't see healing in this life, you'll certainly see it in the next.

God, thank You that healing is a tangible manifestation of what You do on the inside of me – total renewal – and an electrifying reminder of the eternal realities that await. Bring it on! Amen.

# No explanation

> When Jesus saw him and knew he had
> been ill for a long time, He asked him,
> 'Would you like to get well?' (John 5:6 NLT).

As you pray and wait for healing or resolution, remember that God invented decision-making and He doesn't owe us an explanation for His perfect decisions.

At the pool of Bethesda, in Jerusalem, there were 'crowds of sick people – blind, lame, or paralyzed' (John 5:3). Yet Jesus went up to *just one man* amidst swarms of the sick and the dying – and He healed him. Jesus didn't explain why He picked that one man. He didn't owe His disciples or anyone else an explanation. He doesn't owe you and me an explanation either, no matter how sad, cross or confused we may feel.

God has been deciding things since forever. He chose fever trees – not fir trees – to grow in Africa. He chose Abraham's family – not some other family – to bless the whole world. He chose Moses – not some other guy – to lead His people out of Egypt. All this has never bothered me, because it's never been personal. Yet my Heavenly Father is intensely, intimately personal to me. His power that split the sea and raised the dead is alive in me. However He chooses to reveal Himself through me, to the world? Well, I'm ok with that.

> God, You know it all and see it all.
> I'm trusting the decisions to You. Amen.

# Closure opens

> He did not retaliate when He was insulted, nor threaten revenge when He suffered. He left His case in the hands of God, who always judges fairly (1 Pet. 2:23 NLT).

When a friend shared with us that she was sexually abused as a kid, my husband said, 'You need to accept that possibly – probably? – there'll never be justice, in this life, for what's been done to you.' She'd been spilling cold stories over hot coffee at our kitchen table all evening. I'd said all the lukewarm things I knew to say, but that was the white-hot truth she'd come to hear.

She needed a brave someone to say what she already feared: that there may not be earthly revenge or restitution. It brought her *closure* – knowing there may never be closure. Relief sputtered to life. Her expression *opened* – as if she were opening her hands to let go, so she could leave her case in the hands of God.

I pray you'd *open* your heart, stop looking for closure, and start looking for openness. Because to travel light we've got to keep our hearts and lives, our front doors and fridges, *open* to people who deserve our generosity and people who will almost certainly take advantage of it.

God of justice and perfect closure: help me be ok with the possibility that closure may only come when You open up for me the great wide open of eternity. Amen.

# Horizon

'I am the Alpha and the Omega – the beginning
and the end,' says the Lord God. 'I am the One
who is, who always was, and who is still
to come – the Almighty One' (Rev. 1:8 NLT).

When my husband and I did our first scuba dive, the sea was rough, we were nervous, and the boat lurched, dipped and billowed petrol fumes all over our queasiness. Our dive master told us, 'Look at the horizon. Keep your eyes on the horizon and you won't get sick.'

It worked. When I steadied my gaze on a distant shore, my gut-restlessness eased. But when I looked down into the boat to fumble with dive equipment, the nausea surged back.

When we're navigating middle-of-life storms, we mustn't look down into the boat where waves crash over our feet and fears and ask, *Why this storm, God?* We'll seldom find answers in the boat. Mostly, because the story of our suffering is a few sentences in an intricate, sweeping, deeply meaningful and totally un-random plot, the suffering *seems* pretty random, inefficient and ineffectual.

To make sense of suffering, we've got to look up, and we've got to look far – to the horizon of history – where God will roll up all our stories on that final shore. He will refresh, restore and renew all things – and it will be glorious.

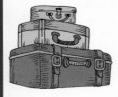

God, thank You that the end
is just the beginning. Amen.

# AUGUST

## Grace and Gravity

Why do you go away? So that you can
come back. So that you can see the place
you came from with new eyes and extra
colors. And the people there see you
differently, too. Coming back
to where you started is not
the same as never leaving.

*Terry Pratchett*

# Stuck by grace

Each time He said, 'My grace is
all you need ...' (2 Cor. 12:9 NLT).

*I* love maps almost as much as I love travel. Maps trace possibility – connecting the dots of flight paths and social media networks. They move us via trains, planes and Google Earth. Maps remind me that there's adventure to chart. History to unearth. A future to discover. Maps *unstick* us from thinking small and free us to live large.

And maps *stick* us. They're reminiscent of gravity – the great equalizer. Developed and developing nations, the rich and the refugee: *no one's floating away*. Gravity sticks us to this planet and there's enough for all of us.

So when I cleared out wads of folded maps from the backpacking of my twenty-somethings, I gave them to my boys. Spellbound, they wallpapered their room from Malawi to Israel, Canada to Scotland. Those maps were a gift of context. I want them to grow up grounded by gravity – *placed* – and set free by possibility – *called*.

Being placed and called goes beyond where we are or might go. We're placed and called – stuck and unstuck – by grace. Grace, more than gravity, holds you in your God-designed on-purpose context. Grace is sufficient for you to stick it out where you are, fighting FOMO when sensational stuff goes down in places you don't live. Grace keeps you supplied and secure where God wants you.

Jesus, Your grace is my mainstay! Amen.

# Unstuck by grace

You then, my child, be strengthened by the
grace that is in Christ Jesus … (2 Tim. 2:1 ESV).

*I*t's comforting that grace *sticks* and secures you. Except, stuck may be exactly what you *don't* want to be. You don't want to be stuck in your circumstances, not getting the mobility, the ministry or the momentum you crave. You don't want to be stuck in the spin cycle of kids and crazy, dinner and deadlines and too often being too tired for sex.

It's refreshing to recall that God's grace is *changing* grace. When grace arrests your heart, it begins to change you. Grace is more than pardon. It's power. Grace is your escape from sin and self. It's God's tenacious love transforming ordinary you into an extraordinary reflection of your extraordinary Redeemer.

You're not the same today as you were yesterday, and you'll be different tomorrow – because grace is changing you. The change might not feel earth-shattering in today's boardroom or frozen-food aisle. But the change is eternal, and that's seismic.

Paradoxically, while grace is our peace and staying power – our *stickability* – on continents and in community, grace also *unsticks* us to move, obeying God's call. And grace unsticks in startling and subtle ways. Grace may move you to another city – or another cubicle. Or it may move you to show up one more time for the friend who hasn't necessarily shown up for you.

God, mobilize me! Amen.

# Deep

> Then Christ will make His home in your hearts as
> you trust in Him. Your roots will grow down into
> God's love and keep you strong (Eph. 3:17 NLT).

On the You-Are-Here map of life, I don't know where God's grace has you today. But I know that it *has* you, and holds you. And while none of us knows the future, I know for sure there's enough grace in all our tomorrows, for daily commutes and vast odysseys. There's enough grace to ground us, and set us free.

Wherever you find yourself grounded, check the stability of your foundations. A tall building with weak foundations cracks and topples. Tall trees with shallow roots blow over in rough winds. And people aren't different. A person may rise high in the world's eyes, or even in the eyes of other believers, but if their rising isn't sustained by the deep foundations of wisdom and humility, their rise will be short-lived, and possibly tragic and destructive to themselves and others.

The deepest foundations that ground us best – that bring us closest to the settling gravitational force we find in Jesus – are often dug by suffering. It's the subterranean spiritual foundations forged in the dark night of the soul – grueling heart work witnessed by God and very few others – that give credibility to the lives we build above the ground.

Lord Jesus, let my roots go deep so my branches can go wide.
Amen.

# Friends in flight

My eyes are ever on the LORD, for only He
will release my feet from the snare (Ps. 25:15 NIV).

Paradoxically, Western culture as most of us experience it seems
to be becoming both more insular and more connected. Social
media with all its flaws and benefits has made us feel isolated and
lonely, and simultaneously part of an intimate global village.

I'm quite sure you can bring to mind friends or family members
who have moved away – relocated to another city, state or country.
Maybe you're the one who has done the moving. I'm trying to
remember – and I'm trying to teach my kids, who have had to say
goodbye too many times – that while it's cool to have video calling
and we should totally use it because it's important to be loyal,
intentional friends or relatives – the greater lesson is possibly about
resilience and adaptability and not finding our security – our spiritual
proprioception – in other people.

Is there someone you need to let go of, because your sense of
direction and gravity is too much caught up in the place they occupy
in your life?

God, I want to go where You ask me to go, stay where
You ask me to stay, and do what You ask me to do,
regardless of where others are going or staying,
and what they're doing. Amen.

# Both

Now may the God of peace make you holy
in every way, and may your whole spirit and
soul and body be kept blameless until our Lord
Jesus Christ comes again (1 Thess. 5:23 NLT).

Flying in an airplane is way different from flying in a spaceship –
because of gravity. Your food doesn't fly off your plastic tray in
an airplane, and on long international flights you can walk the aisles
to stretch your legs. Even though you're actually suspended midair –
in fact hurtling through it at a terrifying pace – your feet are firmly on
the floor of the plane.

Our salvation is kind of like that. We're in a both-and – now-and-
not-yet – space of traveling through time. At the moment of our
salvation we were justified and at the moment of our death we'll be
glorified. But everything in between is our daily sanctification by the
Holy Spirit, and for that we depend on Someone other than ourselves
to keep us grounded at the foot of the cross, and suspended by grace.

You aren't yet all you hope to be and neither is anyone else. We're
all somewhere between grace and gravity, dependent on both for
stability, and mobility.

Jesus, thank You that my future is already
settled and secure – even as You continue to reveal
it in me bit by bit in the here and now. Amen.

# Delight

> So now I am giving you a new commandment:
> Love each other. Just as I have loved you,
> you should love each other (John 13:34 NLT).

It's not melodramatic to say that the global church is in gridlock over some key tenets of the faith. Conservatives and liberals can't seem to get along – and yet we all serve the God of an undivided mind. The God of absolute grace, absolute truth.

Let's get to grips with the Scriptures – and then, *love everyone*. We need to know the depths of the truths of God's Word, living and loving the full counsel of God, and then express it in heartfelt devotion and affection for all around us. Because the truth is that the more conservative our theology is, the more liberal our loving should be. Biblical truth is the gravity that grounds us and steadies us so that we can sincerely and freely offer grace to the travel companions God sends our way for a moment or a lifetime.

And one of the ways we can love people is by only offering our opinion when it's asked for, when it's helpful, or when it's very necessary.

> Jesus, keep working on my heart until I continually
> and unreservedly delight in Your Word and
> delight in the human race You died for. Amen.

# Quit hustling

I have been crucified with Christ and I no
longer live, but Christ lives in me. The life I now
live in the body, I live by faith in the Son of God,
who loved me and gave Himself for me (Gal. 2:20 NIV).

*I*t may feel as if everyone's getting ahead of you. People you look up to, people in your career network, people you don't even know but whose lives you follow on social media – they're achieving the things you dream about. They have the right connections, and all the time, money and emotional energy you lack.

Take heart. Your agenda died with Christ. Thank God and good riddance. Relax now. His ways are so much better than any two-dimensional idea you can dream up. God reaches down and delivers His best plans for your life, in the time and place He has you. No one can rise above gravity. But don't give in to the temptation to create a tall poppy culture – lopping off the blooms of those who rise higher than you.

Celebrate their wins the way you'd want them to celebrate yours. For all you know, they're looking at *your* life with the same sense of longing. Celebrate what God is growing in lives all around you – and in yours.

God, I don't want to exhaust myself chasing second-best stuff. Help me channel my energy into Your purposes for me. Amen.

# Underneath

> The eternal God is your refuge, and underneath
> are the everlasting arms (Deut. 33:27 NIV).

To be securely grounded – so you're free to rise up confidently into anything God calls you to – *figure out the root of your insecurity.*

Maybe you always felt like a hassle – an annoyance, a let-down or an embarrassment? So much so that now it's hard to accept people's friendship. You can't believe people actually *like* you.

Maybe you grew up feeling you were too loud, or too quiet. Maybe you've been emotionally, verbally or physically abused, or you carry financial insecurity – a poverty mindset you're battling to think yourself out of.

No matter what your area of insecurity, or mine, it's always rooted in fear. Fear of failure, rejection, pain, lack, being out of the loop and so many other worries. A wise teacher said, 'All fear is but the notion that God's love ends.' What are you really afraid of? If you knew that God's everlasting love completely surrounded you behind and before, and that underneath were the everlasting arms – would it matter – the thing you fear?

Perfect love casts out fear (1 John 4:18). And our perfect Savior loves you perfectly.

Lord, I'm calmed and comforted, because Your
love is much, much bigger than my biggest fear. Amen.

# Unlikely grace

Satisfy us each morning with Your unfailing love, so we may sing for joy to the end of our lives (Ps. 90:14 NLT).

*I*f we stop expecting our life-travels on this planet to be perfect, we might start seeing more spectacular views. There are moments of unlikely grace all around us if we make even a small effort to notice them.

Walking past a chaotic construction site once, I glanced down at some building rubble – where a mommy mouse had made a safe, snug, happy nest amidst broken concrete, for her half-dozen baby mice. *Unlikely grace.*

My boys tried to grow a lemon tree from seed, in cotton wool on the kitchen windowsill. They figured it hadn't worked, and tossed the seed into the garden – where it began to grow, and is still growing. *Unlikely grace.*

As with every great travel experience, it's often in the unlikely places of life that beauty and grace show up. And like travel, life is never perfect, yet God makes ways where there seem to be none. He gives us the grace to adapt and make the best of the places we find ourselves in. He even refreshes our capacity to extend grace to others, reminding us that grace is less about planning a perfect itinerary and more about being positioned to reflect Jesus.

God, You've infused the universe
with unlikely grace. I'm amazed! Amen.

# Big little world

> He is my loving ally and my fortress, my tower
> of safety, my rescuer. He is my shield, and I take
> refuge in Him … O LORD, what are human beings
> that You should notice them, mere mortals that
> You should think about them? (Ps. 144:2-3 NLT).

To travel light, it helps to remember that the world is very small, and the world is very big.

No one can see us from space. Our existence is miniscule. We're just one of seven billion tiny human specks. Our stories don't occupy tremendous tracts of history. It's so very good to zoom out from all that consumes us and get perspective: it's a big world.

And yet from across the universe and where you find yourself in this very moment, God hears the beats of your heart. No detail escapes Him. He cares about and He *uses* the smallest, most *seemingly* insignificant interactions and events that populate our days. He holds all the big things and the little things in the palms of His hands and He wastes nothing, using even the tiny things we bring for enormous, eternal purpose.

When the crazy mess of life threatens to overwhelm you – zoom out and get perspective, knowing that the Creator is even now zooming in to bring you peace.

> Eternal God, thank You for holding
> the universe, and my hand. Amen.

# Pride protection

> I was caught up to the third heaven fourteen
> years ago … and heard things so astounding …
> things no human is allowed to tell (2 Cor. 12:2, 4 NLT).

**P**aul had mind-bending visions on this third heaven trip. And God said, *Don't tell anyone what you saw.* Right after that, Paul asked God to take away the thorn in his flesh. God said, *No. My grace is enough for you.* (2 Corinthians 12:9) The thorn *was* God's grace. It's the thing that kept Paul's feet on the ground the rest of his earthly life – humble, when he may have felt entitled to name-drop at dinner parties.

When you lose sight of the magnificent wood because of all the very ordinary trees right in front of you, it may be that God's showing you the same grace He showed Paul. Your ordinary life is a hedge of protection – safeguarding you from pride.

So when your laptop crashes or you've run out of coffee and ketchup – when the small, ordinary stuff grows tangled and hedgy, obscuring the big, extraordinary stuff like world change – pause long enough to notice, as Emily Dickinson suggested, that the ordinary hedge is really a burning bush. Take off your shoes, because it's on the humble, holy ground of our ordinary lives that the Father changes us, and through us, the world.

> God, thank You for encircling me –
> protecting me even from myself! Amen.

# Ground friendship

A friend loves at all times … (Prov. 17:17 NIV).

Relationships need to be served up with lashings of hot grace because not one of us is perfect. And relationships are also what keep us satisfied and satiated in the best way. C. S. Lewis wrote, 'Friendship is the moment when one man says to another, "What! You too? I thought that no one but myself …"' So there's gravity and grace in friendships too. They ground us, and set us free.

A while back, #FixWhatsBrokenIn5Words was trending on Twitter. It got me thinking that lasting change happens when we fix in our circle of influence, instead of ranting in our circle of concern. And really, our greatest influence rests in relationships.

Because of the supernatural inside-time-outside-time-all-the-time relevance of God's Word, this five-word generating hashtag has been trending in the Bible for millennia. Take for example, *Friends love at all times* (Proverbs 17:17). *Rejoice with those who rejoice. Weep with those who weep* (Romans 12:15).

Here are some others we could try: *Show an interest; ask questions. Show grace to oversensitive friends. Show grace to insensitive friends. Listen, listen, listen. Then, listen. Don't be cliquey; it's ugly. Don't keep score; it's childish. Don't play the guilt card. Keeping in touch takes effort. Laugh as much as possible.*

Father, fix my broken bits so I can be a safe, loyal, loving friend – gracious, and grounding. Amen.

✈

# Resilience in five words

> I pray that from His glorious, unlimited resources He will empower you with inner strength through His Spirit (Eph. 3:16 NLT).

When life's pace and pressure overwhelm my kids, almost anything they say and do can be translated: 'This Feels Unmanageable.' 'I'm Too Tired.' 'I'm Scared I'll Mess This Up.' 'What's Going On?' 'What If I Can't Be Enough, Do Enough, Have Enough?' 'Stop Making Me Hurry.' And sometimes, 'My Blood Sugar is Way Too Low. I Need a Snack.'

These are sometimes the very things I'm saying beneath the go-go-go of life. I know once my kids dip below their invisible Coping Line, even the smallest thing is massively too much. I know this for a fact because they get it from me.

For the sake of everybody's emotional health, discern where that Coping Line is for you and your kids or co-workers, and manage life so you can kinda-sorta stay above it.

Try doing things in sets of five – because counting to five, or taking five deep breaths, is doable on a wild day, for kids and even most adults. Five-word truths we tell ourselves and others might sound like, 'You'll learn heaps from failure!' 'You're *deciding* to be busy.' 'You can choose your attitude.' 'Let's think of a plan.' 'Do the Next Right Thing.' 'God goes ahead of you.' 'Eventually, everything will be ok.' (Even if eventually is only eternity.)

God, I know You've got this. Amen.

# Politeness in five words

Sensible people control their temper; they earn respect by overlooking wrongs (Prov. 19:11 NLT).

*I*t can take just five well-chosen words to stay polite, even on days when there's a strong chance of everybody freaking out. Let's model for those around us, whether older or younger, what courteous and respectful look like by saying things like: 'Thank you for the supper.' 'Excuse me from the table.' 'It's good to see you.' 'Fine thank you, and you?' 'Can I help with anything?' 'No thanks, I've had enough.' 'Forgive me. I was rude.' 'Please tell me again, slowly?'

Five-minute or five-step habits could also go a long way towards grounding our homes in grace. What if we tried weaving these words into our home-scripts: '*Five more steps* and you'll be *at* the laundry basket.' 'Clean your room as best you can, and as fast as you can, *for five minutes flat*, and while you're doing that we can play music as loud as you like.' 'Of the 1440 minutes in today, it will only take you *five* to unpack your schoolbag (or feed the dogs) (or set the table). 'Let's take *five* minutes to read something (or snuggle) (or pray about tomorrow) (or practice your times tables) (or look for that thing you've lost).'

Lord, it's never ok to be discourteous or disrespectful. Keep me calm and kind, five minutes at a time. Amen.

# Be the green

Your love for one another will prove to the world
that you are My disciples (John 13:35 NLT).

We've got a gray-water system in our back garden, which means our lawn stays more or less green even when everything else is still dry dust, thirsty for summer. It reminds me that there's (metaphorical) brown grass all over the world. There isn't a patch of planet free from sleaze, prejudice or the odd suicide bomber. Then there's the whole abject poverty thing. And any other story you care to scroll through on your news app.

Maybe you look around and you're a little paralyzed. Maybe the jury is still out when it comes to the future of your country, the future of the world. We're all big enough to know that no one can see into next week and next week might be awful.

But I know I also need to be big enough to admit that wherever I go in the world, I take myself with me. There's no getting away from me when I up and go off green-grass hunting. Where there's green grass in the world, it's only because the people right there on that grass are watering it. If I'm not given to watering my grass right where I'm standing – what makes me think I'll bother to water it somewhere else?

God, help me to be for others the
green grass I wish to walk on. Amen.

# Grassroots grace

And His name will be the hope
of all the world (Matt. 12:21 NLT).

What if we decided to get to the root of things? What if we stopped putting our hope in the lawn dressing and the top-soil? What if, right where we're standing, we let God drill holes in us – in our fears and in our comfort zones – so that He can spill out to make the grass green? What if we did everything in our power, with all the resources available to us, in the time we have left, right where God has us?

Let's determine that, today and forever, our hope isn't in politicians or their parties, but in Jesus. And hoping in Jesus doesn't mean being so heavenly minded we're of no earthly good. It means being mobilized from self-preservation to self-sacrifice – compelled to love the world from the grass beneath our feet.

Because no matter what place you've chosen to call home, home is just that – a *calling*. And as God's people, we're called to *be* the safe pasture. What if we welcomed the uncomfortable work of God in us – at grassroots level – and let the Living Water run right out of us, right where we are? I think it would change us. I think it would change our neighborhoods and our cities. It might even change the world.

God, help me water the world,
where I'm standing. Amen.

# Feminists and freedom

> These older women must train the younger women to love their husbands and their children, to live wisely and be pure, to work in their homes, to do good, and to be submissive to their husbands … (Titus 2:4-5 NLT).

Paul's letter to Titus is all about freedom: the gospel sets us free, and that frees us to live healthy lives in the church and out the church – in the big wide communities of the big wide world. It frees us to lead and follow well, and raise others to do the same.

And women get stuck on Titus 2:5, because when wives are told to submit to their husbands it doesn't sound like freedom. History equates submission with oppression – with disrespect, disqualification, disenfranchisement, and all the other ways women were dissed for millennia, and sometimes still are. For too many centuries, culture's pendulum swung dangerously to one extreme. Women were appallingly dominated.

More recently, our fear-turned-anger has swung the pendulum dangerously to the other extreme and everybody's got a bra to burn and a man to emasculate. Yet, the Word isn't a pendulum but the plumb line of truth so it lands this non-issue dead center: marriage is not a competition; it's a communion of lives. It's a one-flesh I've-got-your-back-always-and-forever thing where you can't remember where you stop and your spouse starts. That's not oppressive. It's totally freeing.

Jesus, You died for our freedom,
not our bondage. Thank You! Amen.

# Life laid down

Husbands, love your wives, just as Christ loved the church and gave Himself up for her … (Eph. 5:25 NIV).

*I*f your husband is following his calling, then he'll love you like Christ loved the church. He'll lay down his life for you. That's way harder, way cooler, way sexier than submission. You need not be threatened by that kind of love.

Except, maybe you're thinking, *Easy for you to say. You obviously have a really nice husband. You have no idea the kind of husband I'm dealing with. He lays his life down for golf and for beer. Sometimes he even lays his life down for other women – real or digital. He's definitely not laying it down for me.*

I would *never* assume to minimize the pain or the disappointment of that. I would also never dare to get all preachy and prescriptive on you, where there has been abuse or infidelity. But hear this: even if your husband isn't willing to lay down his life for you, *Jesus Christ already has.* Jesus *already has* laid down His life for you, and therein lies your security. At the cross, Jesus took your shame, and restored your dignity. He's clothed you in righteous robes. Adopted you as a daughter. Gifted you with worth. That gift can't be taken away from you.

Jesus, thank You for how completely and utterly You demonstrate Your love for me. Amen.

✈

# Introvert grace and grounding

But Jesus often withdrew to lonely
places and prayed (Luke 5:16 NIV).

Apparently 42% of humans are introverts. The rest are mostly extroverts. Some are ambiverts (that's me) with one foot in the still waters of introversion and the other kicking cheerfully in the public swimming pool with all the other extroverts.

If you're an introvert, there are things you should understand about how humans run the world. The loudest voices dominate the most important conversations even though, as Susan Cain says, the best talkers don't always have the best ideas. The garrulous appear bravest. Personality trumps character. From social media to Starbucks, from schools to malls to movies – extroversion is held up as the ideal.

All this is totally fine. So long as you know that the world desperately needs leaders and creatives, and leaders and creatives need solitude and space. The most remarkable Leader and Creative *ever*, drew away to quiet spaces to pray. So, it's totally fine for you.

There's more than enough room inside your skin for you to feel completely comfortable. When you realize this, strength and peace are yours. You're not tempted to retreat, pretend to like things you don't, or overcompensate by showing off. The crowds and the clamor aren't a threat. Actually, you begin to *enjoy* them.

God, help me to go quietly inside myself, with You. Amen.

# He knows

Nothing in all creation is hidden from God (Heb. 4:13 NLT).

Fellow woman in the business of mothering kids, friends, co-workers or employees – your Father knows the big loud demands on your time and energy, sunup to sundown and then some.

He knows the fights you fight *with* your kids, under your roof. Fights over homework, screen-time and piano-practicing. Entitlement and set-the-table and *no-soccer-in-the-house!* He knows the fights you fight *for* your kids, in the Enormous Out There. Fights against the bullies and baddies and unbiased who *unthinkably* don't seem to love your child like you do.

He hears the daily barrage of questions fired at you. He knows how many times your sleeves and your heartstrings get tugged, tried, tested and tangled in the furious love of motherhood so that by five in the afternoon – You. Are. Done.

He knows what keeps you up at night – how you're anxious about your kids' anxiety levels. He knows about one kid's wild anger and another kid's social awkwardness. He knows about the office politics and the project tender that was rejected. He sees how some days unstitch into chaos, and some days you straightjacket everyone into submission and you're fighting to control your controllingness.

He knows.

Father, help me rest today, knowing You
know my entire life and You love me
unblinkingly through it all. Amen.

# Satisfied

So if we have enough food and clothing,
let us be content (1 Tim. 6:8 NLT).

God's grace is enough, in the midst of your unraveling or tightly-wound womanhood. And God's grace is *powerful*. It's undeserved, unearned favor and help for days when you're not a fantastic woman – just an average woman who loses your temper and your car keys.

Trust God for grace so at the end of the day, when all your get-up-and-go has already got up and left, there's something – miraculously! – left of you. Something that remembers you and your people are on the same team. Something smiling and spontaneous. Maybe even something sexy.

Trust God for contentment. Because content is what you can be if you have food and clothing, and chances are you and I have too much of both. Trust God to reveal Himself to you today in such a way that you'll know that everything's going to be alright in the end. Maybe soon. Maybe much later. But definitely, *alright in the end*.

Ask God to let contentment settle deep in your bones so that if wish-dreams don't come true, you'll still be comfortably, happily sure that He'll bring you to the fullness He's planned and that your wise, well-resourced, loving God will lead you into all the good works prepared for you (Ephesians 2).

God, thanks to You, I'm happy right here
right now: content despite the crazy. Amen.

# Perspective

> 'There is hope for your future,'
> says the LORD (Jer. 31:17 NLT).

Today, ask God to give you perspective, so you can rest in the truth that the earth is His, and everything in it. The world and all its people belong to Him (Psalm 24:1). That includes your family, wherever He's stuck you by grace and gravity to this planet.

Trust God for perspective on your home, so you'd remember that it will never be perfect, because humans live there. But it can be happy – crammed floor-to-ceiling with love. That way, you'll ease up on trying to fix everything and everyone – ease up on carrying things that aren't yours to carry.

Trust God for perspective so that you don't awfulize and catastrophize the future. Rather, you can make it your daily habit to actualize and normalize, hope and pray.

And ask God to restore your sense of humor. Chill out. Laugh at fun stuff and mostly at yourself. Thank God that He's Emmanuel – God with *us all* – the heart-link and lightness of being between us and our people. What a relief that we don't need to carry all the things because the government rests on His shoulders (Isaiah 9:6).

> God, help me remember that with Your strength
> and wisdom, I can climb these mountains,
> instead of trying to carry them. Amen.

✈

# Rope's end

> I cried out, 'I am slipping!' but Your unfailing
> love, O Lord, supported me (Ps. 94:18 NLT).

Maybe you're in a place where happy, uncomplicated dealings
with colleagues and kids, friends, family, acquaintances and
random strangers, feel impossible, or unmanageable. As you tie up
the loose ends of each day, ask God for closure where uncertainty,
unfinished business or gaping wounds have left you shaky. Lean on
the Prince of Peace to help you finish well.

Ask God to give you real joy in going second. Preferring others.
Not vying for your will, your way. Rather, enjoy being snug and secure
in your own skin as your gladly celebrate God and others in the
busyness of life, knowing you *know* the Wonderful Counselor who
comforts and convicts, as and when we need it.

Perhaps today you could ask God to show you where you're lacking
sensitivity, trusting Him to soften your skin thickened by stress – to
thin it out kind and compassionate so you can feel the frayed nerves
of others as they rub up against you.

> Almighty God, thank You that Your strength-supply
> is limitless, and available to me! Relationally, and in
> every other way, please throw me a rope. Amen.

# Listen

> Plans go wrong for lack of advice; many advisers bring success (Prov. 15:22 NLT).

When my husband and I got a once-in-a-lifetime opportunity to take our kids to Canada for Christmas, I started planning a speaking event with a friend in Michigan, USA. Her hometown is just four hours away from where we'd be, in Ontario.

She was super excited – bending every which way to make sure the gig could happen. But she was also wise – cautioning me – the African who'd never driven on icy highways – that the hostile weather at that time of year might thwart the best of plans. I needed her grace – her excitement and support – and her gravity – the insightful perspectives I lacked. As we travel light through life, we need the angles of others. The Jesus-followers who make a startling mark on this world don't lie to themselves, *about* themselves, even when the truth hurts. They prioritize what they *value* over what they *want*, constantly reminding themselves of what's really important, and what's really at stake. And they don't try to lead themselves, *by* themselves. They lean on the wisdom of a trusted community.

Submitting to the counsel of others is also a way of living with vulnerable dignity, which is the fearless humility of an open heart that says, *I'm here to make a difference, not an impression.*

God, rip off the wisdom-cancelling headphones
of pride! I want to hear You. Amen.

# Character test

> Then David went out of the cave and called out
> to Saul, 'My lord the king!' When Saul looked behind
> him, David bowed down and prostrated himself
> with his face to the ground (1 Sam. 24:8 NIV).

This is a Hollywood-worthy account of David's heroism and humility. He's hiding in a cave. His enemy, Saul, comes into *the same cave* to ... freshen up. Saul doesn't know that David crouches in the darkness. It's the perfect opportunity for David to kill Saul. And he doesn't take it.

He doesn't take it because he trusts God to accomplish God's purposes in His way, according to His will, in His time. David shows tremendous grace towards Saul. He shows *undeserved favor* – because it's safe to say Saul may well have deserved David's revenge. David shows grace because he's grounded: humble, and dependent on his Heavenly Father.

The truest test of my character and yours is when we're given power, position or authority. In what areas of your life is your character being put through its paces, because of the influence you wield? How can you consciously rely on the gravitational force of humility to keep your feet firmly on the ground, and show grace to those under your sway or in your care?

Lord, convict me quickly when I've allowed power
and position to mess with my moral compass. Amen.

# Not here

The women were terrified and bowed with their
faces to the ground. Then the men asked, 'Why are
you looking among the dead for someone who is alive?
He isn't here! He is risen from the dead!' (Luke 24:5-6 NLT).

When Jesus-loving women rushed to His tomb in Jerusalem, the angel who greeted them told them He wasn't there. He'd risen. Jesus defied gravity and the grave – conquering death to rise again. And because of that, He extends His grace to us – His forgiveness and the gift of eternal, gravity-defying brand new life with Him.

Imagine if we lived the truth Paul proclaims in Galatians 2:20. Imagine we lived as if our old self really had died – and been raised with Christ. Then, if sin came knocking, the internal soul-dialogue would go something like, 'Sorry, she's not here. She's *risen*. You can't come and tempt her! She won't do that stuff anymore – the stuff her old (dead) self used to do. Her new living self? She's just not into that.'

Jesus, thank You for conquering death, so I can really live!
Show me where I'm still lugging a corpse. Help me to shake it
off – my old dead self – and enjoy a risen life with You. Amen.

# Sync it up

But don't just listen to God's word. You must
do what it says. Otherwise, you are only
fooling yourselves (James 1:22 NLT).

*A* film director's clapper is used to synchronize the action and the soundtrack. As in, 'Action!' – *clap*. Bob Goff draws the analogy that we should regularly – throughout the course of our day – with every life-scene we film – *sync it up*. We should sync our walk with our talk.

A beautiful way to travel light is to make sure we're not out of step with what we say we believe. Are our footfalls finding gravity – are we being real? And are we walking in grace – are we proclaiming the gospel through our actions and our attitudes? Being constantly out of step – trying to let our behavior or decisions catch up to who we pretend to be – that's unsustainable and will become overwhelmingly exhausting unless we take the time to stop – sync it up – and then graciously get going.

Syncing it up also helps shake off the curse of most high achievers – the voice that taunts, 'Who do you think *you* are to be doing this? You're a fraud, and you'll be found out. They'll realize you don't know what you're doing.' Friend, just sync it up. Sync the sufficient grace of God for your journey, with the gravity that has you grounded in your very real story.

O God, help me to keep it real, and gospel-radical. Amen.

# Chaos, grace and gravity

The commandments of the LORD are right, bringing joy to the heart. The commands of the LORD are clear, giving insight for living (Ps. 19:8 NLT).

There's something in kids – and most grownups – that rebels against regulation. We want to do what we want, the way we want it, because that feels more fun, and more free.

But a soccer match played without rules and refereeing devolves into chaos, offence and certain injury. It's fun for no one. Soccer is designed in such a way that the rules and the ref actually *free* us to enjoy the game as it's meant to be played. Similarly, planes across the globe landing and taking off without air traffic controllers would lead to the deaths of millions. Because the truth about the design of the universe is that the way it's regulated releases us to enjoy the journey of life as it was meant to be lived and explored and relished. The structure that restriction brings liberates our bent towards progress.

The gravity of God's instructions is a grace – not a restriction – that frees us. It's a grace that keeps our feet happily – not lead-weighted – on the ground, which is where they need to be for running, jumping, playing and traveling light.

Jesus, thank You for dying to set me free from slavery to dos-and-don'ts. And thank You for bringing clarity to my chaos and teaching me how to live well. Amen.

# 60 seconds to say it

Instead, we will speak the truth in love, growing in every way more and more like Christ, who is the head of His body, the church (Eph. 4:15 NLT).

Travel is full of brief encounters – some forgettable, others not. And today if we were sharing a cab for a couple of blocks, or if I passed you in the school car park or the grocery store or we rode the same floors in an elevator and I had a minute of your time, you'd think I was weird and intense but I'd say to you,

'God hasn't called you to be successful. He's called you to be fruitful. Stop beating yourself up and trying so hard. Fake fruit falls off, stuck on from the outside. Let God grow the real deal on your branches, *from the inside*.

Practice being in two places at once – the chaos of life, and the quiet of His presence. He knows about all your dreams and disasters. Leave them at His feet so you can do today well and un-distracted, securing tomorrow. You're *so* lovely. (Also, you never *look* as fat as you *feel*.) Get outside. Get more sleep. Eat fresh stuff. Drink water. Sit up straighter; breathe deeper. You're on solid rock in royal robes, barefoot on holy ground. You will not be shaken.'

God, make me brave to take a minute today to say to someone what really needs to be said. Amen.

# Endings

For if we are faithful to the end, trusting God just
as firmly as when we first believed, we will share
in all that belongs to Christ (Heb. 3:14 NLT).

Gravity gets to all of us, eventually. No amount of anti-gravity, anti-wrinkle cream can save us from sagging as time takes its toll. There are serums and surgical procedures that can ward off the tug to the grave, but ultimately, even those will give out.

This is *not* depressing! In fact, you can choose to see it as something rather exhilarating. Daniel Pink talks about the importance of *endings* – and how it's our endings that really *make meaning*. We'll be remembered for our endings – how we finished each job, project, trip, season or relationship. Whether you're in Act 1, Act 2 or Act 3 of your life, you'll come to endings all the time, and the research indicates that whether you're coming to the end of an evening, a contract, a place of residence, a season of studying, or your life – ending with healthy community and strong relationships is monumentally significant.

Edit to the essentials, and end well. Have grace, show grace, depend on grace, and by grace, don't leave anyone or anything, hanging.

Lord Jesus, keep me from ending weakly. Strengthen
me to finish well! I don't want to end as an ellipsis ...
Make an exclamation mark of me! Amen.

# Harness

He led me to a place of safety;
He rescued me … (Ps. 18:19 NLT).

*I*magine hanging by your fingertips, from a ledge on a cliff. There's a sheer wall above you, and a drop-to-your-death below you. You can hold on – for a while. But that's all you can do. Eventually, strength will give out and you'll slip.

But imagine Someone gets you into a harness – securing ropes and fastening you to the top of the cliff. You can't fall! You can lean back, and relax … And then you can *really climb*. You're hands-free, and you're not trying to hold your own weight anymore. You can climb fast, effectively and with great strength, because the pressure's been taken off.

That's living with grace and gravity. We can email, study, work, shop online, discipline our kids, make love, make toast and travel light effectively, strategically, intentionally, consistently and with sufficient energy – because we're not hanging by our fingertips going, *It's all up to me!* We're depending on the Holy Spirit to work in us and through us, so we can keep climbing.

Gravity isn't legalism. It doesn't mean we better pull ourselves up the cliff face *or else*! And grace isn't laissez-faire. It doesn't mean opt out, chill out, flake out. Grace and gravity means we live better. We climb higher, knowing we don't climb alone.

God, thank You for carrying my weight,
so that I can carry on, for Your glory. Amen.

# SEPTEMBER

*Life on a Shoestring*

The traveler sees
what he sees.
The tourist sees
what he has come
to see.
*G. K. Chesterton*

# Empty pockets

For where your treasure is, there your
heart will be also (Matt. 6:21 NIV).

Traveling on a shoestring is the romantic way of saying *traveling with very little money*. It means you're traveling light in every sense of the term. Your *pockets*, in particular, are light. It's the traveling we did in our twenties – and the traveling we're doing now with kids, because there are more tickets to buy, more beds to book. It's youth hostels and backpacks and hitching rides, stretching meals and stretching our budget. And so long as you embrace shoestring travel as pure adventure, it's the very best kind of freedom and fun.

Traveling through life on a shoestring doesn't mean *no strings attached*. It's not an abdication of responsibility. It's not meaningless or frivolous or hedonistic. It's means being willing to give up your comfort and your agenda, giving all of you for all of Him. It's giving up *your* ambitions in favor of *God's*. It's when the only thing tying you down is a burden for the lost.

It's walking the streets of your neighborhood and the world with humility, ever aware that none of us is too important to love and serve in the lowliest of places, in the lowliest of ways.

God, help me let go of the trappings of life,
so I can tether myself to You. Amen.

# Needless

Yes, everything else is worthless when compared
with the infinite value of knowing Christ Jesus my Lord.
For His sake I have discarded everything else, counting it
all as garbage, so that I could gain Christ … (Phil. 3:8 NLT)

What's cool about shoestring travel – backpacking and hitch-hiking and flying budget airlines and generally by the seat of your pants – is that you can only carry so much stuff. It forces you into minimalist living. Which may initially feel inconvenient – even scary – because you have to forgo options and accessories and possibly some comfort – but it clarifies essentials like nothing else does.

Shoestring travel also makes me long for home. I can label any hardship, 'adventure,' so long as I know that at some point it will come to an end, and I'll get to go home.

Really, all of life is that adventure. It's hard, but the more we have to go without, the more we realize what we really need, and what's really important. And the less we rely on what this world has to offer, the more we look forward to the world to come.

Jesus, in You, I've got everything I need to head home. Amen.

# Habit

Jesus knew that the Father had given Him authority over everything … So He got up from the table, took off His robe, wrapped a towel around His waist, and poured water into a basin. Then He began to wash the disciples' feet, drying them with the towel He had around him (John 13:3-5 NLT).

There's a story about a knight who climbs a mountain. The path is rough and steep, winding round … and round … and round the mountain. He slowly follows the contours leading to the summit. He wears a suit of armor with a brass breastplate.

As he climbs higher and higher, his armor grows brighter and brighter, glowing brilliant gold in the sun. *Until just before he reaches the top.* Almost within reach of the highest point – armor gleaming – he dons a monk's brown, rough-sewn habit. He wears the habit of humility so as not to blind others as he makes himself accessible, and available to serve.

As we climb life's steep footpaths, the God-gleam of our lives gets brighter and brighter as we grow more and more like Jesus. And like King Jesus who held the scepter of the creation and stooped to wash feet, we need to carry the shimmer within robes of down-to-earthness, never thinking we've traveled far enough to boast about anything.

Father, no matter how high You let me climb, dress me in habits that keep me living from the ground up. Amen.

# Have title, will travel

> Yet the LORD chose your ancestors as the objects of His love. And He chose you, their descendants, above all other nations, as is evident today (Deut. 10:15 NLT).

*I*'ve fantasized about how awesome it must be to hold a diplomatic passport of sorts. No visa application forms to fill out. No customs, no questions, no queues. I'd be able to travel anywhere, anytime, and I'd probably be traveling first class.

You need some kind of title, for that kind of access to passage. Newsflash: you already have the greatest title you'll ever hold. *Child of God*. Knowing your title gives you ease of travel through life. You can stand firm in the face of the red tape and roadblocks of fear or change or monotony, because you know who you are.

People don't follow titles. They follow courage, kindness and humility. So knowing your title shouldn't breed arrogance or entitlement. Know it for the confidence it brings you, to bring to others the life-changing hope of Jesus.

Jesus, thank You for giving up Your heavenly title,
to give me the all-access privileges of the Kingdom. Amen.

# Inviting extraordinary

The reward for humility and fear of the LORD
is riches and honor and life (Prov. 22:4 ESV).

*I* don't believe that I've ever met someone who *wanted* to be mediocre. Someone who had made it their life's ambition to be average. Make no mistake – we're all just very ordinary humans. Yet we serve an extraordinary God who calls us to be extraordinary reflections of Him – extraordinary conduits of His glory, not our agenda. There's something of the image of God in each of us *ordinary* humans that is drawn to the *extraordinary*.

The world punts ideas of how we can get to extraordinary: the hustle of self-promotion and money and stuff and beauty and who-you-know. God's idea of extraordinary is counter-culture. I heard a preacher say once that humility is always an invitation for God to do extraordinary things.

As Jesus-followers, let's build our reputations on deference and happy self-denial. Let's invite our extraordinary God to do something extraordinary with our ordinary lives, by living lower.

God, from down here on my knees, I'm asking
You to come into my life and do something
remarkable, for Your greatness and glory. Amen.

# Inside out

> For in my inner being I delight
> in God's law … (Rom. 7:22 NIV).

The world operates from the outside in, and sometimes that philosophy works. Like, if you're doing some sort of performance or presentation before an audience? You need to look the part. Because if you *look* the part, you'll *feel* the part; and if you *feel* the part, you'll *be* the part.

But in pretty much every other way, the truth is something different. We need to live from the inner-man or inner-woman *outwards*: living rich, real lives that are rooted in authentic acceptance, and sustained by an ongoing, intimate relationship with the Father. Otherwise, the outer walls we're working hard to build and that we hope will last and look good – those walls built on recognizable achievements – will utterly collapse.

Living outside-in means we're mastered by our circumstances and the fickleness of our emotions. Living inside-out means we take our emotions along for the ride, but we don't let them drive. And we don't let the constant flux of circumstances shift our hope in the unchanging God.

> Lord Jesus, I want what's inside me to spill
> out of me, and I want it to be You. Amen.

# The why and the way

> Don't copy the behavior and customs of this world, but let God transform you into a new person by changing the way you think. Then you will learn to know God's will for you, which is good and pleasing and perfect (Rom. 12:2 NLT).

No matter your line of work or influence, you may experience the fatigue that comes from following too many people – online or in your real world networks – who constantly leave you feeling like you're on the wrong side of the trend curve.

Scott Sauls reminds us that we should study the Word, then study culture. Paul, after all, quoted secular writers from memory (Acts 17:28). So, *study* your society and your civilization. Stay abreast of the leanings and the movements. It's important.

But the fatigue creeps up on you because you're *following* those people or those craze waves or buzz words – instead of following Jesus. You've forgotten to follow the Shepherd's voice in your field. You've heard it said – that if you forget the *why* you lose your *way*. Go back to the last thing God said to you – and keep doing that, until He tells you something different. Keep focusing on *why* you do what you do, and the passion and energy will return.

> God, help me whittle down what I do
> to the shoestring essentials – so I'll
> remember why I do it. Amen.

# Rich man's world

For the love of money is the root of all kinds
of evil. And some people, craving money, have
wandered from the true faith and pierced
themselves with many sorrows (1 Tim. 6:10 NLT).

You don't need to be the brightest bulb in the tanning bed to notice that the world is obsessed with money. Wars are fought over money. Elections are won and lost over money. Marriages are made and messed up over money.

And yet, money isn't wicked. It's like food or sex or gravity or speed or almost any other force or principle in existence: it can be used for tremendous good, and tremendous evil.

To travel light, we need to hold our money lightly too, aware that it's the *love* of money that is the root of evil, and aware that we can't even bank on money in the bank, because our money can be taken from us at any time (Proverbs 23:5). Money isn't who we are – and so *more* money doesn't make us better. More money is simply a tool to make better, wiser choices, and more money comes with even more responsibility.

Carry it carefully. And let go of it generously. In a rich man's world that lusts for stuff, our excellent stewardship and our generous giving are remarkable evidence of the work of the Holy Spirit in our hearts.

God, help me to un-love my money, and shock the world! Amen.

# Human strength

This is what the LORD says: 'Cursed are those who put their trust in mere humans, who rely on human strength and turn their hearts away from the LORD …' ( Jer. 17:5 NLT).

Mark Batterson writes, 'God-given gifts are wonderful things and dangerous things. One of my recurrent prayers is this: *Lord, don't let my gifts take me farther than my character can sustain me.* As we cultivate the gifts God has given us, we can begin to rely on those gifts instead of relying on God. That's when our greatest strength becomes our greatest weakness.'

Like money, we can use our gifts for good, or evil. If you rock at something, you might become proud, relying more on your own mind or muscle or the momentum your gifting has created – and less on the Giver of the gift, who lends you every opportunity to use it.

There's nothing wrong with *enjoying* your gift. And there's nothing quite like operating in your sweet spot and knowing the satisfaction of a job well done. Just ask God to remind you that you did nothing to earn the aptitude He chose to bestow on you. Flying solo, you can do a fair amount with your gift. But surrendered to the Holy Spirit within you, your gift can change the world.

Father, I don't want to move a muscle
without Your strength. Amen.

# All the things

He fills my life with good things. My youth
is renewed like the eagle's! (Ps. 103:5 NLT).

Traveling through life with a shoestring mentality helps us settle more quickly, more easily, in a place of contentment. Ann Voskamp writes, 'The more you let yourself compete and compare, the more you forget your own calling ... The more you push to get in front of others, the more you fall behind in being the best you can be.'

Rather, we can choose to live with a spirit of sufficiency. Satisfaction. Adequacy. Remembering that we get sufficient grace, and our lives are sufficiently supplied, and God has done sufficient good things for us to last us an eternity.

Shoestring travelers aren't afraid to celebrate and enjoy all the riches they come across, because there's an inner serenity – an understanding that they *get enough*. A famed philosopher once said, 'Be content with what you have; rejoice in the way things are. When you realize there is nothing lacking, the whole world belongs to you.'

Lord, I could never count my blessings.
There are far too many. Amen.

# Behind Mr. Angry

And 'don't sin by letting anger control you.' Don't let the sun go down while you are still angry … (Eph. 4:26 NLT).

*A* friend of mine counsels kids who struggle with anxiety. When she talks to them about the things that make them angry, she always says, 'All I see is Mr. Angry. But who is standing *behind* Mr. Angry? I want to talk to *that* person.' She helps the kids see that behind anger is fear, or disappointment, or pride, or insecurity – which has its roots in something else.

Lucius Annaeus Seneca wrote, 'We are driven into wild rage by our luxurious lives, so that whatever does not answer our whims, arouses our anger.' We could travel more lightly if we shed our anger by figuring out what's really behind it – and tackling those things. Things like entitlement or greed or a lust for pleasure, possessions or prestige (1 John 2:16).

When we're willing to look Mr. Angry square in the face – and demand to talk to whoever's hiding behind him – we can make arrangements for *that* person to leave. Mr. Angry usually leaves with them – and a welcome deluge of simplicity, purity and peace washes over our lives.

God, I'm furious! Is it legit, or is there something else behind it? Amen.

# Excellence yes, entitlement no

Whatever you do, work at it with all your heart, as working
for the Lord, not for human masters … (Col. 3:23 NIV).

Travel gives perspective. And traveling through life on a shoestring
– journeying with the values of simplicity and humility – will
give us twenty-twenty vision to recognize attitudes of the heart.

Like, we ought to see to it, if we can, that things in our city or
community *work*. Systems should run smoothly and properly and
there should be a striving for excellence in the powers that be, because
we're paying our taxes and voting rightfully and responsibly. But I
shouldn't allow entitlement to convince me that I *deserve* smooth
sailing – that I *need* perfection – that I'm *justified* in getting irritated
when things *don't* work seamlessly or when I get cut off in the traffic.

Entitlement is insidious, sneaking up on us with its cloying, whin-
ing ways, deceiving us into believing that life owes us a free ride.
Truthfully? We're entitled to hell. Anything short of that is pure grace
on borrowed time. We need to travel lightly, gratefully and joyfully
with that in mind, sowing excellence wherever we can.

God, I want to lift my game, and
inspire others to do the same. Amen.

# Disproportionate

Yes, you will be enriched in every way so that you can always be generous. And when we take your gifts to those who need them, they will thank God (2 Cor. 9:11 NLT).

Data analyzed by Credit Suisse in 2017 revealed that chief executives of the top five global fashion brands made in just four days what garment workers in Bangladesh earn over a lifetime. That kind of gross disparity shows there's something very wrong with the world's economic distribution.

God's not a communist. He owns and distributes the wealth of the universe as He sees fit (Psalm 50:10). He bestows riches on some and not on others. But this doesn't give us license to hoard our resources and clutch close the good things He's given us. The Messiah who said we'd always have the poor with us (Matthew 26:11) also said that in giving generously to the needy, we're giving to Him (Matthew 25:40).

If you're reading this book, I'm guessing you're literate, and you've likely been introduced to Jesus. That makes you more privileged than most people on the planet. Overwhelming gratitude for that reality should spill over into generosity. We can't right all the economic wrongs that sin has wrought across our planet. But we've all got something to give.

Lord, You know my bank balance.
Make me brave, wise and
generous to use it, so that someone
else can travel light. Amen.

# Uncomplicated

Good people leave an inheritance to their grandchildren,
but the sinner's wealth passes to the godly (Prov. 13:22 NLT).

My friends Peter and Wanda have nine kids between them, some biological, some through adoption. And some grandkids. And some sons and daughters-in-law. They joke that their grownup kids shouldn't expect much of an inheritance, because all their money is going into raising their next crowd of kids.

The thing that strikes me about Wanda is that she seems to keep it all together, all ticking over, with the easy grace and uncomplicated faith of one focused on Jesus, and on what will matter in eternity. In a world of damaged baggage and heavy hearts, she's choosing to leave an uncomplicated inheritance.

Are there things you could let go of, to uncomplicate life for those living it in your wake? Could you spend your heart resources on forgiveness and reconciliation, instead of amassing a fortune of bitterness? Imagine for a moment how it might change the world if we spent our time or our money ironing out with easygoing love the rumpled realities of people around us.

God, unravel my stitched-tight heart. Stretch it
out into the simplicity of a legacy of love. Amen.

# Words for years

The glory of the young is their strength; the gray hair of experience is the splendor of the old (Prov. 20:29 NLT).

When I turned 39, I wrote a 39-word manifesto to try to encapsulate my worldview – what I wanted to live for, and how I wanted to live it. It went like this:

*Love the Shepherd-King. Forgive. Own your stuff. Life is relationships. Be humbly, bravely wise. Pray! Laugh! Adventure! Give thanks. Be what you were born for. Compromise comfort, never character. You're beloved, not the protagonist. Everything's going to be ok.*

I'm now forty-something and I've wondered if I shouldn't do this *every* year – and enjoy the privilege of scoring one extra wise word for one extra older, hopefully wiser year. Could you be intentional about writing your own travel guide for life, in the number of words matching your age? The older you are, so much the better! Try scrawling a few words today – even if it's just the things you really hope your kids or friends will learn from you, and take with them on their own life journeys.

Father God, thank You for filling up my years
with teachable moments. I'll never know it all,
but I'm excited to keep learning. Amen.

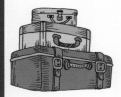

# Priorities

> This is all that I have learned: God made us
> plain and simple, but we have made ourselves
> very complicated (Eccles. 7:29 GNT).

We're all surfing the waves of life-dot-complicated and we need a bit of *simple*.

If we can keep our priorities straightforward and steady, there will be grace for the chaos of lesser things. So here are five areas of life I'm trying to simplify:

When it comes to my *soul*, I'm telling myself, 'The Creator-King wants to meet with you every day. The choice is simple: Either you're going to show up, or you're not.'

For my *marriage*, I'm reminding myself, 'Communicate, communicate, communicate. Keep finding each other.' And for *parenting* my kids? 'It's their hearts that matter. The rest is detail. And beautiful detail develops from soft, strong hearts. Keep praying that God would show you their hearts. Go hard after their hearts, every time.' For *friendships* and other relationships, I'm drumming this simple thought into my head: 'Be a happy, uncomplicated friend. Don't waste an interaction by offering anything other than warm words of life.'

Finally, to travel light and simple through our *careers*, it might help if we tell ourselves, 'Don't add to the noise. As far as possible, only do the things that only you can do.'

God, show me where I'm picking up too much baggage by over-thinking things. Help me prioritize, and simplify. Amen.

# Simple simplicities

> And whatever you do or say, do it as a
> representative of the Lord Jesus, giving thanks
> through Him to God the Father (Col. 3:17 NLT).

Yesterday, we prioritized. But there's much more to life than family, friends and work, right? The complications of all we pile on our plates can totally overwhelm us. Here are five areas we could simplify:

When it comes to *food*, tell yourself, 'Don't worry about it. Don't worship it. Before every meal, treat or temptation, pray: *Choose my weight; choose my plate.*'

You know you need to *rest*, but even that can feel complicated. Simplify rest by setting a nighttime reminder to wind down. Then don't check your phone again until after breakfast. You will survive. So will the world. Part of rest is *exercise*, right? Alleviate the pressure and guilt by simply determining to find ways to be active every day, even it's just ten sit-ups or a walk around the block. Have as much fun as possible.

When it comes to your *home*, keep it tidy. Put things away when you're done. And keep it real. Make space for the raucous and the resting. Finally, simplify your *money* by daily praying for wisdom. Budget. Give. Save. Live. Enjoy. Repeat.

> God, all the parts of my life are
> gifts from You! Help me keep them
> simple, so I can simply enjoy them. Amen.

# God's not done

And this is the plan: At the right time He will bring
everything together under the authority of Christ –
everything in heaven and on earth (Eph. 1:10 NLT)

Sometimes I catch myself feeling a little dazed and startled
that we actually keep spinning through the solar system into
year after new year. Apparently God's not done. He's not done with
humans. He's not done with me. He's not done with you.

There are days when it feels like humanity's plot isn't thickening; it's
curdling. But my brain is so tiny and my perceptions and experiences
so incomplete that I'm trying not to believe everything I think. Rather,
I'm aiming for fearless humility.

Fearless humility doesn't lose the passion of calling, finds peace
amidst confusion, and keeps taking opportunities for as long as God
gives them. Fearless humility says, *I've got nothing to lose except my
life, and Jesus guaranteed it in abundance.* Fearless humility celebrates
the strength and progress, the gifts and ministries of others, for
God's Kingdom and glory. Fearless humility remembers: our origin
determines our destiny. We were conceived by the Creator-King –
that's our origin – to be His image-bearers – that's our destiny. We
can travel with every hope that He's bringing us into that spacious
place.

Mighty God, thank You that I can keep on
living with fearless humility, because history is still
being written, and You're holding the pen. Amen.

# Cookies and simple concerns

> LORD, my heart is not proud; my eyes are not haughty. I don't concern myself with matters too great or too awesome for me to grasp (Ps. 131:1 NLT).

When he was very little my youngest son said, 'When I get to heaven, I'm going to ask Jesus: *How do you make an Oreo cookie?*'

There's a lot to be said for simplicity. For starting each new day with the faith and the guileless dependence of a child. For saying, 'God, this is just little old me. I'm not snooty or stuck-up. I'm not too big for my boots, getting involved in stuff that isn't my concern.'

Child-like faith isn't too insecure to ask the seemingly silly questions, or the awkward questions others are avoiding. Child-like faith says, 'I'll pour myself out as fast as God fills me. And I will delight in the small things – like smiling biscuits that – magic! – have cream on the inside.'

Charles Dickens wrote, 'The important thing is this: to be ready at any moment to sacrifice what you are for what you could become.' The posture of that kind of life is humble, teachable, expectant and never without a sense of child-like wonder.

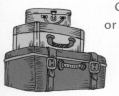

God, keep me from becoming blasé with age
or cynical with the complications of experience.
Let me be ever more wonderstruck by Your
ways, and satisfied with simplicity. Amen.

# Against all odds

Each of you should use whatever gift
you have received ... (1 Pet. 4:10 NIV).

We tried to dissuade our low-vision kiddo from signing up for cricket. We were blunt. (Brutal?) We told him the unpolished truth – that he wouldn't see the ball coming. But he dug his heels deeper. Come hell or heatwave, he was playing cricket.

It was part denial – wanting to be like the other boys against all odds. And part die-hard can-do optimism that we dared not crush because it'll take him far in life – against all odds. We vacillated between we-shouldn't-stop-him-trying-stuff, and are-we-totally-insane because he'll likely get his heart – and possibly his face – broken. When do you cheer for your kids and encourage them to have a go – and when do you tell them the truth about their limitations?

It seems courage simply whispers, *Yes.*

Because it's scary when your kid sobs that he'll *never* be like other kids and you're the grownup who's supposed to have answers but you've come to the end of your good ideas and yourself. And it's a scary kind of happy freedom to release him with the truth that he's right. He won't ever be like other kids. But he can have a crack at whatever it looks like to be the best version of himself, which is, marvelously, his only and highest calling.

Father, against all odds, I'll do my best
with what You've put inside me. Amen.

# Cool courage

Say to those with fearful hearts, 'Be strong, do not fear; your God will come ...' (Isa. 35:4 NIV).

When our visually impaired boy took up rock climbing, it instantly became one of his favorite things to do. Yet this same kid who was scaling walls wrote on his all-about-me worksheet at school that he needs to 'work on his courage'.

Because sometimes he's scared. He thinks being scared means he isn't brave when really, brave only ever happens with simultaneous fear. If we're unafraid, it doesn't mean we're courageous. It means we're comfortable. What we actually need to get comfortable with is the idea that courage *looks* fearless and *feels* fearful, and that's ok.

Without humility, courage never gets off the ground. Humility fuels the bravery that risks rejection and failure. Humility strengthens us to muscle through terror – do it anyway – because we're not so hung up on impressing people. When He went to the cross, Jesus was terrified (Matthew 26:39). But the courage it took to die for the haters – to fight for our hearts and not for His dignity – took more than pushing back fear. It took mind-blowing humility. It was the bravest, scariest, humblest act in history.

It's possible we'd be much braver – much freer – if we remembered *it's not about us*. That kind of terrified, humble courage might have us signing up for all kinds of crazy wonderful.

God, I'm so scared! Pick me! Amen.

# Kid privileges

Never! Can a mother forget her nursing child? Can she feel no love for the child she has borne? But even if that were possible, I would not forget you! (Isa. 49:15 NLT).

My youngest son said to me recently, 'I love my teacher. She treats us like her own kids. I go to her with stuff, and then she talks to me like I'm one of her kids.' I thought to myself, *Whatever they're paying her, it's not enough!*

Because don't we all just want that for our kids? Really, we just want people to *like* them and be *nice* to them and *do for them* as they would for their own kids. That's gospel living. God treats us like His Son – *makes us into* His very own kids through redemption and adoption (Ephesians 1:5). He turns us into heirs. Jesus takes our shame – restores our dignity – and imputes kid-worth to you and me so we get the same royal treatment He does, from His Father.

And God's treatment of us – *because of Jesus* – informs how we live out the rest of our lives, which should be all about our treatment of others – *because of Jesus.*

God, soften and strengthen me to show to others the deep affection and tender compassion You've shown to me. Amen.

# Feelings on a shoestring

Blessed are the merciful … (Matt. 5:7 NIV).

*I* really like other humans. But occasionally my life collides with someone who hurts or angers me. Or knocks me off balance in some subtle way. And sometimes I don't have it in me to muster the inner niceness, which is when I loan love from Jesus who feels all the feelings for all the people, and even feels them for me.

I've tried borrowing His feelings for the sullen cashier or the awkward person at church. Even borrowing His tender feelings for my kids on days I don't like them quite as much as I love them. It changes everything.

In moments when it's all I can do not to stoop and pick up an offence – because I'm irritated, insulted, threatened or hormonal – I say, *Jesus, can I use Your feelings right now? Help me feel for these people what You feel for them.*

This isn't fake. If you're cold and you borrow someone's sweater, you don't hold it up in front of you, pretending to wear it. You actually put it on. And it actually warms you. Wearing Jesus' feelings thaws our icy agendas. There's real joy, real peace, real love. It's impossible to disdain or feel superior when you're warmed by the thought that Jesus had this person in mind when He hung on the cross.

Jesus, my heart's freezing. Please loan
me the warmth of Your love. Amen.

# Travel vulnerable

> Though He was God, He did not think of equality with
> God as something to cling to. Instead, He gave up
> His divine privileges; He took the humble position of a
> slave and was born as a human being (Phil. 2:6-7 NLT).

Much of Brené Brown's research on vulnerability points to Jesus. Brené says, 'It's tough to be vulnerable when we're terrified about what people might see or think.' Jesus risked how people might see Him, receive Him, or crucify Him. Imagine a world where His people borrowed that kind of brave.

She says, 'Vulnerability is the birthplace of innovation, creativity and change.' At a birthplace in Bethlehem, the galaxy-Maker made Himself unspeakably vulnerable – which set in motion the greatest change in history.

She says, 'Vulnerability is the glue that holds relationships together.' If we'll humbly admit we don't have it in us to love like we should, and if we'll see people the way God does, it'll be more than glue. It'll be the elixir that heals marriages, families, churches and nations.

She says, 'Courage starts with showing up and letting ourselves be seen.' Jesus showed up, let Himself be seen, and changed the world. Ordinary us, we don't have that kind of courage. But we could loan it from extraordinary God. In the small spaces of full, frenetic days, we could show up – let ourselves be seen – and change the world.

God, help me to risk loving. Amen.

# Humble not humiliated

Humble yourselves before the Lord, and
He will lift you up in honor (James 4:10 NLT).

There's a difference between humility and humiliation.

When Jesus died on the cross for you and me, He took away our disgrace and re-established our decorum. Even in the Garden of Eden, God had compassion on Adam and Eve, wrapping clothes around their embarrassment (Genesis 3:21). He covers us with His feathers (Psalm 91:4). He clothes us in righteousness (Isaiah 61:10). So it's clear that the culture of the Kingdom isn't humiliation. The currency of the Kingdom isn't shame. The fact that Jesus *was* shamed and humiliated on the cross, on our behalf, saw to that.

So, Jesus was humiliated in our place. But He also showed us how to live humbly. He *did* stand up for the cause He was defending or promoting. He wasn't a pushover for bullies. But He never defended Himself; He only defended His Father's glory. He kept entrusting His case to the One who judges righteously. He taught us how to dive under the wave, every time, when we'd rather be surfing it.

Jesus, I want to give my humble thanks to You
for enduring humiliation so I didn't have to. Amen.

# Take me places

Seven priests will walk ahead of the Ark, each carrying a ram's horn. On the seventh day you are to march around the town seven times, with the priests blowing the horns (Joshua 6:4 NLT).

For years, God provided manna for the wilderness-wandering Israelites. He provided just enough, for each day. They relied solely – humbly – on Him. Then God stopped providing manna (Joshua 5:12). He was leading them into the Promised Land, where there'd be plenty for them to eat, and even to feed others.

But God wanted to keep His people humble. He showed them through the Ark's symbolism that they had to take His presence with them as they took another lap and then another, and another, around Jericho's walls. They needed to do things differently – trusting Him for what may not have been obvious to them.

It takes courage and humility to move on and do things in a new way. But you can trust God to provide. And when your circumstances seem impenetrable – as if you don't have the resources to cope – ask God to help you see as He sees, and take His presence with you as you take another lap. Even just another step. Trust His battle strategy. Then be expectant. Because when Jesus knows He's getting the glory for all you are and do, He'll take you places you couldn't take yourself.

Jesus, I'm ready for an adventure with You. Amen.

# Small fish

All glory to Him who alone is God, our Savior
through Jesus Christ our Lord. All glory, majesty,
power, and authority are His before all time, and in the
present, and beyond all time! Amen (Jude 1:25 NLT).

*I*t's a liberating mercy that you are not irreplaceable. For sure, there's only one you and there will only ever be one you. But it'll help you travel light if you remember that we're all just tiny fish in the vast ocean that is the Kingdom of God: anonymous to pretty much everyone except the One who called us by name and appointed and anointed us for unique works, for His fame and glory.

There's a lot of pressure on big fish, because they have to have big things to declare about themselves. If they run out of big things, they'll no longer be seen as big fish. If you're content to stay a small fish, declaring only the big and everlasting and never-exhausted things of your great God, you'll be swimming happy and free, abundantly able to sustain your small fish existence.

God, I'm so very happy to stay small.
As and when You see fit, make loud my small
voice as I only ever declare Your bigness. Amen.

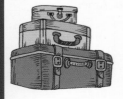

# Recline

> And as Jesus reclined at table in the house, behold,
> many tax collectors and sinners came and were
> reclining with Jesus and His disciples (Matt. 9:10 ESV).

*I*'ve heard and read this story hundreds of times. Jesus ate with tax gatherers, trash talkers and other forms of bad company. He was willing to hang out with the people who desperately needed His restoring touch. But what I've missed is how often the gospel writers mention that Jesus was *reclining*.

Apparently, the Pharisees and other religious leaders of the day would never have dared to *recline* while talking about God. They always stood, as a sign of their power and authority. And yet Jesus reclined. He happily positioned Himself to be approachable. He humbled Himself – Creator-King – Maker of burning stars and smiles and blades of grass – so that those who were still His enemies would feel safe in His presence.

Perhaps as we travel through life on a shoestring – acknowledging unreservedly that it's all about Him – we can find the time and space to recline. We can be amenable and accessible, welcoming others with a posture of humility.

*Jesus, teach me Your ways of flexibility and friendliness,*
*so I can win others over to Your remarkable love. Amen.*

# Brave race to the bottom

Don't you realize that in a race everyone runs, but only one person gets the prize? So run to win (1 Cor. 9:24 NLT).

Traveling through life is not a competition. In fact, we're each encouraged to run our own race (2 Timothy 4:7, Hebrews 12:1). But if all of life *were* a competition, how might we change the world if we saw it all, not as a race to the top, but a race to the bottom? A lifestyle of going lower – preferring others – standing back to let others go first. A lifestyle of humility.

Because you've got to be brave to travel. And the root of brave is always humble. Emily Freeman writes, 'Let's stretch out in the fullness of small and move downward in gladness rather than upward in fear. Let's let go of the constructed life and embrace a connected life, even if it leads to less. Let's remember how our souls weren't made for fame. Let's receive the gift of obscurity with joy, gratitude, and a light heart.'

God, make me the best at getting out of the way of Your glory. Amen.

# Winner

> The night is almost gone; the day of salvation will soon be here. So remove your dark deeds like dirty clothes, and put on the shining armor of right living (Rom. 13:12 NLT).

The fact that we get to travel heavenward through this life is a gift, and a privilege, and not about us. That beautiful truth bomb should keep us traveling light.

Except, sometimes our pride weighs us down ... and slows us down. We start to think life *is* all about us. We start elevating ourselves and when it comes to any known-ness we might enjoy, we forget Who it's from, and Who it's for.

The best strategy to adopt then is to travel light *and* fast. We need to strip off every weight that slows us down, especially the sin that so easily trips us up (Hebrews 12:1). We need to throw off the excess baggage and sprint – reminding ourselves that *the first one to the cross wins*. The first one to ask forgiveness, to show compassion, to make amends, to offer help, to initiate love or service – that person's the winner! And that person's humility-infused influence will likely be extraordinary.

God, help me train hard in humility so I'm fit enough to be the first one to think of myself second, every time. Amen.

# OCTOBER

## Go the Distance

It is good to have an
end to journey toward;
but it is the journey
that matters, in the end.

*Ursula Le Guin*

# Dreams, goals, success

But as for you, be strong and courageous, for
your work will be rewarded (2 Chron. 15:7 NLT).

This month of devotions is about mobility: moving forward with the perseverance necessary to finish strong. It may help you go the distance if you're clear on what you're shooting for. Dreams? Goals? Success? (And what's the difference?)

Dreams are things you hope for – things you long to achieve. Maybe you dream of owning a business or traveling the world, meeting your soul-mate or writing a novel for teenagers. *Give your dreams to Jesus.* All your dreams. Your massive dreams that seem highly unlikely. Your small dreams that seem silly. You can trust Him. Lay your dreams at His feet. Ask Him to keep them safe.

Goals are things you can do to start working towards your dreams. Specific, measureable, actionable decisions you can take within a given timeframe that will begin moving you towards your dreams. Like, commit to a monthly savings plan for business startup capital. Do your research. Exercise. Practice your craft. Be accountable.

Success is daily obedience to Christ. It's simply doing the next right thing, and then the next. If you get to the end of a day and go, 'Was today successful?' You can say a happy *yes* if the inclination of your heart was to obey your King.

Jesus, I give You my dreams. Help me set
wise goals. Move my heart to obedience. Amen.

# Not all fun

> This is why we work hard and continue to struggle,
> for our hope is in the living God, who is the Savior of all
> people and particularly of all believers (1 Tim. 4:10 NLT).

Culture spins the feel-good philosophy that we should just chase our dreams. Pursue our passions. Follow the fun. I definitely believe God's calling on your life will have loads to do with where your passion and aptitude collide. You're in your sweet spot when you're good at doing something that you also love.

It's just important to accept that leaning into the things you're passionate about – following your dreams – doesn't mean you only get to do the fun stuff. Your calling will also be tough. And you shouldn't be afraid of the toughness. For example, it's *easy* to pack grocery bags at a store. It's much *tougher* to read for the degree that fascinates you. But in the long hours of disciplined study there will be a quickening of the spirit – an excitement – real fulfillment – that opting for fun or easy won't deliver.

Paul had an overriding passion to see the spread of the gospel across the world and this was the long-term achievement of his life. But his years were littered with hardships – as a *result* of that same passion. I think he'd be the first to say he wouldn't have chosen differently.

> God, I'm weak, but I'm willing.
> Let's do this thing. Amen.

# Muscle memory

So I run with purpose in every step. I am not just shadowboxing. I discipline my body like an athlete, training it to do what it should. Otherwise, I fear that after preaching to others I myself might be disqualified (1 Cor. 9:26-27 NLT).

Part of what helps us to go the distance and finish strong this side of eternity is the spiritual muscle memory we develop through every hardship we surrender to the power of God. We can trust Him to do in us what we can't do ourselves. We can trust Him for wisdom and strength and insight, growth and endurance.

If we make Jesus our training partner through trials, we build up residual courage which stands us in good stead when it comes to our future responses.

You can probably look back on your life and see where and how God was stockpiling your courage reserves – teaching and maturing you so that down the line you'd be able to cope better. And if you're currently facing overwhelming odds, trust God not to waste this experience. Ask Him to use it to strengthen sinews of wisdom and bravery, so you're well prepared for whatever you'll come across on the roads ahead.

God, please don't waste anything that happens to me. Use it all to get me fit and strong for the stretch of road ahead. Amen.

# Courage to cut

Those who left Egypt had all been circumcised, but none of those born after the Exodus, during the years in the wilderness, had been circumcised … So Joshua circumcised their sons – those who had grown up to take their fathers' places – for they had not been circumcised on the way to the Promised Land (Josh. 5:5, 7 NLT).

*I*n Joshua 5 we read that God instructed Joshua to circumcise a new generation of Israelite men. The wilderness generation – about to enter the Promised Land – couldn't ride on the momentum of the previous generation, and call it courage. God had different plans for their generation and they had to continue to be courageous, step by new step into a new future.

Circumcision is an actual (painful) cutting away. Sometimes we need to be courageous to cut away things we've built into our lives – or things we've carried with us from previous generations, and never questioned – so we can walk into the land (actual or metaphorical) that God is opening up to us. There's fresh grace for every generation (Isaiah 41:4), but every generation also has to make its own clear-cut sacrifices, depending on the traps or temptations of its contemporary culture.

Father, make me brave to cut away what's holding me back so I can step into what You require of my generation, for the fame of Your name. Amen.

# Weights

You say, 'I am allowed to do anything' – but not everything
is good for you. You say, 'I am allowed to do anything' –
but not everything is beneficial (1 Cor. 10:23 NLT).

*I*f we're going to go the distance, we have to travel light, throwing
off the heavy things that have us dragging our feet (Heb. 12:1).

Maybe the weight you carry is the need to prove a point. Cast
off that weight by occasionally keeping your opinions to yourself.
Let's build up, not tear down. Let's stop venting, and start living and
leading by example.

Then there are the weights of comparison and staying angry and
social media addiction and eating too much. Be honest with God and
yourself about the things you need to drop. And if those things are
sin, call them what they are and repent.

Maybe you're too focused on carrying equally weighted dumbbells
in each hand – living a balanced life. It's been said that no one living
a balanced life ever changed the world. It's possible we'd be more
striking in our Christ-likeness if we focused less on finding balance,
and more on bearing fruit.

God, please show me what I need to drop,
so I can stay strong and go far. Amen.

# Loving and leading

> Children, always obey your parents, for this pleases
> the Lord. Fathers, do not aggravate your children,
> or they will become discouraged (Col. 3:20-21 NLT).

Everyone needs to forgive their parents for something. We've blown it with our kids countless times, and doubtless we'll blow it countless more. Because we're all making up this kid-raising gig as we go along (Right?) (Or is it just us?). We *definitely do* need their forgiveness – retrospectively, today, and in advance.

But two things you and I should want our kids, and others in our care, to know in the marrow of their bones, despite what we may or may not get right or wrong:

We are resolutely committed to loving them. We'll leverage all we are for all they're becoming. They are well loved, and loved well.

And we are passionately resolved to call out the potential God has placed in them. We should want our kids to be the best possible versions of themselves and leave the planet better than they found it. Part of that potential is to lead, because we're all called to lead our own lives, and lead others to Christ. Also, it's exactly in uncertain times (now!) that the world needs the clear vision of tenacious leaders.

> Father, as a parent I can't tick all the boxes
> all the time. Help me to simply love and lead
> my kids, so we can go the distance. Amen.

# Currents

I will refuse to look at anything
vile and vulgar (Ps. 101:3 NLT).

*A* reader of mine got in touch with me once, explaining: 'The reason for my email is I have been finding it very disturbing and disconcerting how it's so hard to find a movie or series to watch that isn't full of sickeningly gross violence or sexual depravity (pretty much porn) or messed up twisted concepts. It bothers me that believers find it ok to fill their minds with such horrible things and even worse, *enjoy* it. According to Philippians 4:8 we are supposed to fill our minds with what is pure and lovely. I think watching this stuff is completely in opposition to that. How do we as Christians deal with this as well as keep our children safe from numbing their minds to such terrible things?'

To go the distance – to finish well without getting sidetracked along life's road by the very real evil described above (because haven't we all struggled with various degrees of entertainment-related guilt, frustration and disgust?) – let's admit that the undertow of cultural currents will take us to dark places. It'll be hard work – swimming upstream – but it'll make you fitter and stronger than those drifting downstream. Let's keep searching for something wholesome to watch. Read a book. Talk. Hug an actual human. We'll be glad we did.

Jesus, make me immovable on my resolve to keep it clean. Amen.

# Pack and plan

Be ready and keep ready, you and all
your hosts that are assembled about you,
and be a guard for them (Ezek. 38:7 ESV).

Sometimes I think if we put as much time and effort and energy into planning and packing for life – as opposed to only planning and packing for trips we're taking – we'd enjoy more peace and a greater sense of accomplishment.

Take parenting for example. If we *planned* our parenting the way we plan a trip, we'd picture where we're going – and pack accordingly. We'd pack the right kind of truth. We'd begin with the end in mind and that would steer our goals and expectations. We'd ask ourselves, 'What kind of person do I want to grow, in this child?' Then we'd make decisions with that in mind. Your answer might be, 'A person who is fruitful, exposed and aware, able to rest, able to be alone, able to listen. A person who doesn't panic, who doesn't think busyness equals success,' and so on.

Where do you feel your life is going at the moment? Are you planning for it? And what are you packing for the ride?

God, I want to travel strategically. I pray for
insight and discernment. Help me to pack and plan
for the kind of life's journey that will exalt You. Amen.

# Travel slow

> Please, my lord, go ahead of your servant.
> We will follow slowly, at a pace that is comfortable
> for the livestock and the children (Gen. 33:14 NLT).

Jacob wasn't perfect. But he wasn't too proud to walk towards his brother, Esau, and ask forgiveness. Also, he wasn't too proud to walk slowly. He wisely went at the pace comfortable for the littles in the procession of his family and servants.

I used to piggyback my youngest son when we walked around the block in the late afternoons. Now he runs happily ahead. If I'd forced him to walk on his own little legs before he was ready, I might've killed it for him – the joy that is walking through leafy streets at twilight.

To go the distance, discern whether you're on a stretch of road best for running or walking. Or walking *slowly*. Or even allowing someone to carry you. Or slowing down for the sake of someone traveling with you. Sure, that can *feel* like time wasted. You *could* go faster without that person and capitalize on something else in your life. But going slower might benefit that relationship – and ultimately, that will matter more.

There's an African proverb that says, 'If you want to go fast, go alone. If you want to go far, go together.'

> God, set my pace. I don't want to get ahead of myself,
> or anyone else who needs my hand to hold. Amen.

# Grit and grace

Dear friends, you always followed my instructions when I was with you. And now that I am away, it is even more important. Work hard to show the results of your salvation, obeying God with deep reverence and fear (Phil. 2:12 NLT).

Jesus came to earth as one hundred percent God and one hundred percent man. My brain short-circuits when I try to assimilate the two – because how can both be one hundred percent simultaneously true? But I've come to accept this *both-and* reality as one of the beautiful God-mysteries permeating the universe.

Something similar happens in us. Much of life is walking the tightrope of grit and grace – working as if it's one hundred percent up to us, and praying as if it's one hundred percent up to God. He lends us every breath and infuses our muscles and brain cells with energy and potential: without Him we are nothing, and we can do nothing. And yet concurrently He holds us accountable to decide to use our gifts and opportunities – our money, time, abilities and relationships – for His Kingdom and glory.

And there's nothing quite like the exhausted satisfaction of accomplishment: knowing that you gave it your absolute human best, and that God was supernaturally empowering you.

Grit and grace go the distance.

Jesus, help me harness every fiber of my potential even as I depend fully on You. Amen.

# Great leaders go the distance

> Getting wisdom is the wisest thing
> you can do! And whatever else you do,
> develop good judgment (Prov. 4:7 NLT).

*I*f we're going to go the distance as leaders – leading organizations, or classrooms, or families, or leading our own lives and others to Christ – we're going to need to ask ourselves some questions, and give ourselves some honest answers. Andy Stanley explains that asking great questions reveals and reinforces our values and behaviors.

For example, ask yourself daily – hourly? – 'What would a great leader do?' That kind of question instantly clears the fog of emotion that's always part of any big decision.

Asking 'What would a great leader do?' unmasks your motives (because at some point what's good for everyone around you might conflict with your personal ambitions, and you'll need to make a tough – humble – call).

Asking, 'What would a great leader do?' shows up your weaknesses, challenging and inspiring you to reach beyond the limits of your personality, temperament and leadership style.

> God, I want to lead myself and others well,
> as I follow You. Help me to ask myself and
> answer myself, honestly, the right questions. Amen.

# Spiders

Oh, what a miserable person I am! Who will
free me from this life that is dominated by sin
and death? Thank God! The answer is in
Jesus Christ our Lord … (Rom. 7:24-25 NLT).

You've lived with yourself, and you've probably lived with other humans. So you'll know there's no denying we all have besetting sins that repeatedly trip us up.

Maybe for you it's substance abuse or gossip. Overspending or overeating. Envy or materialism or lust or irresponsible escapism. Maybe you've tried over and over and over to deal with your sin. You've prayed and repented, repented and prayed. You've memorized Scripture, read books, gone for counseling.

Those are all good things to do. Keep doing them. But Carlos Whitaker suggests there's no point continually cleaning out the cobwebs – sweeping out the corners of your mind where a tangled transgression mesh collects. *You have to kill the spider* – or it'll keep spinning its webs of sin.

Perhaps the spider is fear or pride or the lie you've believed about yourself which has led to your unhealthy habits. Perhaps you're really assailed by debilitating insecurity and that's what has you lashing out in all sorts of hurtful, hateful ways. Ask God to show you the spider. Waste no time. Kill it.

Lord, give me a holy arachnophobia. Exterminate
whatever's spinning webs to snare me. Amen.

# All sides

This High Priest of ours understands our
weaknesses, for He faced all of the same testings
we do, yet He did not sin (Heb. 4:15 NLT).

*I*f you and I are going to finish strong, we need to be intentional about how we carry and cover ourselves. To live wholeheartedly – which is a healthy, sustainable, admirable way to live, yes? – soft-science researchers suggest we need to have a strong back, a soft front, and an heroic heart. That means, marshaling the courage to stand up for ourselves and for others and for the truth; being vulnerable (which takes inordinate courage too); and borrowing all the inner brave we need from our soft, strong Savior.

A place to start is to ask God to show you if any of those three things is lacking in your life. Is your heart soft and open to those around you – but you're too easily manipulated or mismanaged? Or are you relentlessly courageous and principled – without the compassion necessary to temper your stance?

Not one of us will ever be perfectly brave or perfectly loving – but as we go the distance from birth to death, the Holy Spirit transforms us more and more into the likeness of perfectly brave, perfectly loving Jesus. We can lean on Him as we learn His ways.

Jesus, You lived perfectly, and You perfectly
understand my imperfection. Make me both supple
and sturdy on all sides – built for brave. Amen.

# Shovel coal

Whoever pursues righteousness and unfailing love
will find life, righteousness, and honor (Prov. 21:21 NLT).

We've all seen Christian leaders going strong for a while – then flaking out of a failing ministry. And we've all seen Christian leaders who get wiser and humbler and godlier – gentler and stronger – the older they get.

What's the difference? Why and how do some go the distance, and others not?

A steam train keeps going for miles, just on momentum, after its engine has cut out. People are the same, and none of us is above trundling on for a while without real power. If we stop shoveling the coal of prayer, truth, fellowship and accountability, we can keep going for quite some time, with no one the wiser. But eventually the impetus peters out. We grind to an embarrassing halt.

An older, wiser man of God said to me once that to go the distance, 'do God's bidding for your life. Do it resolutely, humbly, no matter the cost.' That translates into our lives as: daily time with God; journaling our prayers and convictions; not Band-Aiding the heart-sepsis of sin; and remembering that our Father sees and rewards every little thing – every small act of obedience to the Spirit's prompting.

Keep refueling your resolve to go the distance.

God, don't let me get lazy – cruising through
life on momentum. Help me travel well by daily
leaning on and learning from You. Amen.

# The snuff of dreams

Don't be afraid, for I am with you. Don't be discouraged, for I am your God. I will strengthen you and help you. I will hold you up with My victorious right hand (Isa. 41:10 NLT).

Fear can so easily hinder God's work in our lives. We fear failure. We fear what others will think of our endeavors. We fear that what God is calling us into will cost us more in prayer and pressure than we want to pay. And so we snuff out the dreams that spark to life in our souls.

God is bent on inspiring you with ideas of where and how He's working, and where and how you can spend your one life in the best and fullest possible way. Yet because of fear or laziness or self-doubt born of lies, we push those ideas quickly away before they can grip our hearts.

To go the distance and make Kingdom waves big enough for others to surf, decide today to be brave enough to pay attention to the glimpse God gives you of what could be if you were to lean into the still-fragile idea He is birthing. Write it down. Pray about it. Don't ignore it.

God, help me to pause to really picture the dream that flickers across the screen of my soul. If it's from You, please confirm it. And lend me wisdom to know how to pursue it. Amen.

# Heights

> The Sovereign LORD is my strength!
> He makes me as surefooted as a deer, able
> to tread upon the heights (Hab. 3:19 NLT).

*A*s you continue to go the distance in this life – heading for heaven – there will no doubt be valleys and sheer cliffs – some harsh, some beautiful. Success can have you standing on heights with magnificent views – and adverse circumstances or your own sin can have you standing on scary, slippery heights. In every case, God is able to make you *stand* on those heights.

Whatever breathtaking, exhilarating altitude you reach, or whatever pinnacle of pain you find yourself standing on, God will have the final say in your life. Not circumstances. Not another person. Not your success. Not even your sin. All those things might be impacting you, but they can't define your destiny, because God is sovereign even over our waywardness and His purposes cannot be thwarted (Job 42:2).

Yahweh, thank You that no matter what precarious place I find myself teetering on the edge of – I needn't crouch and cling all alone. You are with me, and You make me able to stand. Amen.

# Daughters go the distance

God decided in advance to adopt us into His own family by bringing us to Himself through Jesus Christ. This is what He wanted to do, and it gave Him great pleasure (Eph. 1:5 NLT).

*I*t's unlikely that a child abandoned on the streets will amount to much – if she survives for any length of time. But a child adopted – cherished and nurtured in a home where she belongs and is beloved – will flourish.

You are not abandoned, and never will be. You're adopted. More than that, you're adopted by a King – which makes you royalty. And *even more* than that – you're adopted by the King who signed the papers for your adoption with His own blood, securing your belonging for eternity.

Why then, do you and I still sometimes behave as if we're scraping together an existence on the streets outside the palace – as if we haven't been invited in, clothed, given our own room and a place at the table?

You are no longer an orphan. You're a daughter in the house – warm, clothed and fed – and your wise, excellent, loving Father will give you all you need to go the distance He has mapped out for you to travel.

Father, thank You for calling me into Your courts so that I'm equipped to go back out into the streets, carrying Your name. Amen.

# Temporary extension of travel

And this is what He promised us –
eternal life (1 John 2:25 NIV).

Believers and non-believers (who are angry at the God they don't believe in) struggle to accept that sometimes God heals, and sometimes He doesn't. We stare hard at our difficult circumstances as if they're an autostereogram – a magic eye puzzle – and if we stare for long enough an image will emerge from the chaos of dots or random patterns – a *reason why* God hasn't answered our prayer the way we wish He would.

When we hear stories of miraculous healings – and there *are* stories of miraculous healings – it bolsters our faith. Readies us a little more for life's road. But for our faith to go far despite what happens or doesn't happen, we need to accept that, for any of us, healing is just temporary. It's putting off the inevitable. Buying us more time this side of eternity. We can and should pray for healing, for ourselves and others, because it's a blessing to be spared pain, to have energy and capacity for Kingdom work, and to have more earth-time with loved ones.

But it's healthy to know that eventually, at the end of our lives, healing as we're hoping for it to roll out won't work for any of us. It's then that God gives us the ultimate healing of eternity: the biggest miracle of all.

God, I can't wait for heaven, and perfect healing! Amen.

# Have mirror, will travel

> Now we see things imperfectly, like puzzling reflections
> in a mirror, but then we will see everything with perfect
> clarity. All that I know now is partial and incomplete,
> but then I will know everything completely, just as
> God now knows me completely (1 Cor. 13:12 NLT).

To travel far and light, pack a mirror. Decide to become more self-aware, even if it makes you uncomfortable. Note: not self-centered, self-sufficient or any other kind of egotism. Just self-aware: willing to ask yourself some probing questions as you brush teeth and notice new wrinkles.

Like, 'What did I disagree with today?' Because sometimes I slide through days peaceably enough without ever thinking critically. 'Where did I fail today? What would it take to get this thing right?' Because God has given us imagination for solution. 'Have I believed a lie about myself? Have I let that lie become my label and that label become my limit?' Or maybe, 'If I'm jealous of what someone else has, is it because I don't believe my Heavenly Father will be generous with me?'

The crazy pace we choose makes it hard to carve out time for introspection. But to go the distance, we've got to slow down – and take a long hard look at our reflections.

Father, I can hide from myself but never from You. Help me to be honest, for my own growth and the greater good. Amen.

# Mobilize

> So now there is no condemnation for those
> who belong to Christ Jesus (Rom. 8:1 NLT).

My friend Brett leads a far more interesting life than I do. After time with him, I'm always left questioning how willing I am for God to move me – and make me uncomfortable – for His Kingdom.

Over coffee once, we discussed the transformation of society, conquering animosity and reconciliation between groups of people who have traditionally had little to do with each other. We talked about how politics and ideologies and religions are entrenched around geographical lines and that healing and understanding will come when we muster up the movement necessary to cross back over those lines, not just philosophically but physically too. We talked about generational guilt – if it's real or relevant or if we should stop feeling it already? He reminded me that guilt and conviction feel exactly the same. But guilt paralyses; *conviction mobilizes*.

Maybe God is challenging you to cross over some lines and embrace someone whom you've always seen as 'other'. Maybe you could mobilize your discomfort the way you'd mobilize stiff muscles: by stretching, and moving.

God, where I'm mud-stuck in guilt, move me to repentance,
then mobilize me for world-change. Amen.

# Live like it's new

> Place me like a seal over your heart, like a seal on your arm. For love is as strong as death, its jealousy as enduring as the grave. Love flashes like fire, the brightest kind of flame (Song of Solomon 8:6 NLT).

For your marriage to go the distance, you sometimes have to pretend you're just starting out. Pretend like you're vibing. So, if you're newly married, *do fun stuff!* And if you've been married for eons, *pretend* you're newly married, and *do fun stuff!*

Don't constantly host hordes of people in your home – at the expense of your alone time. Switch off your phones sometimes and savor the ultimate, intimate *us*-factor of being newlyweds – or better, *experienced* weds. Take time to see where your boundaries fall, then fling wide the front door.

Find excuses to celebrate anything, like the fact that it's Tuesday. Go out, go away, stay home, be alone. *Plan* for spontaneity. Scheduled romance is better than no romance. Always have something to look forward to.

And make a lot of love. He might need it more. You might need it less. That's just how God made us, and He called it good. Do the dance of compromise and compassion and lay yourselves down for each other's needs. (Sometimes literally.)

God, whether our marriage is brand new or worn in,
help us live it all like it's the first time. Amen.

# Protect the pillars

> This explains why a man leaves his father
> and mother and is joined to his wife, and
> the two are united into one (Gen. 2:24 NLT).

*I*n marriage you may find the things that initially attracted you to each other become annoying. Revisit *why* you fell in love. Conjure up those first feelings until you remember that the frustrations are part of the chemistry.

Make an effort. Apologize *immediately*. Forgive *quickly*. Say, 'I love you' *a lot*. Kiss him *longer* than necessary on the lips. Tell him *all* about your day, even when you're tired and it's easier to say, 'Fine.' Pray together, *out loud* and *often*. And when the kids come, don't transfer all your affectionate vibes from each other onto them.

These are all ways to build and protect the Genesis 2 pillars of your marriage: severance ('This explains why a man leaves his father and mother'), permanence ('and is joined to his wife'), unity ('the two are united into one') and intimacy ('the man and his wife were both naked, but they felt no shame').

Lord, give me awesome ideas of ways to remind
us both that we're building this marriage together. Amen.

# Not the man you married

> Always be humble and gentle. Be patient with each other, making allowance for each other's faults because of your love (Eph. 4:2 NLT).

You'll hear women say, 'But he's not the man I married!' He shouldn't be. If he's exactly the same as he was on your wedding day, he hasn't grown at all. You can't predict what life will throw at you guys in the years ahead, but throw things it will. Accept that experiences change us, and that it would be weird and time-warpy to have a static spouse.

That said, don't start living separate lives. Keep finding each other. Talk for long enough to get to the laughing part. Stay friends. Behave more like his lover and less like his mother. Fight to uncover and rediscover each other's sense of humor and hope.

Don't humiliate each other, and don't enable each other. In a good marriage, you know each other *so* well – you're *so* one-flesh – that you can start compensating for each other's weaknesses to the point that there's resentment or an unhealthy shift in responsibilities. Don't stop challenging each other and calling each other out on stuff. You're life partners, not co-dependents.

Your stress will affect him, and his stress will affect you. Again, the whole one-flesh thing. Remember: *us against the problem*. You're allies, and you can go the distance.

God, keep us doing all we can to help each other go further. Amen.

# Everyday love

Submit to one another out of
reverence for Christ (Eph. 5:21 NIV).

*Y*ou have today, and eternity. That's all you can be sure of. If you die tonight, being at peace with your man will be more important than filing the lights-and-water accounts. (Though filing is useful. And long-term planning is brilliant for saving up to make memories, and for syncing your decisions and directions.)

Marriage is the beautiful symbiosis of mutual submission, which asks, every day: 'What does love require of me? What can I do to help? What burden can I carry for you so that you can go further in what God has called you to?' Leverage all of you for all of him, every day. He'll be falling over himself to do the same.

The Big Day of the wedding itself is crucial (duh). It's fantastically special – deeply significant. But your Big Day was just Day 1 of many, many Days. There are even more special and significant days ahead. Mostly they happen on average Thursdays when you're flossing and you catch yourself thinking you're the luckiest girl alive.

Jesus, show me every day what love requires. Amen.

# Old people have got it going on

The way of the righteous is like the first gleam of dawn, which shines ever brighter until the full light of day (Prov. 4:18 NLT).

*I* once spoke at a Seniors Fellowship. The folks were in their late-eighties and nineties. They wore shrieking hearing aids. They had chin hairs, chesty coughs and all the other things that go with decades of earthly wear-and-tear. And they were a far greater inspiration to me than I was to them.

It's tempting to patronize elderly peeps – to feel superior to the old because from the outside, their worlds have shrunk. Their lives have turned small. Yet we'd be fools to dismiss them, because on the inside their lives have turned big. Their worlds have expanded – so much so that they're almost touching eternity. Their time isn't running out; it's running *towards*.

I looked out at that room of arthritic hands and compression stockings and thought, *They're ages younger than me, inside.* Though their bodies are dying, their spirits are being renewed every day (2 Corinthians 4:16). They bruise dark from every bump and maybe it's because they've lived long enough to know real compassion – to feel the world's pain with readiness to bleed for it – like Jesus. Maybe their paper-thin skin is evidence of the thin places they live – where heaven meets earth. It's possible that, really, this is their finest hour.

God, I want to age exquisitely, to glorify You. Amen.

# Kids who go the distance

Surely there is a reward for the righteous … (Ps. 58:11 ESV).

When he was tiny, our youngest son signed up for mini-soccer. His enthusiasm plummeted a few practices in when he realized all the other boys in the swarm of dust and boots were better and faster. He got hot and thirsty and tired. What he *never* got was the ball. He wanted to quit.

As parents, we could've taken the path of least resistance and let him quit. Or we could've justified his quitting from a contrived moral high ground. Or we could've made him play.

We decided to make him play. He called us the Meanest Parents Ever. But the message we wanted to send him was, *Life's going to be hard as it is, but it's going to be unplayable if you give up when things are difficult, or quit before you really even start. If something's worth your time, energy and attention, it's probably going to take hard work and commitment. If you don't learn now to finish what you start, when and where will you learn it? And then, will it be too late?*

Incredibly, after a soccer practice mid-season, our boy tackled my kneecaps in a fierce hug and blurted softly, 'I love you more than anything!' And I thought, being the Meanest Parents Ever isn't half bad.

Father, help me and my kids not to
give up, and not to give in. Amen.

# Hit the tree

So let's not get tired of doing what is good.
At just the right time we will reap a harvest
of blessing if we don't give up (Gal. 6:9 NLT).

John Maxwell maintains that consistency wins. He explains his 'Rule of Five' by saying that if you have a tree in the garden that needs to be chopped down, and you take an axe out into the garden every day and smack that tree in the same place five times – *one two three four five* – day in and day out for a long time – eventually that tree will fall down.

It doesn't help to run around the garden hitting every tree you see a couple times for good luck. And it doesn't help only to hit the tree once or to skip a day or a week or start over on another tree.

To go the distance, ask yourself, *What is my tree?* Then keep smacking that tree. Five times a day. Consistently. With structure and strategy and commitment. Don't give up. Don't lose focus. Just keep smacking that tree. The rewards of compounded consistency are always astounding.

God, give me staying power where I'm prone to
flaking out. Help me commit to chopping down
the right tree, no matter how long it takes. Amen.

# Words that go the distance

Take control of what I say, O LORD,
and guard my lips (Ps. 141:3 NLT).

We're shaped by the language we use, and if we want to go the distance for God it's crucial that we exercise verbal precision – as opposed to verbosity or exaggeration. Because surely God is strong enough through us, with the actual truth. We don't need to inflate it or embellish it.

This challenge is not just for writers or speakers or teachers or radio presenters. We all use words every day, and God will ask us to give an account of each one (Matthew 12:36).

Let's travel light by offloading a bunch of unnecessary words. Ill-timed conversations. Gossip, slander and any other maliciousness. God's Word has gone the distance through all of human history, so His words are a good place to start if we're wondering how to shape our own.

Creator of communication, choose the words I send
out into the world today. Let whatever comes out
of me be wise, life-giving, timely and true. Amen.

# Dogs go the distance

… a real friend sticks closer than a brother (Prov. 18:24 NLT).

Our golden retriever, Lola, can teach humans a thing or two. Lola only barks when she has something to say. Her barks say, *'I want to go out.' 'Now I want to come in.'* Sometimes my bark isn't even meaningful. I should at least save my barking for moments when it adds absolutely necessary value.

Lola loves unquestioningly. Unreservedly. And she doesn't allow her imperfections to get in the way of her unrivaled devotion. She comes, always with the slow wag of great affection. Always with the bad breath and the muddy paws. And she doesn't fear the rejection that her imperfections might herald, because she utterly trusts that we love her anyway. Us humans, too often we fence ourselves in behind insecurities, unwilling for others to see how we're damaged and deficient. Maybe we'd let people in more easily – love them and lean on them – if we unconditionally accepted the truth that we're *unconditionally accepted.*

Lola is a well-wisher, not a point-prover. And she's relentlessly patient. Whether we're gone five minutes or a week, the welcome is equally gracious. How might culture – the world? – change if we kept score a little less? If we all waited and welcomed people with unwearied, happy mercy?

God, help me travel uncomplicated paths of loyal love. Amen.

# Friends go the distance

It is not an enemy who taunts me – I could bear that. It is not my foes who so arrogantly insult me – I could have hidden from them. Instead, it is you – my equal, my companion and close friend (Ps. 55:12-13 NLT).

There'll be days when your friends don't get you. At times they'll feel threatened by your success. At other times, you'll be the one feeling left out or behind. The ebb and flow of emotion and circumstance is part of life on the planet, and we shouldn't be shocked by it. We should, however, manage it.

Lean in, don't lean away. There's always a temptation to protect ourselves by withdrawing or pretending we don't need our friends because no one wants to be known as needy. Instead of acting hardcore and indifferent, we might try resting in the finished work of Christ – which means there's nothing left for us to do or prove; all that's left for us to do is love. It really doesn't matter if you're the one making all the effort. Friendship needn't be a one-for-me-one-for-you competition.

If you're sensing that a friendship has landed in unhealthy spaces, be brave to face the awkwardness. Have an honest chat. To go the distance, it's also ok to set boundaries, so you've got stamina for the long haul.

Jesus, let my friendships be lit cities on hills – our mutual love drawing weary travelers to You! Amen.

# Your Guide
# to go the distance

Even when I walk through the darkest valley,
I will not be afraid, for You are close beside me. Your rod
and Your staff protect and comfort me (Ps. 23:4 NLT).

*A* tremendous truth about traveling light through life is that we don't ever travel alone. We have the ultimate Guide who knows the pitfalls and the stunning views of every road. What's more, even when we get tired, He never does (Psalm 121:4).

It's also some kind of marvelous that Jesus – faithful Shepherd and Sherpa – didn't die so we could *cope* with the road we're on. He died so we could be *free*. He died so we could walk comfortably and well and with deep peace and genuine contentment – no matter how rough (or tragic or grief-stricken or frightening) the terrain we encounter. There may be boulders that scrape our boots and loose shale that makes us slip and the treachery of jagged crags – but God's steady hand never lets go of ours.

John Newton – who sailed slave-trading seas before God gloriously interrupted his wayward life-voyage and rerouted him – wrote:

*While I am a pilgrim here, Let Thy love my spirit cheer; As my Guide, my Guard, my Friend, Lead me to my journey's end …*

Jesus, I'm putting all my hope in You alone to guide me
along the paths You've picked out as perfect for me. Amen.

# NOVEMBER

Walk Off the Map

Not all those who
wander are lost.

*J. R. R. Tolkien*

# Unfold

All Scripture is inspired by God and is useful
to teach us what is true and to make us realize
what is wrong in our lives … (2 Tim. 3:16 NLT).

There's an app for everything, though it's still kind of exciting, when you're traveling, to get yourself an actual real paper *map*, so you can live yourself into an area with better spatial perception. But you could buy yourself the best map of the city or country you're traveling through, and leave it folded in your backpack – where it will be of no use. To use a map – to make it *useful* – you have to open it, find your You-Are-Here, study the map, interpret it – and then *go*.

God's Word is our ultimate life map. There are instructions, timeless principles, narratives and examples for every aspect of life in any and every culture and any and every time in history. But if we leave our Bibles closed on our bedside tables, in our drawers or on our shelves – the power of God in those pages lies dormant. His Word is rendered useless.

Northrop Frye wrote, 'The Bible should be taught so early and so thoroughly that it sinks straight to the bottom of the mind, where everything that comes along later can settle on it.' It's never too late to get your bearings.

God, thank You that You didn't leave me
directionless. Help me unfold Your truth. Amen.

# Never a dull movement

His lightning flashes out across the world.
The earth sees and trembles (Ps. 97:4 NLT).

Perhaps as you read this you're on an exotic adventure. You just pulled this book from your backpack. You're settled into a seat on a train through Europe or east Africa. Man, I hope so! But it's likely you opened this book with a sigh born of duty or obligation because you know it's in your best interests to try to have a 'quiet time' though you're exhausted and stressed about the meeting later today or your toddler's high fever or the fact that the washing machine's spin cycle isn't working and the laundry comes out dripping. There's nothing exotic or adventurous about your life today. You're going nowhere.

I submit to you that you're wrong.

Because you're traveling through time, all the time, and though you don't know the day, once each year you pass the advance anniversary of your death. Some travel days feel exotic and adventurous, and some travel days feel frustratingly slow, even pointless. *But you're still moving.* If God didn't still have somewhere for you to go and be, He'd have already taken you to your journey's end.

Ask Him to help you see as He sees, so you'd see the glory in the boring and regain your energy to make the most of the ride.

Lord, open my eyes today to the scenery passing me by. Amen.

# Off the map, into the mire

I praise God for what He has promised.
I trust in God, so why should I be afraid?
What can mere mortals do to me? (Ps. 56:4 NLT).

The people of each generation are both blessed and tainted by the unique time in history that they occupy. Like, kids who live through wars or famine might one day raise *their* kids either to hoard or to splurge – a reaction to the deprivation of their own childhoods.

It's no exaggeration that we're traveling into difficult days. Every media stream broadcasts how the world has gone all sorts of senseless and it's going to take a fight for us not to lose our joy in these dark days. It's a fight worth fighting because it sets us apart as believers. The world should watch our lives and go, 'There's something weird – and compelling – about those Jesus people. They're in serious trouble. It looks like they're in quicksand like the rest of us. They seem to have lost their maps in the mud – *but they haven't lost their hope.*'

Perhaps the greatest gift we can give to the next generation is not to let these complicated times – politically, economically, ideologically or culturally – mar our children. We could let our kids and others see that they needn't fear death. Also, they needn't fear life.

God, even as the mud squelches between
my toes, I'm declaring that You are
my joy for the journey. Amen.

# Grounded for change

My heart is steadfast, O God! I will sing and
make melody with all my being! (Ps. 108:1 esv).

To travel light, we need to get comfortable with change. Life is never static nor should it be. The whole point of our existence is to *change* – to become more like Jesus – so change isn't something we should fear. We live for the changeless God who changes us.

So we need to accept and assume that God *will* call us to walk off the map. We will know failure and weakness and surprise attacks. He will challenge our thinking, our attitudes and actions. We'll feel the tremors of revolution and He'll lend us the wisdom to measure them and investigate their source. It's ok – in fact it's expected of us – to be curious and open to how life around us is advancing. We can accept, embrace and welcome transformation.

*So long as we're grounded.*

Let's study the Scriptures so we'll know the truth. It will set us free. Let's be still, so we'll recognize the unchanging voice of our Heavenly Father, even when all around us is changing.

Lord, tie me to Your truth, so I'm free to travel. Amen.

# Always afloat

> … upon this rock I will build My church, and all the powers of hell will not conquer it (Matt. 16:18 NLT).

Living life for Jesus can seem risky. If we look at our lives the way others might – others who don't know and trust and *believe* Jesus the way we do – it can seem like we've lost the plot. Like, why would we *give away* chunks of our income when times are tough? Why would we put ourselves or our families in danger by traveling to hostile parts of the world to tell people about God's love? Why would we say no to sex now and wait for sex later?

People might sneer that Christianity is a sinking ship in the backwaters – but it's simply not the truth. The world is peripheral to the church, not the other way around. The storm is outside of our boat, not in it. God promises to provide and protect. He *made* the sea and He holds it together. If you're seeking Him first (Matthew 6:33), you can sail any kind of sea, expectantly and with great peace.

Jesus endorsed His church, guaranteeing its survival and making it the only ship that comes with any kind of no-sinking guarantee. Ships of state or commerce may well sink, but if you're in a ship with Jesus, you'll survive the storm.

Jesus, thank You for keeping me and every molecule and meteoroid, afloat. Amen.

# Lost and found

> If you try to hang on to your life, you will
> lose it. But if you give up your life for My
> sake, you will save it (Matt. 16:25 NLT).

Jesus asks us to lose our lives for His sake, and in so doing, we'll find *real* life – the *abundant* life He came to bring. He's not calling us to some kind of crazy suicide mission. He's just reminding us that calling Him Lord means that He's the ultimate source and authority of our lives.

The life we're losing is the (false) sense of security we get from our stuff, our relationships, our governments, our economics, and all the other things onto which we can be tempted to fix our hope.

Losing our lives doesn't mean losing our way. Your colleagues or varsity friends might scoff that you've 'found religion' and lost your way – that you need a real GPS to navigate the complexities of life. The liberating truth is that you can navigate just fine, because Jesus says, 'I am the way, the truth, and the life' (John 14:6). He *is the way* – and you *know* Him – so you *know the way*. Follow the way, and you'll reach your destination.

Jesus, You don't just know the route I should take.
You *are* the route I should take. Thank You! Amen.

# Walk off the map for others

Mark out a straight path for your feet so that those who are weak and lame will not fall but become strong. Work at living in peace with everyone, and work at living a holy life, for those who are not holy will not see the Lord (Heb. 12:13-14 NLT).

*I*t's easy to talk the warm-fuzzy talk about loving people, and we probably all like to think of ourselves as kind and compassionate folks. But to love the human race the way God does and to navigate relationships excellently, we need to know that love is almost always inconvenient. Love will cost us time out of our hectic schedules. Love will cost us detours from our focused to-dos. Love will often cost us money.

But the cost is worth it because at the end of our lives how we treated others and managed our relationships is all that will really matter, and all that will really be remembered. And perhaps the closest thing to perfection this side of heaven is to love others well. We can do this by making a sincere effort to listen, and to translate our intentions into other people's realities. It will take courage and conviction, but in traveling the bypasses of inconvenient love we'll happen upon beauty we wouldn't otherwise have seen.

God, show me who I need to love today, by walking off the map of my plans and preferences. Amen.

# Currency conversion

> You used to do these things when your life was
> still part of this world. But now is the time to
> get rid of anger, rage, malicious behavior, slander,
> and dirty language (Col. 3:7-8 NLT).

My husband uses an old Zimbabwean dollar bill as a bookmark. He can't spend it anywhere, because years ago the Zimbabwean dollar lost all value and went out of circulation. If he tried to use that dollar bill in a store, he'd get strange looks. Someone might even call security.

Wherever we are in the world, we need to use the currency of that country. And as believers – living, moving and having our being in God (Acts 17:28) – we need to use the currency of the Kingdom, which is love, joy, peace, patience, kindness, goodness, faithfulness, gentleness and self-control (Galatians 5:22-23). We can also pay in forgiveness and self-sacrifice, obedience and prayer. We can extend grace-credit to others, whether or not they qualify for the loan and whether or not they will ever pay us back.

The Kingdom's currency isn't offence. Why then, do we still trade in it? The Kingdom's currency isn't unforgiveness, jealousy or slander – and yet we invest heavily in those high-risk commodities. If you've picked up some foreign currency and you're carrying it around in your case? Exchange it, and travel light.

> God, help me simplify my life by only
> dealing in Kingdom cash. Amen.

# Have future, will travel

> Surely there is a future, and your hope
> will not be cut off (Prov. 23:18 ESV).

*I*'ve read about a renowned entrepreneur and life coach with a huge platform. He's in his early seventies, and he has a 25-year plan for his life. Apparently he's sharper than he's ever been before. He believes that your future has to be bigger than your past, and he lives it.

Do you feel as if your time is running out, or running *towards* something bigger and better than you're living now? Bigger and better doesn't mean richer or more successful or more influential (though I guess it might). It means deeper devotion and greater dependence on God. It means growing more and more familiar with His ways and His purposes in the world.

Don't let the passage of time turn your life small. We all probably must get to a point one day where we downscale financially. We might move into a smaller home. Sell a car. Shift some investments. But may it never be that we downscale spiritually. That our vision shrinks and we settle for small when it comes to the purposes of God in our lives and our circle of influence.

> Father, with You, the best is yet to be. I want
> to go big before I go home, for eternity. Amen.

# Dot to dot

Many are the plans in a person's heart, but it is the LORD's purpose that prevails (Prov. 19:21 NIV).

We're all moving into an unknown future. None of us can see past the next five minutes – or indeed the next breath that God lends us. It may feel pointless even having a map – making a plan – picking a route – because there are no guarantees and God alone knows where we're really going and how much time we have left.

Choose today to celebrate God's sovereignty, providence, love, wisdom and power. All of life's burning questions have actual answers, and God knows them. Praise Him that, sure, you don't have a clue what tomorrow will bring, but *He does*.

Thank Him that He's connecting the dots, all the time. Enjoy the truth that anywhere you go, you're *sent*. And as your dot-to-dot journey is disclosed – dot by God-ordained dot – you'll get to discover more of the mystery of His eternal kindness.

God, some days I really have no idea where
I'm going. I'm so grateful that You do. Amen.

# Reach out

Keep on loving each other as brothers and sisters.
Don't forget to show hospitality to strangers, for
some who have done this have entertained
angels without realizing it (Heb. 13:1-2 NLT).

When I travel alone, I get to speak to people I wouldn't necessarily speak to if I was traveling with friends or family. I'm far braver and more inclined to strike up conversations with strangers – *Is this seat taken?* – when I'm on my own. It's a way I can walk off the map socially or relationally and forge new, diverse, interesting connections – as opposed to sitting alone and with my own thoughts, or loving the friends or family with me.

And sometimes we need to walk off the map socially or relationally or from a career perspective, even when we're not road-tripping or catching planes and trains. That could mean: don't always wait to be invited to sit at the popular table. The *happening* table. The table full of people you want to be like. Instead, find your own table, lay it, and invite others to join you. You might be surprised to find a plethora of fascinating and refreshing life links.

Lord Jesus, make me brave to make things happen.
Help me spend less energy hustling to fit in and
more energy reaching out to others. Amen.

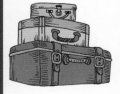

# True, regardless

The very essence of Your words is truth; all Your just regulations will stand forever (Ps. 119:160 NLT).

Lisa Whittle points out, 'Even as we're told by the world that God is not in charge, *we walk in His authority*. The world doesn't have to understand that for it to be true. This position doesn't change without the world's endorsement.'

The world will try to sell you all sorts of maps and apps that pinpoint your apparent location. You're under no obligation to believe that that's really your position. You're under no obligation to follow the directions they offer. Jesus prayed to His Father, for us, saying, 'Make them holy by Your truth; teach them Your word, which is truth' (John 17:17).

The great adventure of faith is that we get to turn culture's map upside down and read it counter-culture. Plus, we have the freedom to walk right off it to follow Jesus into something far grander, and far more meaningful. That might mean potholed roads, tough choices, sacrifice and obedience – but man, the adventure will be worth it.

Jesus, when things are shaky remind me that
Your Word stands firm and true, and so can I. Amen.

# Braving

> But to you who are willing to listen, I say, love your enemies! Do good to those who hate you. Bless those who curse you. Pray for those who hurt you (Luke 6:27-28 NLT).

Brené Brown has turned BRAVING into an acronym for developing trust – which always involves the risk of walking off your emotional or relational map. BRAVING stands for: Boundaries, Reliability, Accountability, Vault (confidentiality that goes both ways), Integrity (choosing courage over comfort, and choosing what's right over what's fun, fast and easy), Non-judgment and Generosity.

She says, 'People are hard to hate close-up. Move in.' Perhaps it's time we moved out and away from the walls we've erected to keep us in and others out – in an attempt to safeguard ourselves emotionally – and travel towards others – braving unchartered areas of life and relationship. Jesus braved relationships with humans He knew would let Him down in the worst way. And He says to us, *Go and do likewise.*

God, I'm fairly horrified even at the thought of approaching certain people, never mind opening my life to them, and trusting them. Help me get over myself. Amen.

# Walk off well

> Make it your goal to live a quiet life, minding your own business and working with your hands, just as we instructed you before. Then people who are not Christians will respect the way you live, and you will not need to depend on others (1 Thess. 4:11-12 NLT).

Our earth-years are full of endings and beginnings. Fresh life-semesters and new directions. Our journeys take us places we didn't imagine, and sometimes they come full circle.

If you're coming to the close of something – and November is usually full of all sorts of endings – finish off with excellence. If you're walking off the map into new things, walk well. When we leave anything, there should be joy, not guilt, anxiety, excuses or defensiveness. There should be joy, because we've traveled well, traveled light.

There should be joy, because we're excited and expectant for the journey's next leg. If what you're feeling as you approach an ending is resentment or exhaustion or bitterness or anger or good-riddance – do what you can to make right with those involved.

With all the faith and sweat it takes, tie up the loose ends of what you've woven in this time or place, as neatly and securely as it's in your power to do.

Father God, help me walk away or say goodbye or put down what I've been carrying, with grace, gratitude, dignity and great love. Help me give honor where it's due. Amen.

# Joy pursuit

The prospect of the righteous is joy, but the hopes
of the wicked come to nothing (Prov. 10:28 NIV).

*I* tend to over-think things. I over-analyze motives, projecting possible costs and consequences. Obviously weighing up pros and cons, and seeking wisdom and insight – those are all good things. But sometimes I over-complicate the decision-making process.

Provided our thinking hasn't devolved into abject selfishness or hedonism, then *joy* (real, fruit-of-the-Spirit joy) should be a major marker for deciding things. As in, 'Is there joy in this opportunity or option or relationship or place? Does it bring me *joy*?' Because His yoke is easy and His burden is light (Matthew 11:30) and the Kingdom of God is not a matter of what we eat or drink, but of living a life of goodness and peace and *joy* in the Holy Spirit (Romans 14:17) and maybe, to travel light, and with the freedom to walk off the map should God call us to do so, we don't have to complicate things with over-analysis. Decisions really can be as simple as joy.

God, keep me from splashing ineffectually in the
shallow waters of convoluted decision-making. Help me
identify where the deep joy lies, and assure me of the
freedom I have in You, to dive in accordingly. Amen.

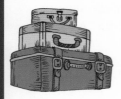

# Daily future mercy

Great is His faithfulness; His mercies begin
afresh each morning (Lam. 3:23 NLT).

*I*t's often easier to live with your own pain, than to watch a loved
one living with theirs. If you look to the future and unrest tugs at
your gut, perhaps it's because you can't imagine there's a hope and a
future for your kids. It may seem as if they will certainly have to walk
right off the known map, and not knowing what that will look like
can be scary.

Take a deep breath, and take heart. God has promised that His
grace is sufficient for the travels of each adult – each child – each
grandchild (2 Corinthians 12:9). He will make a way for *each one* –
even when it seems the road runs out. His plans are perfect and He is
perfectly powerful to fulfill them.

Almighty God, I'm grateful that, even if tougher times
lie ahead, You're already in the future and You'll lend
us and our kids capacity to carry whatever comes. Amen.

# Not complicated

Anyone who wants to do the will of God
will know whether My teaching is from God
or is merely My own (John 7:17 NLT).

A couple years ago our youngest son collected his pocket money in a ziplock bag and kept pestering me about giving it to a group of homeless, jobless men who hung out every day on a sidewalk near our home.

Eventually I capitulated and said, 'Ok, today's the day.' I drove up and pulled over in the dust. My son got out the car and ran to a man who leapt to his feet smiling wide. It was like he'd been *expecting* this blonde kid on a hot, random Tuesday. There was no awkwardness or condescension. No need for explanation. It was just a God thing. The mystery of simple faith and straightforward faithfulness, received.

I underestimate the Holy Spirit's power in my kids' lives. However immature their understanding of faith, if they've accepted Jesus they've received His Spirit (Romans 8:9). He'll guide them into all truth (John 16:13), lay His desires on their hearts (Psalm 37:4), and prompt them to do His will (2 Thessalonians 1:11). You and I can trust all that for us too. We talk about *finding* God's will – as if it's lost. But really, figuring out what's next for you on His agenda is not that hard, and not that hidden.

God, help me relax, and do Your bidding. Amen.

# You just don't know

Oh, how great are God's riches and wisdom and
knowledge! How impossible it is for us to understand
His decisions and His ways! (Rom. 11:33 NLT).

Centuries ago, a man who went to China as a missionary was
a total failure. Not a single convert. He was persecuted and
rejected. His wife and all six of his kids died in China. All he'd managed
to do there was purchase a small plot of land, so he could bury them.

Then he died too. The title deed of the land ended up with a family
member in England, and was passed down a couple generations. A
hundred years later, another missionary set out for China. By now,
China was closed to foreigners – unless you owned land. Turns out,
he'd inherited the title deed of a small plot of land …

*You just don't know* where and how God is threading your life
into the tapestry of a much bigger story. It must have sucked to be
the first guy, who died along with his family in a state of wretched
disappointment. But if he kept his faith to the end – hoping in the
finished work of Christ and eternal glory – he would've died content,
with great reward.

When things seem fruitless but God says, *Keep at it*, He's up to
something bigger than you and your life.

Lord, I'm excited to see the finished product
of what You're making with me! Amen.

# Bash down the door

'All right then,' Jonathan told him. 'We will cross over and let them see us. If they say to us, "Stay where you are or we'll kill you," then we will stop and not go up to them. But if they say, "Come on up and fight," then we will go up. That will be the LORD's sign that He will help us defeat them' (1 Sam. 14:8-10 NLT).

For Jonathan, determining God's will wasn't as easy as waiting for an open door to amble through. It was choosing the *hardest* of two options. Keith Ferrin writes, 'The most common answer to *What's God's will for my life?* is "If it's God's will, He'll open the door. If it's not, He'll close it." That sounds good. But I don't think it's biblical. Sometimes God opens the door. Other times, He wants you to kick it down.'

God does open and close doors. Often, that's an indication of His will for us. But He seldom calls His people to paths of least resistance. All sorts of crazy, stupid, tempting, easy-as-pie doors stand wide open and it's *so* not His will for us to slide through them. And sometimes a door is locked and you think, *Why pick the hard way?*

Let's pray for wisdom around which open doors to walk through, and which closed doors to kick down.

God, thank You that Your purposes
can't be stopped by a door! Amen.

# City peace

And work for the peace and prosperity of the city where I sent you into exile. Pray to the LORD for it, for its welfare will determine your welfare (Jer. 29:7 NLT).

*I*f the map of your life has taken you to – or left you in – a place you'd rather not be, pray for the welfare of the city (or the backwater town) you're in, because *its* welfare will affect *your* welfare. That's not to say you'll stay there forever. God may alleviate your angst by moving you somewhere more comfortable or more exciting.

But maybe He won't. Maybe God will get maximum glory from your life on earth by leaving you where you are. Pray that He would open your eyes to the beauty and opportunity that you've missed.

Pray that He would grow rich, ripe, low-slung fruit from your branches, and make you a place of shade and rest for the people around you. You never know: you may suddenly realize that you're unbelievably satisfied with the life you already have.

Lord, bless the streets and the citizens surrounding me. Make me an agent of peace and productivity in this place. Amen.

# Lost in life's supermarket

If you look for Me wholeheartedly,
you will find Me (Jer. 29:13 NLT).

My mom used to tell me and my sisters that if we got lost in the mall or the supermarket, we were to *stay where we were*, so she could find us. 'Don't try to find me,' she'd say. 'Stay right where you are and I'll come looking. If you're looking for me and I'm looking for you, we could be going in circles.'

That's good advice. When you're lost, stay where you are. God says that if we seek Him, we'll find Him. So when you're lost, seek God. But know that sometimes seeking God isn't hurtling through aisles, knocking things to the floor in a frantic attempt to figure out where you are and making such a din you wouldn't hear Him if He was standing right in front of you, calling your name.

Sometimes seeking God means just staying put. And instead of asking flustered and frightened, 'Where am I?' Simply stop – slow down – and say, 'I'm here! Please find me.' Yours is a kind, good Father. He'll hear that prayer. He'll come running. And you'll know it's Him.

God, I'm unsure and afraid. I don't want to
make big decisions, or try to go it alone. I can't
trust my panicked judgment. I'm going to stay where
I am – bide my time – and wait for You to find me. Amen.

# Way out

The temptations in your life are no different
from what others experience. And God is faithful.
He will not allow the temptation to be more than you
can stand. When you are tempted, He will show you
a way out so that you can endure (1 Cor. 10:13 NLT).

*I* have days that unravel. The fibers whiz loose from my happy mom ensemble. I'm stripped of kind composure and my kids are tripping over tangled heaps of angry words at my feet. There are loose threads lying ugly to end the day threadbare – leaving them hanging. I desperately want to fix those days. But how do I pick up dropped stitches and tie tight the slack strings with truth and love?

That's when I hear Paul's heartening reminder – that what I'm experiencing isn't different from what others go through. God won't push me beyond my limits, and He'll show me a way out.

God doesn't give us a loophole. Not an easy out. Not an *opt* out. He shows us a *way* out. Jesus said, 'I am the way …' (John 14:16) So, I'm not looking for a way out on my own. The way into the truth about how to do life and live it for the Father – He's right here with me in the mess. He *is* the way out, from the mess of me.

Jesus, You're the lit exit sign from
my sin and myself. Thank You! Amen.

# New paths

For I am about to do something new. See, I have
already begun! Do you not see it? I will make
a pathway through the wilderness. I will create
rivers in the dry wasteland (Isa. 43:19 NLT).

Sometimes I catch a shocking glimpse of the pathways being
furrowed and webbed in the brains and hearts of my kids –
and I wonder about the pathways already formed in me. I see how
I've been forcing their thoughts down the emergency exit. Because
my boys fight and I yell, 'Don't fight.' They whine and I threaten,
'Don't whine.' They flush moths down the loo and I say, 'Don't. Don't.
Don't.' So they reverse down those same roads, making the grooves
deeper. And we're back where we started.

Yet bad habits are beaten by good ones and I need to be showing
my kids *new* brain-paths – and finding new paths of my own. Ways to
walk away from the ruts we're grinding with heels dug in. *A way out.*

So they gripe and bicker and I say, 'Tell me three things you're
grateful for!' or 'What made you laugh at school today?' *Take a new
road.* Let's choose to detour from the trudge-trudge of old actions
and attitudes to plough unchartered heartland where our souls can
breathe easy and run free.

God, keep me from reversing my
thinking and ending where I began. Give me
courage to take wise, life-giving off ramps. Amen.

# Worth the living

Your faithfulness extends to
every generation … (Ps. 119:90 NLT).

'My daughter shot herself. She was seventeen.' A woman told me this at a ministry morning, with the matter-of-fact sobriety that comes from walking through grief. She told me how vivacious her daughter had been. How somehow the lie had seeped and settled into her young bones – *that life wasn't worth the living.*

I drove home from that event, slow and quiet through mist, keeping my eyes on a meter of wet tar edging out in front of my car. I thought, *faith is like driving through mist.* We can't see what's coming but we edge onwards anyway because we know that somewhere up ahead the mist will surely clear.

If you're staring down the barrel of a gun at a future that holds no promise and you don't know what lurks round the bends of tomorrow's misted road: remember our Creator-King is on the throne. He's faithful. His mercies are new every morning. He answers prayers for wisdom. He has our kids on their own journeys, and there's grace enough for the steps they're taking into a future we won't necessarily live to see. They can face uncertain days, as the old song goes, *because He lives.* And life is worth the living. Oh, it is so very much worth the living.

God, I can't see what's coming, but You can,
so I'm going to keep going anyway. Amen.

# Shrink

He heals the brokenhearted and
bandages their wounds (Ps. 147:3 NLT).

As Christians, we need to get over the idea that therapy or counseling is a sign of weakness, or not trusting God. Too many people find themselves at the end of frayed ropes because they refuse to get help – even though refusing to get help is *so* last century. They expect a kid or spouse to hold together the emotional health of the family. It's not possible, and not fair.

Let's face our hearts, and be brave enough to drag into the light whatever hides there – understanding how our *thinking* affects our *feeling* and our feeling affects our *doing*. We could turn the tide of loneliness and anxiety which is fast reaching terrifying global soul levels. Because if we've processed some of our own pain, we'll be better at helping others do the same.

There's nothing courageous about hiding our embarrassment or pretending to be indestructible, to impress the people we think are watching. Nothing courageous about hurting the people we love most, because we were too proud to ask for help. It's ok to let people see we're willing to journey with them as we lean on the only One who can fix us – redeeming our pasts, securing our futures and sustaining us in all our todays, in gritty, glorious, unexpected ways.

Holy Spirit – Counselor – help me let
others in, to help me let the pain out. Amen.

# Water and wilderness

> Then Jesus was led by the Spirit into the wilderness
> to be tempted there by the devil (Matt. 4:1 NLT).

*J*esus was baptized (Matthew 3:16) – then led into the wilderness to be tempted. He went straight from the water, into the wilderness: straight from being refreshed, set apart and imbued with calling and courage – to being sabotaged by ridicule, doubt, hunger and thirst.

In the water – the faith-building place of acceptance and commissioning – the Word of God came *over* Him: 'This is My dearly loved Son, who brings Me great joy.' (Matthew 3:17) And in the wilderness – the desolate place of danger and fear – the Word of God came *out* of Him: 'The Scriptures say … The Scriptures also say …' (Matthew 4)

For the rest of our lives, it's going to be all about the water and the wilderness. Pre-eternity life-on-earth is pretty much one big wilderness experience. We need to get ourselves drenched as much and as often as possible in prayer, church, accountability friendships and podcasts in the car. We've got to get over ourselves, and into the Word. So that when we leave the water where the Word comes *over* us – when we're back in the wilderness of office politics and school runs – the Word will come *out* of us. *Powerfully.* With conviction and the deep-seated faith that isn't dependent on circumstances.

> Jesus, refresh me so I'm ready for the
> rough roads of the great wide open. Amen.

# Turn around

But the Lord is faithful … (2 Thess. 3:3 NLT).

Some wild flowers grow always only facing one direction: the sun. And if you're *also* facing the sun, you won't see their full, fiery brilliance. *You have to look back to see their splendor.*

As you crest another hill of your road – looking ahead – facing forwards – eyes fixed on the Son and the path ahead – mobilized by the momentum of another frenetic year – maybe you could –

Stop for just a minute. And look back.

Because as you keep putting one foot in front of the other to finish the year well – you might be struggling to see the point of it all. You're leaving in your wake the year's ups and downs and life happening in fantastic, grueling, disappointing or serendipitous ways. But the beauty of it – the faith that God will use it all for His glory and your ultimate good – escapes you.

Take a moment. Turn around for the view. There are victories, convictions, adventures, laughs and hugs crammed colorful into minutes and months. God can do immeasurably more than we imagine (Ephesians 3:20). He imagines from seed bright miracles of petals and tall trees. And He imagined from eternity past the masterpiece of you, preparing the good paths you'd walk (Ephesians 2:10). Keep on keeping on. Every now and then, look back.

Father, open my eyes to the
kaleidoscope of Your glory. Amen.

# Don't walk alone

How good and pleasant it is when God's
people live together in unity (Ps. 133:1 NIV).

I remember celebrating the happy wedding of wonderful friends, a couple of weeks after learning that our newborn baby was blind. It was a surreal moment in which my emotions walked right off the map.

The reality of life is that much of the time we walk parallel roads. Heartache and happiness can coexist, and normally do. We don't need to separate the pain of the world from its beauty, in order to live a full, exquisite, meaningful life. It's ok to live in the tension of rejoicing with one person and sincerely feeling the pain of another.

Walking off the map also doesn't mean walking off alone with your pain. We're wired for connection and community, and I believe loneliness is one of the enemy's preferred strategies in our generation.

Don't ever believe his lie – that you have no option but to travel solo. In fact, you might question whether you're heading in the right direction at all, if no one you know and love is willing to head there with you.

God, thank You that no matter what conflicting
or confusing emotions rise in me, You've designed
us to be carried by community, so I don't have
to figure everything out on my own. Amen.

# Find them

For God loved the world so much that He gave His
one and only Son, so that everyone who believes
in Him will not perish but have eternal life. God
sent His Son into the world not to judge the world,
but to save the world through Him (John 3:16-17 NLT).

Most of the people who fill my days are fellow believers. I'm acutely, uncomfortably challenged by that. I don't have so many of the proverbial tax collectors and sinners coming over for dinner at our place.

And yet, if I'm not deeply burdened for the lost – *that's a problem*. While I can pray and trust God to bring people across my path – people who need to rub up against the love of Christ as it manifests through me – sometimes I absolutely must walk off my map to *find* them.

Are you seeking out the lost? It might be horribly uncomfortable. You definitely won't always know what to say. But if you trust God for wisdom in the moment, you'll have it. And if you fear that your timing is off, know that it's *always* a good time to demonstrate love, joy, peace, patience, kindness, goodness, faithfulness, gentleness and self-control (Galatians 5:22-23). Love never fails (1 Corinthians 13:8), which means you can't possibly get it wrong. Start there.

Jesus, Mission Earth was to seek and save
the lost. Help me get with the program! Amen.

# God knows your name

So he returned home to his father. And while he was still a long way off, his father saw him coming. Filled with love and compassion, he ran to his son, embraced him, and kissed him (Luke 15:20 NLT).

Perhaps it feels to you as if you've wandered too far off the map. You feel lost and alone and you're speculating whether God still has your best interests at heart, and if He's really guarding your steps (1 Samuel 2:9). Perhaps you're ashamed, because you walked away from God on purpose.

Please seize this truth, and let it settle your soul:

Your Heavenly Father knows your name. He loves you. He has plans for you. No matter where you go or what you do, He will chase you down and bring you home (Psalm 139:9-10). Nothing is too difficult for Him. He conquered sin and death for all, and for all time, by handing Himself in and giving Himself up to the punishment that should have been meted out to me and you. He shed His blood so you didn't have to. No sin is too heinous or shocking or disgusting for Him to forgive.

Turn around and run back to him, friend. You'll find He's already running to you.

God, it's impossible to escape Your never-ending, everywhere love. Thank You! Amen.

# DECEMBER

## Sky's the Limit

Certainly, travel is more
than the seeing of sights;
it is a change that goes on,
deep and permanent,
in the ideas of living.

*Miriam Beard*

# Finest hour

*He alone is my rock and my salvation, my fortress where I will not be shaken (Ps. 62:6 NLT).*

As another year winds down, let's not forget that if God is for us, who can be against us? Let's trust Him to remind us that overwhelming victory is ours, and that *nothing* – neither death nor life, neither drought nor downpour, neither sleazy politicians nor violent riots – *nothing* seen or unseen can separate us from His love (Romans 8).

Let's not forget that nothing is beyond God's Kingship. Nothing undermines His majesty or throws off His plans for His glory. Let's not forget that we have this treasure – *Him* – in jars of clay – *us* (2 Corinthians 4:7). And *so much greater* is He in us, than anything, anyone, on offer from the world (1 John 4:4).

Let's live radiant with expectation – eager to see Him show up in splendor to lead, protect and provide. Let it never be said that the church of Jesus Christ drowned and floundered and clutched at wreckage. Rather, let the records reflect that when storms raged and waves drenched, we got braver and happier in the hope we possess. Let us, His people, be the starlit way that leads the world to Christmas and into an unlit New Year. Let's let Jesus make a miracle of us. And let this be our finest hour.

Jesus, strengthen our faith.
Make us the peace, not the panic. Amen.

# All aboard

> The LORD has established His throne in heaven, and His kingdom rules over all (Ps. 103:19 NIV).

Maybe we – the global church – need to start asking Jesus to make a miracle of us. Because the world's a sinking ship and we hear it from every continent: *there's nowhere safe or solid. Nowhere left to jump.*

Except, Jesus said that on a rock He'd build His church, and all the powers of hell wouldn't conquer it (Matthew 16:18). So we need to stop thinking that it's up to us with our bands and our baristas to build His church. We should stop embarrassing ourselves and Him with doom-and-gloom fear-mongering because a watching world mocks, *Where is your hope?*

We should stop *wasting* energy on doctrinal one-upmanship instead of *spending* it on getting Kingdom dirt under our fingernails. We need to ask God to break our hard hearts so we can love like Him. Where there are incriminating emails, accusations, secrets and lies, we should be light and truth, integrity and stability. Where there's ignorance, arrogance, injustice and poverty, we need to be wise, humble, fearless and generous. Jesus is no sinking ship, and we need to get *all aboard.*

Mighty King, I'm with You! And
with You, anything's possible. Amen.

DECEMBER 3

# High jump

I will walk in freedom, for I have devoted
myself to Your commandments (Ps. 119:45 NLT).

No matter how fit or strong you are and how much you practice jumping – you'll only ever be able to jump so high off the ground. But if you've got a trampoline or a springboard beneath you – different story. If your feet have something to push off from, you can get a *lot* more elevation.

To live as if the sky's the limit – to reach high and far, to maximize your influence and leverage every opportunity in the time you have and the place you are – you've got to be intentional about what's beneath your feet.

What's your launching pad? How are you gaining altitude? Without the proper grounding of Word study, prayer, fellowship and accountability, we won't get the traction we need to be able to tread upon the heights God intended for us (Habakkuk 3:19).

With the right footing, the sky's the limit.

God, get me fit, so I'm free to run steep
slopes or scale cliffs for Your Kingdom. Amen.

# Limitless

*Your unfailing love, O LORD, is as vast as the heavens; Your faithfulness reaches beyond the clouds (Ps. 36:5 NLT).*

The sky's the limit when it comes to God's grace and faithfulness. It's hard for us to get our heads around anything fathomless and eternal – trapped as we are in a temporal, tangible world where time, vision and resources are always finite. But God isn't running out of steam as history wears on through the ages. He's actively pursuing purposes that press towards His final summing up of His glorious story.

So it's seriously the best news ever that grace got us where we are; there's enough grace for today; and there will be more grace – and then some – for all the tomorrows. We needn't fear that our generation or the ones coming after us are too far gone – that our case is hopeless – that evil has swept across the pages of our lives and societies wreaking irreparable destruction.

God's grace extends to every generation. Even ours. Even the ones coming after us.

> God, don't let me ever forget that I live in
> the wide-open spaces of limitless hope. Amen.

# Doubt

> You have taught children and infants to
> tell of Your strength, silencing Your enemies
> and all who oppose You (Ps. 8:2 NLT).

Perhaps you had sky's-the-limit kind of dreams but now you're wondering if you're kidding yourself. You cringe and squirm and reckon folks must think you're properly weird and it's easy to convince yourself you don't have what it takes and the thing you thought God was saying – about a life's work – about the passion and peace of a calling – you're positively, embarrassingly sure you heard wrong. You lie awake some nights gripped by the terrible thought: *What if my very best is really just very average?*

You're right about some things. You're right that God doesn't need you and that there are others He could call. Others better educated, equipped and experienced.

But you're wrong to think you didn't hear right. He delights in using our weakness to show His strength (1 Corinthians 1:27). You may just have been listening to the wrong people. Whatever your calling is, it will play out in community and touch the lives of others – so how others receive it is part of how it will be revealed. Just remember that your mandate is from God. *He* calls you – those people don't.

Lord, it's incredible to think that You use babies and children and *even me*, to spread Your fame. I stand in awe. Amen.

# It takes all sorts

> This is why I remind you to fan into flames
> the spiritual gift God gave you when I
> laid my hands on you (2 Tim. 1:6 NLT).

Thank God for people who make you doubt your calling. Relax into the truth that sometimes it's people very close to you – people who know you exceptionally well – who can't see the fingerprints of God on your life because you've smudged them with your imperfections.

They can't see the wood for the trees because they're too up-close-and-personal to the tree (you). They see the gnarled bark and the termites noshing bits of the trunk. Those people are a gift. They keep you humble – mindful of your fallibility and that you're not all you should be or could be, just like everyone else. God uses those people to confirm your conviction because if they *never* recognize God's call on your life – will you still follow it?

And then thank God for the people who make you believe. Ask God to identify and surround you with those people, as much as possible. They're the folks honored to pray for you and with you because they can see that you've been planted for a purpose.

God, thank You for the gift of every person
You've sent to sand smooth my rough edges. Amen.

# Seeing and being seen

As they talked and discussed these things, Jesus Himself
suddenly came and began walking with them. But God
kept them from recognizing Him (Luke 24:15-16 NLT).

There were moments when those closest to Jesus, and total
strangers, caught a shadowed glimpse of who He really was –
*God!* – and what He was about. But mostly He was taken for granted,
sidelined, mocked and reviled. Incredibly, He never felt sorry for
Himself. Never mentioned His achievements to get attention. Never
tried to steer the conversation His way. The only name He dropped
was His Father's. He never doubted His calling, and He lived for God's
greatness, not His own.

Wouldn't it rock the world if we adopted that kind of demeanor as
we lived out our respective callings? Humbly, mindfully, confidently
taking opportunities for as long as God keeps sending them. Enjoying
doing what He's asked us to do.

It would be equally phenomenal if we asked God to open our eyes
to the amazing-ness He's put inside those around us and closest to
us – those whose imperfections we know better than our own.

Let's ask Him to help us see people, whom perhaps we've intentionally or subconsciously written off, the way He sees them.

Jesus, I'm so glad I get to set free what You've put inside me. Help
me cheer for those around me who are doing the same. Amen.

# Plan A: Success

> At the same time, God's hand was on the people
> in the land of Judah, giving them all one heart to
> obey the orders of the king and his officials, who were
> following the word of the LORD (2 Chron. 30:12 NLT).

Failure is an inevitable part of life. We needn't fear it or be shocked by it or allow it to paralyze us from ever even trying. It's so often a catalyst for growth and change and can even be an indication of God's will (or what God's will is *not*). You can always pray for wisdom, trusting God for help to recognize and navigate failure with grace, dignity, genuine humility and a teachable spirit.

But know that God doesn't *want* you to fail at what He's called you to. His plan is for your *victory* over sin and self. You needn't put on airs of false humility and think that that makes you hyper-spiritual. Instead, take legitimate, unadulterated pleasure in His work in your life, and the work He's doing through you. We serve a happy God.

God, give me guts to fail forwards, always leaning
into the victory You died for me to take hold of. Amen.

# Total release

Instead of your shame you will receive a double portion,
and instead of disgrace you will rejoice in your inheritance.
And so you will inherit a double portion in your land,
and everlasting joy will be yours (Isa. 61:7 NIV).

Perhaps to travel light – as if the sky's the limit – you could ask God to release you completely from old grief, or new grievances.

Ask Him to release you from racism, sexism, or any other ugly, ungodly *ism*. Ask Him to release you from fear of what others think of you, and what they think about your gifts, your dreams, and the direction God is taking your life. Ask Him to release you completely from scarcity thinking that makes you wonder if there's room for your contribution to the Kingdom.

Ask Him to release you completely from the fear of shining too brightly and risking having others feel threatened by you. Ask Him to release you completely from the knee-jerk tendency to shrink back from brilliant ideas, because you're afraid you'll fail at them. And ask Him to release you completely from the shame that has you hamstrung.

We're body-bound here on earth. Yet still, for all of us, the sky's the limit because we serve the King and Creator of unmerited, unlimited kindness.

God, You're the great chain-breaker!
You split the sea and raised the dead and I know
You can release me from shackles of shame. Amen.

# Discern to deliver

Discretion will protect you, and
understanding will guard you (Prov. 2:11 NIV).

Maybe you're someone who *notices* things. You have the gift of prophecy – or discernment – or insight – or gut feel – call it what you will. You're seldom wrong about the emotional vibes you pick up in a room. You're seldom wrong about what you sense beneath polite conversation. You detect people's pain or insecurity or anger – which is when it's good to remember that mercy triumphs over judgment (James 2:13).

If you perceive something negative in your boss, your husband, or your best friend from school, rather pray the positive opposite for him or her. Ask God *why* He may have highlighted for you another person's challenge or crisis. For sure, it's not for you to judge. It's not necessarily for you to confront that person. It's definitely not for you to share with anyone else.

Rather, ask God to use you to call out the gold in that person. Ask Him to help you counter the negativity with words of wisdom and compassion. No situation is beyond His redemption.

Great Deliverer, nothing's impossible for You!
Lend me discernment so I can see Your
Kingdom come. Amen.

# Small is the new big

Share your food with the hungry, and give shelter
to the homeless. Give clothes to those who need them,
and do not hide from relatives who need your help.
Then your salvation will come like the dawn,
and your wounds will quickly heal. Your godliness
will lead you forward, and the glory of the LORD
will protect you from behind (Isa. 58:7-8 NLT).

When I was at university, a couple of my friends used to write tiny notes of encouragement that they would surreptitiously leave in the pockets of coats and pants on the racks of department stores in malls. Unsuspecting shoppers would buy those clothes – and possibly only discover, the first time they wore them and put a hand into a pocket – a small scrap of love left by a stranger.

Whether or not something like that would be considered destruction of property or crossing some other line, I'm not sure. But I like to think those notes could have changed someone's whole day, whole world, whole life.

You just never know when your smallest act of kindness or courtesy – seen or unseen, rewarded or ignored – could make an enormous difference.

God, enthuse me with the importance of
small things! I don't want to put off doing a single
good thing, if it's in my power to do it. Amen.

# If you knew you couldn't fail

What shall we say about such wonderful things as these? If God is for us, who can ever be against us? (Rom. 8:31 NLT).

Once my boys used their give-away pocket money to buy bread for some jobless, homeless people in our neighborhood. I explained the whole teach-a-man-to-make-a-sandwich-and-you-feed-him-for-life concept, and that handouts wouldn't solve poverty in our city. *But they were convinced they couldn't fail.*

That same week, I got a nasty blog-related social media message. I wanted to go to bed with a lot of chocolate and stop writing forever. *I was convinced I'd failed, and would fail again.*

But then a friend's question re-surfaced: *What would you do if you knew you couldn't fail?* It's the most brilliant, fear-stripping question. It makes me gut-honest with myself and reveals whether any restlessness I feel is dissatisfaction – the discontent of ingratitude and entitlement – or dissonance, which is an inconsistency between my current reality, and my potential.

Dissonance is inspiring and encouraging. It's the opposite of complacency, which is boring and disappointing. It stirs me to lift my game and makes me brave to keep doing what I do – less hung up on failure and more intent on God's glory.

Great God, make me fearless to do for
You what I'd do if I knew I couldn't fail. Amen.

# Jesus plus nothing

He is before all things, and in Him
all things hold together (Col. 1:17 NIV).

Jesus gave us abundant life. That means there's too much of it. It overflows from us. We don't need anything else to go our way to be able to say, '*Now* I've got enough life.' This is just the truth of the great success story that is the cross: God's gift of life is *Jesus plus nothing*. We need to do, earn and achieve exactly *nothing* to get it, which means there's no risk of failure when it comes to our ultimate, eternal future.

So, why the fear of *what* others will think or *how* things will pan out or *if* we'll make a difference? Why the fear of failure?

Of course, it's not about whether or not we'll fail. This side of heaven, we will fail. A lot. That's life. (We'll also, I feel quite sure, get bunches of things right.) But keeping in mind what we'd attempt if we knew we couldn't fail should keep us showing up at laptops, microphones, boardrooms and other potential failure fests. It should keep us sane. It should keep us happy. It should make us brave. And it should give us hope.

Jesus, keep me living like the stakes are low,
the dreams are big and the risks are worth it, so that
I'll be a conduit of who You are in a hurting world. Amen.

# Hope-realism tension

So each generation should set its hope anew
on God, not forgetting His glorious miracles
and obeying His commands (Ps. 78:7 NLT).

For his sixth birthday, our youngest son wanted a submarine. A real one. I loved that he believed a submarine was a viable option. He had so much hope. But it made me think of Psalm 78 – how we're called to set our hope *on God*. Not on submarines.

Solomon said hope deferred makes the heart sick (Proverbs 13:12). If your hope is set on a submarine and you don't get one, reality bites and punctures your inflated expectation. Disappointment leaks – sets like concrete – and you get cynical.

There's a tension you have to deal with then, because some tell you to Just Have Faith. All things are possible with God (Matthew 19:26) – even submarines. And others tell you to Stop Being Silly. They've seen how sixth birthdays typically play out, and you should get over yourself and your submarine.

Sometimes what we hope for is groundless, unrealistic, unwise, or obsessive. And when God doesn't deliver, we blame Him for the disaster or disappointment. We stop hoping and praying altogether. Rather, let's trust God to sustain our optimism and guide our hopes even as we ask smart people's advice, do our research, think and pray.

Father, keep my hoping heart un-bitter,
and lend me Your wisdom. Amen.

# Cynicism antidote

Plant the good seeds of righteousness, and you will harvest a crop of love. Plough up the hard ground of your hearts for now is the time to seek the LORD, that He may come and shower righteousness upon you (Hos. 10:12 NLT).

*I*t's a sad day when misplaced hope hardens our hearts. To avoid the dangers of pipedreams and pessimism, we could try this reality check:

If you've stopped praying that God would grant you your heart's desire, you know you're cynical. When you no longer bring dreams before God, you're pretty much saying you don't believe He can make them come true. If you've stopped praying for others, you know you're self-obsessed. Your dreams have become idealistically, idolatrously too big when your heart no longer breaks for the broken hearts of others. If you've stopped praying entirely, you can't hope for God to lay His dreams on your heart or make you wise to the practicalities of how those dreams will walk around in the world.

Whatever it is you long for – *ask God to grant that desire*. Keep hoping in our Miracle-Maker. Ask Him to reveal His wise, wondrous plans. Then leave your dreams with Him, and see how you can spend yourself for the sake of others. Life will send you regular reminders that it doesn't always work out. But nothing's impossible, least of all hope.

Jesus, keep me soft, not cynical – hoping, not hard. Amen.

# Cheering

Be happy with those who are happy … (Rom. 12:15 NLT).

Perhaps 'sky's the limit' is seriously not something you'd apply to celebrating the success of others. In fact, your celebrating can hardly get off the ground. If you're honest – and really life is too short and too important to be anything other than honest, especially with yourself, and especially before God – you're jealous. You're angry with God because He hasn't blessed you the way He's blessed your successful friend or colleague or acquaintance. Essentially, your sour grapes say that you don't believe God has it in Him to bless you in the same way.

Try telling yourself this truth: the sky's the limit when it comes to God's resources. He's your *Father*. Why would He not, *how could He not*, only ever have your ultimate wellbeing at heart, even if that ultimate wellbeing isn't what *you* had in mind?

Don't worry about what God is doing in other people's lives. Seek Him first, and seek first His Kingdom, and everything else will be added, as and when and all in good time (Matthew 6:33). Then enjoy making much of your successful friends, associates and family members, knowing that God will take full responsibility for the consequences at play in a life fully devoted to Him.

God, I know You can make a cheerleader of me yet! Amen.

# Stronger

We also pray that you will be strengthened with
all His glorious power so you will have all the
endurance and patience you need (Col. 1:11 NLT).

Holly Gerth says she's not a fantastic runner, but she runs anyway, challenging the inner voice that tells her she's pathetic or slow.

She writes, '… when we want to give up … when we think we can't do it … we're actually getting stronger. We're not tired because we're failing; we're tired because we're fighting. We're not weary because we're weak; we're weary because we're winning the battle to go to the next level in our lives. This is the scandalous secret: when we want to quit, it really means we're making progress … Let's not allow the enemy of our hearts to convince us to stop because we think we're not doing well enough. Instead, let's recognize the effort and pain for what they are – signs of growth. Yes, sometimes the hurt means we are injured and need to rest. But often it simply means we are breaking through what has held us back and pushing with all our might toward what God has for us. In the place between what is comfortable and what seems like it will surely kill us is often where we become all we're created to be.'

Don't be afraid. Your struggle might be evidence that you're getting stronger, and the sky's the limit.

God, keep me from quitting! Amen.

# In step

Since they are no longer two but one, let no one split apart what God has joined together (Mark 10:8-9 NLT).

*I*f you're married, you obviously want to keep in step with your husband, spiritually and emotionally and in every other way.

You don't want your husband rushing ahead of you and leaving you bewildered in his wake – forgotten or left out. Ask God for energy to keep up with his excitement. Ask God to help you better understand his decisions and motivations.

Also, you don't want to be flying high without your husband. Keep communicating your ideas and your passions, all the while re-membering that he's not a ceiling on your potential or God's call on your life. He's your covering – never to stifle, but always to protect.

Maybe you're worrying needlessly about this aspect of your one-flesh lives. If you're both believers, then what's of God for you is of God for your husband. You both have the Holy Spirit, and even if one of you takes longer to process a new direction or opportunity, if you both keep praying and talking, God will sync your hearts. And if your husband hasn't yet met Jesus, ask God to give you extraordinary wisdom to navigate your joint decisions, and eyes to see how your relationship with God influences him.

Father, help me and my man to speed up or slow down, to find a common, comfortable pace. Amen.

# Soul audit

> To Him who is able to keep you from stumbling
> and to present you before His glorious presence
> without fault and with great joy … (Jude 1:24 NIV).

Towards the end of one particular year, our then-five-year-old asked if we could go out for pizza. We said no. 'I don't like your attitude,' he reproached. Familiar words, because they were words I'd said to *him*. And words I'd said to myself in those last weeks. *I don't like your attitude.*

I preach the Finish Strong doctrine on all the racetracks of life, but *strong* is too strong a word to describe how I limped across the line of that year. No photo finish.

So I did a soul audit: making space to decide what to take with me into a new year, and what to leave behind. I asked God to give me one word for the new year. One word through which to filter my actions and attitudes – so that I could live the next year as if the sky's the limit.

Don't let the potential Christmas chaos eclipse the importance of auditing your soul – somewhere in the next couple weeks – so you can travel light. Who knows? Maybe all you'll need to pack for next year is a word.

Lord, adjust my attitude. Assess my soul, so I can finish
this year well, and begin next year even better. Amen.

# He's God. I'm not

Great is our Lord and mighty in power;
His understanding has no limit (Ps. 147:5 NIV).

*I*f you're nearing the end of this year and you're tired or confused or disappointed or at a loss as to the next step – pray for wisdom. For every decision, take Andy Stanley's advice and ask yourself, 'In light of my past experiences, my current circumstances, and my future hopes and dreams, what's the *wise* thing to do?'

Ask God to help you see as He sees. Ask Him to bring into the light anything hidden in darkness. Ask Him to help you see danger coming before it gets to you – and ask Him for the wisdom to know how to courageously run from it, or courageously confront it. Pray daily, *You are God. I am not. Show me what is wise.*

You don't have to know everything. You don't have to know all the answers and outcomes and curveballs and consequences. There's a wise King who sees and knows and controls all the things, completely. He reigns, and He's not abdicating ever.

God, I can't begin to tell You how relieved I am that
we're ending the year with You still on the throne. Amen.

# Love-filtered life

And may the Lord make your love for one another
and for all people grow and overflow, just as our
love for you overflows (1 Thess. 3:12 NLT).

The sky's the limit when it comes to love. There'll never be a surplus.
Never a flooded love-market in this world. So let's determine to
sift life through this question in the coming year: *What does love look
like, right now?* You won't have to think hard. The answer becomes
evident even in the busiest of brains, quickly and clearly. Love doesn't
need deliberation and analysis. It simply compels us to take what is
obviously the right road.

In this or that situation, does love look tough, or tender? In the
gap between expectations and experience, how do I believe the best,
instead of assuming the worst? How do I best position myself to love
God, and others? How do I live with what C. S. Lewis called the child's
heart of faith and the adult's head of reason? Because love keeps on
being brave enough to forgive and to stay connected to a hurting,
hating world.

Lord, help me to keep on allowing all of life to
fall through the filter of love, choosing to show
others the love I would hope for, from them. Amen.

# Leverage your opportunities

Whatever you do, do well (Eccles. 9:10 NLT).

One way of traveling light – out of this year and into the next – is to simply focus on leveraging the opportunities God gives, for His Kingdom and glory.

Leverage says, *I want to be prepared for whatever God has planned.* So, we don't wait for the big break. We treat every opportunity like it's *the* opportunity. We treat every end result like it's *the* end result – not a means to some greater, more significant outcome. Obedience is always the tick of success. We needn't buy into the celebrity culture that has made our Christian living and loving a thing of elbowing for a place on the podium.

Let's rather make it our ambition to lead a quiet life (1 Thessalonians 4:11). Let's put our heads down and work hard to dig and seed and water in faith – then look up amazed to see what God has grown, in us and through us, in these current crazy grace-laden days.

If you're waiting on God because you don't see any opportunities on the horizon or anywhere else, do what waiters do: serve. There's always someone who can benefit from your unspent energy while you wait for God to reveal something of the next stretch of your journey.

God, I want to make much of You,
with the best of me. Amen.

# Leverage your average

So where does this leave the philosophers, the scholars,
and the world's brilliant debaters? God has made the
wisdom of this world look foolish (1 Cor. 1:20 NLT).

*I* wouldn't have picked most of the obscure, ordinary people in
the Bible, if I was the Creator-King, spreading my name and
fame. I wouldn't have used random shepherds. Rough fishermen. I
would've used influencers and frontrunners. Big names shaping
culture.

But He's the last-shall-be-first God of upside-down Kingdom and
He can leverage obscurity. He can leverage ordinary. So instead, Jesus
arrived in a quiet corner of history. Sure, the Romans were rapidly
and ironically building the roads that would carry His message to the
known world and beyond. But it's as if God was saying, *I don't need
big bands, or bandwidth. I'll use a teenage girl. A stable. I'll use some
grassy hillsides and some villages and sometimes I'll slip unseen through
the crowd. And I will change the world, and the eternal destiny of the
human race.*

If you're like me, you're 5% aptitude, 95% keen. Thank God, He
sees the keen. He sees the small raw talent and the big eagerness to
obey – and He uses that for His greatness. God leverages our ordinary,
obscure capacity. Our ordinary, obscure lives. He uses us to bring
world-changing hope.

God, leverage all that I have, all that I am, all that
I do, for Your Kingdom and Your glory. Amen.

# Wonder

Suddenly, an angel of the Lord appeared among them, and the radiance of the Lord's glory surrounded them … They hurried to the village and found Mary and Joseph. And there was the baby, lying in the manger. After seeing Him, the shepherds told everyone what had happened and what the angel had said to them about this child. All who heard the shepherds' story were astonished … (Luke 2:9, 16-18 NLT).

When our son is happy, he twirls, skips and hums. Because he's visually impaired, he hasn't noticed that no one else really does this. Everyone else is too cool to sing and spin delirious.

We've decided not to point this out, because the fruit of the Spirit is joy, not cool. There's such purity in the uninhibited wonder of his actions and reactions – such a true gauge of how kids the world over might leap about if they didn't know that anyone was watching, or if they hadn't already learned aloofness and reserve from all the cool people.

Our boy's candid, unconstrained ways have made me determined never to lose my sense of wonder. I want to find Christmas wonder woven into moments lived slowly and wholly every day of the year. Wondrously un-cool, I want to keep on delighting in, and being satisfied by, the wonder of the Living God.

Lord, like You did for those Christmas Eve
shepherds long ago, awaken in me
the wonder of You. Amen.

# O holy night

For a child is born to us, a son is given to us.
The government will rest on His shoulders. And
He will be called: Wonderful Counselor, Mighty God,
Everlasting Father, Prince of Peace (Isa. 9:6 NLT).

*I* don't know where you find yourself on this Christmas Day, or how this year is ending for you. You might be elated. Exhausted. Expectant. Dejected. Content. Entitled. Invincible. Numb. Neutral. Shocked. Maybe you've been a Kingdom casualty – hit by the shrapnel of another's selfish agenda. Maybe you've experienced extraordinary victory.

Whatever the differing spaces we find ourselves in this Christmas, we all carry the same hope that bloomed over Bethlehem so many Christmases ago. The hope of freedom, birthed in a barn.

So, we could be gentle with each other, maybe? And magnify God's great name above the mess, to remember that because of the mess Jesus was birthed into, our mess is not forever. The lights of eternity are on the horizon even as we work and rest, wait and hope.

Jesus, I'm so grateful for Christmas. How can I ever thank You for breaking into our darkness with Your heavenly light? Amen.

# Despite disappointment

As for me, I will always have hope; I will
praise You more and more (Ps. 71:14 NIV).

Maybe your sense of hope has an element of nostalgia to it –
like taking a sip of your childhood. Your heart twinges when
*that* song plays. You're surprised by sadness when you smell what
used to thrill you – like country dust or ocean salt. You remember
how when those things first filled your senses the world was your
playground of every big dream and possibility. Now those sounds and
smells remind you that life sometimes sets you up for disappointment.

Nothing in this life satisfies us forever, or completely. We'll know
the blessing of moments, and decades of deep fulfillment, but even
the best circumstance, happenstance or relationship is in some way
flawed – just like us – because this is a damaged world.

*That's no reason to grow cynical or settle for disappointment!*
Actually, it's all the more reason to relish good gifts. Grab beautiful
moments and live them! Seek out beautiful people and love on
them! Disappointment is inevitable – like growing hungry or tired.
It's bound to happen again, no matter how much you've just eaten
or rested. That's really ok. It needn't stop you from making today
brilliant.

God, even in the aftermath of Christmas wonder,
help me hold loosely the things of this world,
so that inevitable disappointments don't crush
my soul or unseat my hope. Amen.

# Heavenly minded
# for earthly good

Point out anything in me that offends You, and lead
me along the path of everlasting life (Ps. 139:24 NLT).

*I*t took giving birth to two humans – God gifting me with new-forged souls to supervise – to give me the bifocals of eternal perspective and earthly urgency. Because all this – the physical and the temporal – will pass away and I need to focus the lens of my heart on *what is to come* so that I can be more effective in *what is*.

People disdain Christians for being so heavenly minded they're of no earthly good. That's junk. If your mind is really set on eternity, you'll be a force for seismic change. Your priorities will shift and free you of negligible concerns. You'll be moved to speak hope in a world of broken bodies and shattered souls. And because you're fearfully and wonderfully made, God will use you in a distinct, remarkable way, according to your passions and opportunities, to take Kingdom ground, and change the world.

So to make a lasting difference? Embrace how God has shaped you – your gifts; your physical, emotional and intellectual quirks; and your obvious shortcomings. Bow low before Him. Surrender your spiritual deficiencies to the scrutiny of the Spirit. As He convicts, forgives and restores, your life will be different. And so will the world.

Father, fix my heart on eternity, so it helps me fix earth. Amen.

# Crowned

And you will be My kingdom of priests,
My holy nation. This is the message you must
give to the people of Israel (Ex. 19:6 NLT).

Our identity is this: we go to God – hat in hand – *and He gives us a crown*. When the reality of that identity becomes more deeply entrenched in our hearts – this paradoxical identity of *bow low* because you're an object of mercy but *walk tall* because you're a child of the King – we begin to start moving energetically and intentionally into all God has for us. We can travel light with a spring in our step because we don't need to carry bags proving who we are.

The Queen of England doesn't have a British passport. She doesn't need one. She's allowed to travel wherever she likes, *because she wears the crown*. She doesn't have to prove who she is and why she deserves to be allowed to travel. She just goes.

We can travel confidently through life because we've been absolutely accepted by the absolute authority of the universe. We belong in God's Kingdom. We've been declared royalty. Knowing those things about who we are makes it far easier and more obvious to know where to go, and what to do, and how to travel light.

God, the sky's the limit! I can go wherever You send me, because You've crowned me with Your kindness. Amen.

# Forever young

> For you died to this life, and your real life is
> hidden with Christ in God (Col. 3:3 NLT).

As you grow older, it may feel as if you're heading downhill, and in many ways you probably are. Your body will sag and soften – accept it. But our culture tends to idolize the young and advertising will have you obsessing and over-spending on products and other fake elixirs promising eternal youth.

You shouldn't make a wrinkle-free face an idol of your heart. But you need never live with the defeatist attitude that your best years are behind you, because as time barrels on, God grows you *backwards*. You're being renewed (2 Corinthians 4:16), and if you're walking with Jesus, day in and day out, decade in and decade out, you're getting more and more beautiful on the inside. And inside beauty tends to spill over as outside beauty.

When it comes to the beauty of your soul, the sky's the limit.

God, thank You that for every extra day You've got
me walking around on earth, I get to reach higher and
further into the spectrum of Your beauty, growing
more and more into Your likeness. Amen.

# Slow-burn joy

> I have told you these things so that you will be filled with
> My joy. Yes, your joy will overflow (John 15:11 NLT).

Slow-burn joy is different from unbridled happiness. When Jesus sweated blood – then spilled it out for people who hated Him – I reckon He wasn't happy. We have it on good authority that He said, 'My God! My God! Why have You forsaken Me?' (Matthew 27:46) We also know that, 'for the *joy* set before Him, He endured the cross.' (Hebrews 12:2)

Did He *feel* joy as they hammered metal through tendons? Certainly, *He didn't lose sight of it*.

So maybe, slow-burn joy is the calm content of keeping your wits about you – knowing everything's going to be ok in the end – in the *very* end. Knowing the game is won, even if right now you've been red-carded or benched.

Realistically, joy cools in moments of trauma, grief and fight-or-flight fear. But it doesn't disappear entirely. Joy is a fruit of the Spirit and if we're saved we're also Holy-Spirit-filled and He's always there – whether we *feel* Him or not. If we practice surrendering to Him even in the anger or disappointment, the slow-burn will glow bright again. Maybe it won't *feel* like 'joy' but more like the serenity of knowing we're held. The soul equilibrium that takes the edge off stabbing pain.

> Jesus, help me never lose sight
> of the joy set before me. Amen.

# Unbridled happiness

Come, everyone! Clap your hands! Shout
to God with joyful praise! (Ps. 47:1 NLT).

Slightly different from joy, rampant happiness is the ecstasy
of the fun or the funny, the thrilling and delicious. It's in-the-moment amnesia that forgets hurt. It's enchanted and elated. It's the splendor of a gasp-worthy view. It's wedding days and babies born and first summer swims.

But perhaps we struggle to enjoy joy – and we keep happiness from happening – because we feel sorry for ourselves and entitled to a better deal. We feel guilty for relishing good gifts when so many others have so much less. Or we're afraid of the future – waiting for the other shoe to drop instead of staying in the happy here-and-now.

Truth bomb: in this crazy world beautiful *and* terrible things happen. And you don't have to be a sunbeam for Jesus 24/7. But sometimes, it's ok to smile anyway. Fake it 'til you make it. Decide to let the life God's poured into you spray out like fountains kids run through. You might find you quite enjoy it.

We humans are always buoyed up and happier if we have *something to look forward to*. So maybe Jesus-followers *should* be happier than most. Maybe we *should* be able to see the shafts of light in dust or gloom or other people. Because we look forward to a lasting hope.

Jesus, I praise You that I can travel light. Amen.

### The End.
(Which for us, is really just the beginning.)